BUILDING FOR GOVERNMENT

First published in 1999 by
Town House and Country House
Trinity House, Charleston Rd
Ranelagh, Dublin 6

in association with
The Office of Public Works
St Stephen's Green, Dublin 2

ISBN: 1-86059-074-8

A CIP catalogue record for this book
is available from the British Library

Designed and typeset by Jason Ellams

Printed in Italy

BUILDING FOR GOVERNMENT
The Architecture of State Buildings
OPW: Ireland 1900–2000

With essays by Terence Brown,
Arthur Gibney & Michael O'Doherty

Researched by Caroline Pegum

Contents

Acknowledgements

Martin Cullen TD, Minister of State at the Department of Finance with responsibility for the Office of Public Works, would like to thank the following for assisting in this publication:
Architectural Services OPW; Professor Terence Brown; Kevin Connolly; Noel de Chenu; Tony Roche, John Scarry and Con Brogan, Dúchas Photographic Unit; Arthur Gibney; relevant government departments; Valerie Ingram and Nicola Maher, Library OPW; Yvonne Jackson; Jennifer Lonergan; Rachel MacRory; Jacquie Moore; Frederick O'Dwyer; Organisation Unit OPW; Avril Percival; Personnel & Development Services OPW; Project Management Services OPW; Registry OPW; Town House & Country House.

Special acknowledgement is made to the following:
Brian (Barry) Murphy, Michael O'Doherty, Klaus Unger, Mary Heffernan, Treasa Coady and Caroline Pegum

With thanks to the following bodies for research assistance and the provision of illustrative material:
Aer Rianta
An Post
ARC Survey Photographic Ltd
Arthur Gibney & Partners
Barretstown Gang Camp
Peter Barrow, Photographer
Barry Mason, Photographer
Benson & Forsyth
Michael Blake, Photographer
Burke-Kennedy Doyle
Country Life Picture Library
Costello Murray Beaumont
G & T Crampton Ltd
David Meehan Photography
Davison & Associates Ltd
Desmond FitzGerald, the Knight of Glin
Department of Foreign Affairs
John Denby, Carrick-on-Suir
Dublin Castle Conference Centre
Dúchas - The Heritage Service of the Department of Arts, Heritage, Gaeltacht and the Islands
Eamonn Duffy (Rosemount) Ltd
Kevin Dunne, Photographer
Frank Crowley & Partners
Frank Fennell Photography
Gem Joinery, Longford
The Glebe Gallery, Dúchas The Heritage Service
Gilroy McMahon Architects
Gulfstream Aerospace Corporation, USA

Anthony Haughey, Photographer
Henry J Lyons & Partners
Horan Keogan Ryan Associates
Hugh Lane Municipal Gallery of Modern Art
The Hunt Museum, Limerick
The Irish Air Corps
Irish Architectural Archive
The Irish Times
Jones & Kelly, Architects
Kings Inns Library
Knight Frank International, London
Leinster House
Liam Lyons, Westport
Mark McCall Photography
Seamus Monahan & Partners
Mary Croke Photography
Michael Quinn Photography
Matthew Murray
Narrowcast Ltd
National Archives of Ireland
National Botanic Gardens
National Concert Hall
National Gallery of Ireland
National Library of Ireland
National Museum of Ireland
Aisling Ní Bhriain
Nick Gleiss Photography, California
Norton Associates
David O'Mara
Finbarr O'Connell, Cork
Donal O'Donovan
P & A Lavin Associates
Grace Pasley, National Botanic Gardens
Photo Display Images
Raymond E Chaplin, Netherfield Visual Ltd
Reuters Ltd
Robert Allen Photography
Royal Commission on the Historical Monuments of England
Royal Dublin Society
Royal Society of Antiquaries of Ireland
John Searle, Photographer
John Sisk & Son
Steve Stephens Photography, London
Stuart Smyth, Photographer
Studioworks
The Board of Trinity College Dublin
Trustees of the Ulster Museum
Victoria & Albert Picture Library
Vincent Vidal, Photographer
Warner Corporate Photography
The Whitworth Art Gallery, University of Manchester

Preface

This publication has been commissioned with two purposes in mind.

On the eve of the millennium it affords us the opportunity to account for the work in building construction and refurbishment with which the Office of Public Works has been entrusted by government over the past one hundred years. We believe it is right and proper also to acknowledge the confidence which colleagues in government and the public service have placed in the OPW during that time.

Secondly, we wish to record our appreciation and thanks to our colleagues in the OPW, past and present, for their contribution to this work. Their skill and expertise is well demonstrated by the work featured in this book.

As the new century and millennium approach we look forward to working with our staff to meet the challenging targets we have set for the OPW in the future.

Martin Cullen Minister of State at the Department of Finance with responsibilty for the Office of Public Works

Brian (Barry) Murphy Chairman

Foreword

Government policy on architecture was clearly articulated in 1997 by a policy statement which includes the objective to 'promote high standards of design and construction in building works for which it is responsible'. As an operational arm of government, the OPW implements government policy and is committed to providing high-quality services to meet policy objectives. The OPW also has an advisory role to government on architectural matters.

As the state architectural practice, the OPW has been responsible for a vast range of buildings for government departments and offices, both new building and architectural conservation projects. The variety of building types is immense, including government offices, cultural institutions, courts, prisons and Garda stations, visitor centres, as well as the conservation of important historic buildings such as Dublin Castle, Leinster House, the Custom House, the Four Courts and a range of Historic Properties. At different stages during this century, the OPW also had responsibility for post offices, national education buildings, airports, military barracks and National Monuments.

This book is presented in three parts. Part 1 highlights a selection of major projects, in approximate chronological order. Part 2 focuses on a number of other works, such as Garda stations. Part 3 is a listing of all the OPW's major twentieth-century projects and various OPW personnel.

Completion dates are generally given at the start of each entry. Where no date appears, this indicates that projects were undertaken at the site on several occasions over the course of the twentieth century.

BUILDING FOR GOVERNMENT

Reviewing the Century
Michael O'Doherty

The reasons for undertaking this publication at this time are twofold. It is firstly to provide to the twenty-first-century generations a record of the architecture created by the Office of Public Works (OPW) throughout the twentieth century. Secondly it is to acknowledge the work, skill, talent and imagination of all those individuals who, having served with dedication and often under difficult and challenging circumstances, passed quietly into the shadows.

The classical definition of architecture rests on three cornerstones: utility, durability and beauty. These foundations, being as valid today as ever, have been the guiding principles for the successive generations of architects who passed through the OPW and are evidenced in the numerous projects and construction programmes undertaken throughout the century.

Utility in architecture embraces functionality, practicality and efficient use of resources essential to enabling the user (in this instance government and the organs of state) to function efficiently. Durability reflects a permanence and stability in its physical framework which has to be maintained over the years by successive generations. Beauty or aesthetics provides that additional enriching quality which, while placing buildings in time, also reflects national well-being and culture. The buildings created by the OPW as a government agency are particularly expressive of the aspirations and identity of the state.

The OPW was never a single corporate entity which marched to the tune of a particular architect's personality, but throughout the twentieth century was made up of individuals from diverse architectural backgrounds and schools who had the opportunity to express their individual personalities based at all times on the three stated cornerstones. It is this diversity at the core of twentieth-century state buildings that enriches the cultural value and heritage of our towns and countryside today.

But if it was the three-fold principle of utility, durability and beauty that motivated the forms of particular buildings designed by the OPW over the century, it was government and its specific policies that provided, decided and articulated the specific needs.

As the century began, the main factors impacting on the work of the OPW were the industrial economy, relative national prosperity and a domestic political calm. While in this climate there was vigorous investment throughout the thirty-two counties in industry and the country's infrastructure, government, on foot of its various social, educational, economic and security policies, was investing, through the OPW, in public education at all levels, in civil and national security and justice, in cultural institutions and in the postal and communication services. In the years before World War I, these policies gave rise to the prolific construction programme of national schools and universities as well as post offices, urban and rural police stations and coast guard stations.

In addition to building this necessary infrastructure, existing institutions were being extended and maintained. The National Gallery was having its first wing added at this time, to house the gift of pictures from the Countess of Milltown, and the wonderful chapel ceiling at the Royal Hospital Kilmainham was being meticulously reconstructed. The maintenance and care of the government building stock also formed a major part of the work of the OPW in the first years of the century, with works to Dublin Castle and the Royal Hospital appearing regularly in annual government estimates. The Four Courts, the GPO and the Custom House were similarly cared for.

As state-sponsored buildings, these programmes reflect recent government policy in various fields. In terms of education, the first significant development of the new century occurred in 1908 when the OPW published new rules for the design of national schools. These guidelines reflected an advance in thinking on the part of the Board of National Education in providing for the schoolgoing population. They demonstrated particular concern for the health and physical well-being of the pupil and teacher, with new standards of space per pupil, natural light, ventilation, heating and sanitation being defined. Permitted maximum distance between teacher and pupil was also defined, as well as a minimum ceiling height of 13 feet. Window sills were prescribed at 4 feet and it was stipulated that windows should reach as near as possible to the ceiling.

What emerged on foot of the new thinking and comprehensive rules was a new school type that remained current until the thirties, before giving way to the high-windowed architecturally conscious corridor schools which remained until the mid-sixties.

Government policies during those early years of the century are legible also in those building programmes from which emerged the countrywide classically composed post offices, the new and robust police station at Pearse Street and the construction of George's Hall at Dublin Castle for the visit of King George V and Queen Mary in 1911. Worthy of note also in this context was the design by J Howard Pentland of the Royal Dublin Fusiliers Memorial at the entrance to St Stephen's Green, which was built to commemorate those who died in the 1899–1900 South African war.

The Labour Exchange Act was passed in 1909 and resulted in the setting up of labour exchanges throughout the country. The urgency in providing for the implementation of this legislation arose from growing unemployment, reflected in the OPW's proposal to procure the new buildings through developers on a lease-back basis, with an option to purchase after a term of years. The first purpose-built exchange was in Werburgh Street and was designed in 1914 by Andrew Robinson, assisted by MJ Burke and Harold Leask.

Subsequent exchanges have been built by the OPW throughout the century.

The 1914–18 war, along with the 1916 Rising and subsequent civil unrest, diverted the focus of government away from its capital programmes, resulting in a drop-off in the work of the OPW, and matters remained like this until 1922 and the transfer of power to the new Free State government. During this time there was a drop-off also in architectural staff numbers, with many leaving to participate in the war effort.

With the new independent Free State status and cessation of overt civil disruption came new government policies, new challenges for the OPW and a new generation of architectural talent into the OPW. The combination of this new talent with the experience of the remaining existing staff members like Byrne, Leask and Burke provided a resource with skill and scholarship in restoration of existing buildings as well as the talent to enable the emergence of a new architecture in the new building programmes which were to follow.

While the new Free State government tended to promote 'Irish Ireland' cultural policies in the difficult post-civil war political climate, continuity and stability were emphasised. Understandably, the thrust of the new government's policies, insofar as they affected the OPW, was towards the restructuring of government departments and the service agencies that were essential to the running, economy and cultural well-being of the state. For the following years, the OPW was, as a consequence, largely occupied with works associated with the provision of accommodation for departments whose offices had been destroyed, the provision of barracks and residencies for the new civic guard force and the reconstruction in particular of the three important Dublin buildings – the Custom House, the Four Courts and the GPO.

With regard to the latter, the skill and manner of their reconstruction must stand as the single finest individual achievement of the OPW Architectural Services over the century. The work was carried out over a period of eight years – 1924 to 1932 – with the greatest consideration to both the classical detail and the subtle design and integration of the modern services and fittings. The wealth of experience gained in these three reconstructions has carried through successive generations and informed the confident reconstruction projects carried out later in Dublin Castle and Kilkenny Castle and contributed to the consolidation of a conservation expertise within the OPW which can be evidenced today in the restoration of the nation's heritage buildings such as Castletown House and Rathfarnham Castle.

The architecture of the thirties, forties and fifties is evidence of a government and its departments more confidently constructing the new democracy, notwithstanding the limitation of financial resources and the impact of the 1939–45 war. This confidence is expressed in the new purpose-designed rural government offices begun in the 1930s, and the new headquarters for the Department of Industry and Commerce (1939–42) to be followed by the Raymond McGrath scheme of offices at Dublin Castle (1946), the configuration of which may well have been influenced by the Hugo Häring 1927 grand plan for a new government office opposite the Reichstag in Berlin. While the McGrath Dublin Castle scheme did not proceed, it was in part replaced in the early sixties by the modern Stamping Branch building in the Lower Castle Yard by Frank du Berry.

The confidently modernist new Dublin Airport terminal building, for which a special team was assembled within Architectural Services under the direction of Desmond FitzGerald, probably symbolises more than any other single project this century the rising confidence and ambition of the new nation. Architecturally, it was a pioneering building and while reflecting the spirit of a nation, instilled also a confidence within the OPW for future challenging developments.

Accommodation for legations abroad was also a significant element in the construction of the new state. In the early thirties diplomats and their support staff were accommodated in rented premises and, in accordance with government policy, the premises were furnished as far as was practicable with Irish-made furniture and fittings to act as a showcase for Irish design and craft. Later, during the forties and fifties, government policy was to change to permit the purchase of embassy premises. This change was to result in the acquisition of important premises in Madrid, the Hôtel de Breteuil in Paris and the Villa Spada in Rome.

Government policy was to impact again on the school building programme and on school design during these years. Through its education policy, government was committed to ensuring that primary education was available throughout the country and in its most remote regions. With a corps of architectural staff, Basil Boyd-Barrett developed a comprehensive typology of standard school plans of varying sizes and for varying site conditions. The buildings were designed to withstand the most exposed weather conditions and were planned using the earlier principles of providing pupils and teachers with maximum natural light, ventilation and general comfort, hence the tall-windowed classrooms with traditional sliding sash windows and clerestory windows for cross ventilation. Construction and finish materials were traditional, robust and simple so that availability of either materials or skills throughout rural Ireland would never be an issue. This standard school type lasted until the early sixties when Boyd-Barrett acquiesced to the development of a new school type, which responded to the changing demands of the curriculum and the availability of a wider range of building materials, including modern heating and artificial lighting systems.

The new school type design was low-ceilinged with a flat roof supported on crosswalls and with panel infill windows to the classroom. While seen as modern and progressive, this building-type was not without its problems, particularly in the maintenance of the flat roof and window panels, and remained no more than a decade before being supplanted by the more contextual Malachy Daly type of school, which saw the return of the pitched roof and the replacement of the infill panel with a conventional window

wall, which has been seen as a more sensitive response to building in the Irish landscape.

In the sixties the success of the government's programmes for economic expansion, which focused mainly on industrial and tourism development in the private sector, brought with it a spirit of national economic well-being which was reflected in the nature of the work being undertaken by the OPW. As well as the ongoing work programmes in schools, Garda accommodation, post and telecommunication and other state services continuing on an accelerated basis, a number of grand projects were authorised by government. Arguably the most dramatic of these was a proposal for a new 2000-seater concert hall to be located at Beggar's Bush and to be dedicated to the late American President John F Kennedy. For a number of years government had been exploring other options for establishing a venue for symphonic concerts, one of these being an auditorium located in Parnell Square to be accessed through the Rotunda cinema at the north end of O'Connell Street. It was eventually decided, however, that a national concert venue should be sited in the university premises at Earlsfort Terrace, which were soon to be vacated. The National Concert Hall opened in 1981.

The other important projects sponsored by government in the sixties were the reconstruction of the State Apartments and the East Cross Block at Dublin Castle and also the new Stamping Branch building in the Lower Castle Yard, the latter being one of the outstanding modern buildings of the decade. A new exhibition wing was added to the National Gallery which was designed also by Frank du Berry. Worthy of mention in this same context is the establishment of the John F Kennedy Arboretum and Forest Park in County Wexford, which features a very sensitive design by Fred Hilton for the public reception and information building (1968).

Throughout the following three decades policy in the area of public services changed dramatically, influenced by a perceived need to reorganise a much enlarged government and civil service structure as well as work practices in a world that was rapidly changing and beginning to engage with developments in technology. Radical improvements in services to the community were demanded by government, with quality, speed of service, courtesy, efficiency and privacy of the customer becoming paramount. Arising from this, a campaign was launched by government, in which the OPW played a central role, to improve the general appearance and image of public service buildings both new and existing and also the manner of meeting, managing and dealing with the public. Computerised information technology was to be a central component in serving the public more effectively.

Coinciding with government's thrust in the modernising of public services was an increased requirement in national security arising from paramilitary activity associated with Northern Ireland and also an increase in unemployment arising from a general downturn in the national economy. The combination of all three elements resulted in a very significant increase in building activity in government office accommodation, new Garda stations and new and larger employment exchanges. By the mid- to late seventies a new generation of young architects had joined the OPW and, as in the twenties, the combination of this young talent with the existing experienced corps provided a potent resource to meet the architectural challenges embedded in government's programmes and succeeded in creating a new and modern public image for its various agencies.

Ireland's entry into the EEC (now the EU) in 1973 brought with it structural funding programmes that were to have a profound effect on the OPW and its architects over the last three decades of the century. Under the tourism-related funding programmes drawn up by government, monies became available for capital investment in national and historic parks, protection of national monuments and all the national cultural institutions, including the National Botanic Gardens. This led to the development of specialisation of many of the architects in conservation, restoration and museum, gallery and exhibition design. Community membership also opened up dialogue with professional and managerial counterparts in other member countries and the opportunity to participate in developing common strategies and approaches in the conservation and management of the architectural and national heritage.

With European membership also came an obligation on government to provide locally for the hosting at intervals of the European Presidency, a task which became increasingly complex during the eighties, as more countries joined the EU. The practice of converting old buildings for new uses, which had been successfully achieved and demonstrated with the opening of the National Concert Hall at Earlsfort Terrace, was the formula to be adopted by government with its decision to create a modern conference facility in the historic precinct of the Upper Castle Yard at Dublin Castle, which successfully and eloquently accommodated the 1990 Presidency. Following on from this came the restoration of the Treasury Building at Dublin Castle to house the offices of the Comptroller and Auditor General and later the Ship Street range of

buildings to house a section of the Revenue Commissioners. The National Museum and the National Library were also to avail of old buildings to meet modern demands with the conversion of the military barracks at Collins Barracks to house and display the Art and Industry collection of the National Museum and the College of Art to provide additional space for the National Library.

During the eighties government also undertook a programme of decentralisation which required the construction of a series of departmental office buildings throughout the country. These were initially in six locations: Letterkenny, Sligo, Cavan, Galway, Ballina and Killarney. Such was the priority placed by government on the programme that the OPW engaged with developers on a design-build-and-finance basis to deliver the projects. A methodology developed that provided for lease-back and purchase after a term of years, reminiscent of the method employed in 1909 for delivery of labour exchanges. The process was successful in terms of efficiency, cost and quality, and was adopted for the entire programme, which is still extant.

In the nineties a variation of this procurement process (client-led design-build) was developed to meet government's accelerated prison programme. This variation provides for the building design concepts being developed by the OPW architects before tendering takes place, thus permitting developers with their own architects to assume responsibility for production details.

The Office of Public Works began the century with the construction of the new Milltown wing at the National Gallery and the restoration of the chapel ceiling at the Royal Hospital, Kilmainham, and it ends it with the construction of the new Clare Street extension to the Gallery and the restoration of the National Museum façade at Kildare Street – projects that act as fitting 'bookends' to a century of skill and quality in design by successive generations of OPW architects.

Continuity and Change in
the OPW, 1900–2000
Arthur Gibney

The origins of the Office of Public Works can be traced back as far as the seventeenth century to the office of the Engineer and Surveyor General of the Royal Works. The responsibilities of this office included the design, construction, repairs and maintenance of forts and fortifications (as Engineer General) and (as Surveyor General) state buildings such as the Royal Hospital, Kilmainham, the Royal Barracks, Dublin Castle and the Irish Parliament House. Notable holders of this office included architects of distinction such as Sir William Robinson (1671–1700), Thomas Burgh (1700–30) and Sir Edward Lovett Pearce (1730–3).

The terms of engagement of these Surveyors General were remarkably liberal. They were appointed by royal patent and they were only accountable to the crown through the viceregal administration. This allowed them considerable independence from parliamentary control, especially in the handling of building finance. They received a substantial salary and they were paid an additional sum to cover staff and office expenses. They also (up to the mid-eighteenth century) maintained a customary right to receive discounts from building contractors based on a percentage of their accounts. They were, as Edward McParland[1] has pointed out, directly engaged in the contractual process with the tradesman who carried out the work, acting in a sub-contractual capacity.

By the mid-eighteenth century the independence and lack of accountability of these Surveyors General had aroused resentment within the Irish political establishment. Accusations of misconduct in the management of an expensive regional barrack-building programme (1748–50) provoked a parliamentary enquiry which resulted in the disgrace and resignation of the Surveyor General, Arthur Jones Neville, in 1752. This provided the political initiative for reforms in the 1750s and the eventual abolition of the Surveyor General's office. This came in 1762 when the engineering responsibilities for fortifications were vested in the Board of Ordnance, and responsibilities for military and civic buildings was given to the former Barrack Board, which was then reconstituted under the new title of the Barrack Board and Board of Works.[2] This is recognisably the predecessor of today's Office of Public Works.

This Board was governed by seven commissioners who were mostly Members of Parliament, but day-to-day executive functions of the office were carried out by architects and surveyors. The architect Thomas Cooley filled the post of clerk and inspector of civil buildings from 1776 until 1784, and Francis Johnson occupied a similar position from 1805 until the 1820s. An important aspect of the reforms that accompanied the reconstitution of the Board was the pressure on fiscal control. The commissioners and the architects involved were engaged on a salaried basis and they received no payments from tradesmen engaged in the contractual process. This was an important step in the evolution of the architectural profession in Ireland and a code of practice based on a truly professional ethic.

Further reforms in the nineteenth century saw the removal of the Board's responsibility for barrack construction, a marked increase in engineering responsibilities and its reconstitution in 1831 – under three commissioners instead of seven – as the Board of Public Works. This title was in common use until the middle of the twentieth century.

Senior architects in the Board of Works have traditionally been involved in the advancement of the professional role of the architect since the 1830s. Jacob Owen, appointed Principal Engineer and Architect to the Board in 1833, became one of the first members of the Royal Institute of the Architects of Ireland in 1839 and acted as its vice-president from 1849 until 1867. In the twentieth century a considerable number of RIAI presidents were either Principal Architects or senior architects in the Board of Works. These included WH Howard Cooke in 1940–1, JM Fairweather in 1950–1, Gerald McNicholl in 1956–7, Oscar Richardson in 1978–9 and Martin Burke in 1982–3.

Our interest in this background is not solely historical but lies in a need to establish traditions which have influenced the OPW's operational policies over a long period. One persistent influence on professional staff was the Board's strong sense of accountability for cost estimates and budgetary controls because of the intense scrutiny of expenditure from the public purse. Another equally powerful pressure was the perceived need for high constructional standards in buildings which inevitably, over the years, have to be maintained and repaired by successive state architects out of that same purse.

This constructional ethic is particularly visible in many OPW buildings commissioned during the first half of the century. The massive solidity of early works such as Andrew Robinson's police station at Pearse Street (1915) is maintained in Howard Cooke's telephone exchange at Clontarf (1925), JM Fairweather's Garda stations at Donnybrook (1931) and Drumcondra (1933), JR Boyd-Barrett's Industry and Commerce Ministry in Kildare Street (1942) and Sydney Maskell's post office at Andrew Street (1940s). It is also reflected in the rational construction of generations of rural national schools built under Basil Boyd-Barrett's direction from the 1930s until the 1960s.

The prediction and control of building costs is not easily achieved, particularly in contracts where high building standards are strongly in demand. However, the huge volume of building work processed by OPW architects, the recurrent use of methods and materials and the repetitive building types produced can provide quantitative data which should contribute considerably to cost control. Outside the OPW there is a tendency among architects

1. Edward McParland, 'The office of the surveyor general in Ireland in the eighteenth century,' *Jour. Soc. Arch. Hist. G. Brit.* vol.38, (1995), 98.

2. *Ibid,* 92, 96.

to envy their state-employed colleagues the amplitude of their building budgets and the architectural opportunities these state budgets present. On the other hand, OPW architects must at times have resented the appointment of private consultants for the design of important state buildings.

On occasions the commissioners – or their political masters – felt that the special nature or importance of certain projects required the appointment of outside architectural consultants. This occurred on two occasions in the early part of the century. In 1904 the commission for the design of the College of Science/Government Offices complex in Merrion Street was given to the well-known English architect Sir Aston Webb, with TM Deane acting as local consultant. In 1912, following a competition limited to local architects, the commission for the design of University College Dublin, at Earlsfort Terrace, was awarded to RM Butler.

These external commissions and the obviously political basis for the appointment of an expatriate architect at Merrion Street may well have frustrated state-employed architects in the Board of Works. Under normal circumstances these design responsibilities would have been entrusted to senior architects such as Robert Cochrane, John Howard Pentland or Andrew Robinson. However, with hindsight, it is obvious that the subtle compositional refinements and civic qualities of both Webb's Merrion Street opus and Butler's university have fully vindicated their choice as designers for such important public works. The choice of JR Boyd-Barrett as architect for the Ministry of Industry and Commerce in Kildare Street in 1936 was also the result of an architectural competition.

Looking back at the buildings associated with the state over the first half of the twentieth century we can see a considerable uniformity of design approach in spite of a widely eclectic choice of expression. The early buildings up to the mid-1920s were remarkably confident in their handling of a full and varied repertoire of classical detail and ornament. Later buildings of the 1930s were more restrained in their architectural language often relying – like the Garda stations at Donnybrook, Drumcondra and Athlone – on compositional massing and axial planning to indicate a classical pedigree. By the 1940s the presence of classical motifs was almost vestigial and embedded in an architectural language which by this stage had merged into vernacular idiom.

Although state-employed architects were probably trying to come to terms with the spirit of the times we can find few direct references to the prevailing European zeitgeist and the modernist ideals which had emerged so strongly in Europe during this period. One exception, however, was Howard Cooke, who as Sean Rothery[3] points out, made strong use of art deco patterns in his post office in Rathmines in 1933. There were few examples of modernist inspiration among the works of private architects either. In 1935 the Commissioners of Public Works decided that the requirements of a proposed new ministry at Kildare Street were important enough to justify the involvement of a consultant architect and the project became an architectural competition. This must be seen

both as a means of securing another important civic building for the city, but also – as in all such competitions – an attempt to look at new ideas.

The results were disappointing. The winning scheme, designed by J R Boyd-Barrett, was conservative in character and its six-storey steel frame was hidden behind a pseudo-classical façade. The designs placed second, by Jones and Kelly, and third, by the architectural student Elenor Butler, were also based on classical precedents.

It is this immediate background which makes the sudden and unexpected quality of the 1937 design for a new Dublin Airport terminal at Collinstown so surprising. Only about a year separates the acceptance of Boyd-Barrett's competition-winning scheme for the Kildare Street ministry and the commissioning of designs for the airport. The Board of Works – disappointed, perhaps, at the routine result of the recent competition – decided to set up a special internal department to handle the airport terminal and the project was entrusted to a team of young architects under the leadership of the 26-year-old Desmond FitzGerald.

The design that emerged in 1937 was a perfect paradigm of the principles which governed the modernist aesthetic. The exposed concrete structure, the cantilevered slabs, the glazed curtain wall and continuous railed balconies proclaimed the terminal's immediate affinity with the International style. The plastic and structural characteristics of its concrete frame were fully exploited in its design; its internal volumes and surface cladding were free from structural constraints and its external form was a rational expression of its operational functions. This daring and imaginative building must have made a marked impact on local sensibilities at many levels. To many young architects it represented an elegant and rigorous expression of principles that brought Ireland into line with the forefront of European culture. To the public its hovering slabs and tapered cantilevers must have presented a metaphor for the freedom of flight itself and the future felicities of a better world.

To the OPW and to the architectural profession in Ireland, the airport terminal was a watershed and a threshold to a new era. Its design team leader, Desmond FitzGerald, was awarded the Triennial Gold Medal of the RIAI for the period 1938–40. Unfortunately, as Frederick O'Dwyer[4] points out, its completion on the eve of the second world war in 1939 prevented it getting the international recognition it deserved. However, it is recognised today as the only building of quality in an otherwise dull complex, and it remains as a monument to the idealist aspirations of its time and the team of young designers who produced it. FitzGerald's strong and forceful personality was obviously a key factor in the building's development but the later work in his long career in private practice never replicated the airport's elegant architectural language and he became known for his conservative architectural viewpoint.

Building activities were curtailed in Ireland during most of the 1940s because of shortages of materials, but planning and design

3. Sean Rothery, *Ireland and the new architecture 1900–1940*, Dub. (1991), 182–183.

4. Frederick O'Dwyer, 'The architecture of the Office of Public Works. 1831–1923,' in *Public Works*, Eds. Ciaran O'Connor and John O'Regan, Dub. (1987), 37.

of state projects continued. In 1940 Raymond McGrath, a well-known proponent of modern architectural theory, joined the Board of Works as a senior architect. McGrath, an Australian of Irish extraction, came to London on a fellowship in the 1920s and in the 1930s achieved an international reputation as one of the foremost designers in Britain. His talents and experience were quickly recognised by his superiors and he was entrusted with some of the most important projects under commission at the time.

His success as a designer and his remarkable skill as a draughtsman quickly earned his promotion and he was appointed Principal Architect on the retirement of JM Fairweather in 1948. He continued in this position until 1968.

In spite of McGrath's powerful position and the respect he enjoyed among his architectural colleagues, his career in the state service was somewhat unsuccessful. He was unfortunate in the fact that his most important projects were conceived during an era of economic gloom, and that their realisation was controlled by pragmatic politicians who were oblivious to the cultural values he espoused. He had a foretaste of such problems early in his career. In 1946 he became involved in the design of a national concert hall in the Rotunda Assembly Rooms and the adjoining gardens. This proposal was promoted by ministers in the ruling Fianna Fáil government, but they were voted out of office in 1948 and the project was abandoned. He started work on a major redevelopment plan for Dublin Castle in 1947, based on a range of modern buildings envisaged as a foil to the eighteenth-century precinct. On this occasion the scheme was approved by the new inter-party government in 1948, but abandoned by a succeeding Fianna Fáil administration in 1951. The most important opportunity in his career came in 1964 in the commission to design the 2000-seat Kennedy memorial concert hall. This was sponsored by a Fianna Fáil government under Sean Lemass, but supported by an all-party committee set up to ensure its delivery. This project took longer to die than its predecessors but its rejection was finally confirmed after the next change of government in 1974.

On the other hand, McGrath enjoyed great success as a decorator and interior designer and he excelled in the assembly of specially designed carpets, furnishings and fittings in period interiors. He had splendid opportunities in the 1950s and 1960s to exercise his skills in historic buildings in Ireland and in Irish embassies in London, Washington, Paris and Rome. He became involved in Áras an Uachtaráin in 1944 and over the next decade he acted as mentor and consultant to such architects as Percy le Clerc and Oscar Richardson in the considerable refurbishment of this state residence. In the 1960s he was consultant to Oscar Richardson and JB Maguire in the rebuilding of the State Apartments in Dublin Castle and he co-ordinated the decorative reinstatement of the eighteenth-century interiors in the apartments.

A new generation of Irish architects trained in the modern tradition joined the Board during the late 1940s and early 1950s and many traditional proposals prepared during the war years were updated and modernised prior to their construction. These included buildings such as the veterinary college in Ballsbridge and the post office in St Andrew's Street. The simplicity and dignity of the Curragh church, designed by Gerald McNicholl and Michael Curran, anticipated the new church architecture of the 1960s and 1970s. The involvement of Ronald Tallon and Bertie Banahan (working under the direction of A Seymour Rice) on post offices in Drogheda, Letterkenny and Cootehill in the mid-1950s introduced a new modernist idiom into these provincial towns. However, the slow progress of the Irish economy during these post-war decades did not encourage optimism and several talented architects such as Tallon and Banahan left the state service to pursue successful careers in private practice.

The repair, renovation and conservation of historic buildings have been an important part of the state architect's traditional role for over two centuries. The accumulated experience gained over the years by architects within the Board of Works have developed special resources and in the twentieth century architects such as Harold Leask, Percy le Clerc, David Slattery and Frederick O'Dwyer have emerged as specialists whose skills have been in demand by the state, by local authorities and by private clients.

One of the first tasks facing the newly established Irish Republic in 1922 was the restoration of public buildings such as the General Post Office, the Custom House and the Four Courts, which had been badly damaged during the 1916 rebellion and the civil war. This reconstruction work started in 1923 under the newly appointed principal architect TJ Byrne, but the considerable scale of the rebuilding programme prolonged these contracts until the mid-1930s.

The first stage in the ambitious OPW reconstruction programme for Dublin Castle started in 1961 with the rebuilding of the Cross-Block (1717) and the renovation of the adjoining early eighteenth-century State Apartments in the Upper Castle Yard. Oscar Richardson and JB Maguire received an RIAI Conservation Medal for this work in the 1970s. The first stage of the conservation programme of Kilkenny Castle – the Picture Gallery – also started in 1969 under the control of Martin Burke and John Cummings. In 1974, following the decision to abandon the Kennedy memorial hall, the OPW was asked to establish the feasibility of converting the Great Hall of UCD into a concert hall. Approval was given to proceed with the proposal in the late 1970s. The hall and the adjoining university foyer on Earlsfort Terrace were elegantly refurbished by a team led by Michael O'Doherty and the National Concert Hall held its first public performance in 1981.

In the 1980s two important historical restoration programmes were entrusted to private consultants. John Costello handled the massive restoration contract for William Robinson's Royal Hospital, Kilmainham (1680–5) and Austin Dunphy worked on William Chambers' neo-classic Casino at Marino (1758–76). Both architects were awarded RIAI Conservation Medals (1984–6) for the quality of their work. Serious problems with the Portland stone facing of Gandon's Custom House (1781–91) initiated a rigorous survey and a major restoration contract in 1984. The survey revealed that Gandon's use of the French system of iron armatures (to stabilise thin ashlar facings) had caused serious damage (due to expansion and corrosion of the iron) in the aftermath of the fire of 1921. The complicated task of stabilising and restoring the masonry and the cleaning of stone and statuary was handled with considerable success by David Slattery and Alastair Lindsay. Slattery and Lindsay were also involved in part of the second development programme in Dublin Castle involving the restoration of eighteenth-century buildings in the northern range.

This programme was a highly complex scheme to develop Dublin Castle as a national conference and exhibition centre and its fast-track contract was geared for completion in time for Ireland's EC presidency in 1990. The proposal involved the restoration of the eighteenth-century ranges to the north and west of the Upper Castle Yard and the addition of new buildings to house conference, exhibition and catering facilities. The rebuilding of the Bedford Tower and Guard House block has restored these buildings to their eighteenth-century configuration and ensured the symmetrical organisation of the entrance area by reinstating the use of the Gate of Fortitude to balance its neighbour, the Gate of Justice. The architects involved were Klaus Unger, Angela Rolfe and David Byers.

Working on historical monuments such as Charlesfort in Kinsale, the Royal Barracks or the ranges of Dublin Castle – all designed by former state architects such as William Robertson, Thomas Burgh and Thomas Eyre – must promote a strong sense of a received tradition within the OPW. In recent years the state has also been asked to take responsibility for a large number of private monuments such as Castletown House, Ross Castle, Portumna Castle and Trim Castle. This has developed a strong specialisation in the conservation process involving OPW architects such as John Cahill and David Wall and OPW architects who have been absorbed into Dúchas, the newly established heritage service, such as Paul McMahon, Grellan Rourke, Aighleann O'Shaughnessy and Willy Cumming.

The 1980s will be remembered in the OPW as a golden era of exciting development opportunities and enlightened government patronage which continued into the 1990s. Notable early projects were Klaus Unger and Michael Carroll's laboratories at Abbotstown, Stephen Kane and David Byers' government offices at Thurles and Geoff Johnston's elegantly designed telephone exchange at Priory Park. Admirable also were the experiments with native timber construction resulting in the rigorously designed holiday complex at Killykeen Forest and the twin timber pavilions in St Stephen's Green designed by Noel de Chenu and Ciaran O'Connor.

A notable characteristic of OPW architecture during the 1980s was the emergence of new stylistic ideas based on the changing architectural images projected in the work of some international architects. This was particularly noticeable in the work of younger designers. The practice of entrusting important projects to young architects was not unusual in the OPW and we have already seen the successful results of such a policy in the design of the Dublin Airport terminal in the late 1930s.

Like the modernist designers of the 1930s, this generation of young architects promoted new cultural ideals imported from Europe and America. They were strongly influenced by design theories exemplified in the work of post-modern architects such as Robert Krier, James Stirling and Michael Graves. The emergence of these stylistic images in OPW buildings during this period was undoubtedly due to freedom given to the *jeunesse dorée* to express cultural preferences. The most successful use of this post-modern imagery is probably seen in the Children's Court at Smithfield, where the combination of fine materials, carefully chosen details and a monumental expression make a powerful architectural statement, although its choice of visual expression is hardly appropriate for a children's court. Less successful architecturally are buildings such as the regional Garda headquarters in Cork city. Here the difficulty in reconciling the classical monumentality of its composition with contemporary scale and materials is apparent.

We might also question the use of a post-modern language in the new contemporary extensions (Castle Hall and the conference centre) in Dublin Castle. The use of decorative ironwork, two-toned ashlar facings, cornices and column capitals make interesting architectural statements on their own, but they share an uneasy relationship with the classical syntax of the eighteenth-century surroundings. A more austere and less assertive architectural language might have been more successful.

Recent buildings completed in the 1990s are particularly interesting and some have made a considerable public impact. The magic of Mary MacKenna's visitor centre at the Céide Fields has captured the popular imagination and won the RIAI Triennial Gold Medal for 1992–4. The conversion of Sir Aston Webb's imposing College of Science into the Taoiseach's office in Merrion Street has added a new civic dimension to the state's identity and provided Dublin with an imagery associated with the Elysée Palace and the Fauburg St Honoré. This has resulted in the award of the RIAI Conservation Medal for 1989–92 to Noel de Chenu and the architectural team of Klaus Unger, Angela Rolfe and David Byers. There are other, later projects, such as the restored glass houses at the Botanic Gardens and the new museum at Collins Barracks which are equally exciting. These buildings and other millennium projects nearing completion may well ensure the OPW's dominance of the architectural award system until well into the first decade of the twenty-first century.

Architecture in Independent Ireland
Terence Brown

In the Lestrygonians episode of *Ulysses* (the episode which employs architecture as a preoccupying motif) Leopold Bloom allows himself a jaundiced reverie on his native city and on Ireland's architectural inheritance in general. Bloom ponders

> Houses, lines of houses, streets, miles of pavements, piled up bricks, stones... Piled up in cities, worn away age after age. Pyramids in sand. Big stones left. Round towers. Rest rubble, sprawling suburbs, jerry built, Kerwan's mushroom houses, built of breeze. Shelter for the night.

His apparently random stream of consciousness in this passage is deceptive, for through Bloom's interior monologue in this episode Joyce is entering not only a critique of Dublin's burgeoning twentieth-century suburban blight, but highlighting some of the challenges the architectural imagination had to confront in an independent Ireland. (*Ulysses* was published in 1922, the year in which the Irish Free State came into existence.)

Architecture in this passage is associated not only with the crass opportunism of the jerry-built, but with the grand state projects built on a foundation of slavery. Babylon, Pharaonic Egypt, dynastic China are analogues here of Ascendancy power, which gave the city of Dublin many of its principal buildings but left an abiding sense among the island's majority population that Augustan grandeur and Georgian elegance of manner in Ireland were memorials of historic suffering, stony reminders of helotry and imperial power. And when the architectural imagination ranged the Irish landscape for guidance as to what might constitute a more fully indigenous public building style than that bequeathed by the Georgian age it met, as well as ubiquitous ruination, only standing stones, round towers, which together had offered the nineteenth century the possibility of an architectural Celticism and, in the latter case, the inspiration for a local expression of the medieval revivalism of the age. The problem with the Hiberno-Romanesque, however, was that it had become wearisomely hackneyed by the early twentieth century, with public houses as well as cathedrals asserting their national credentials in an Irish florescence of the medieval mania. Again Joyce was alert to architectural history. Barney Kiernan's pub in Little Britain Street (in the Cyclops episode of *Ulysses*) is the object of withering satire as it is blessed by the Reverend Father O'Flynn in the saintly company of Malachi and Patrick:

> ...the celebrant blessed the house and censed the mullioned windows and the groynes and the vaults and the arrises and the capitals and the pediments and the cornices and the engrailed arches and the spires and the cupolas and sprinkled the lintels thereof with blessed water...

To add to the difficulties Ireland faced in developing inherited idioms in the 1920s there were those ready to make architecture sharply political. W B Yeats, for example, in defiance of national sentiment and in face of much incendiary violence unleashed against the Ascendancy's houses during the troubled times, chose in the early years of Irish independence to celebrate the 'big houses' of the Irish countryside as sites of self-delighting civilisation, for all the political noxiousness of their origins. His vision of architectural exploit in the circumstances was grandly offensive as he imagined in his poem 'Meditations in Time of Civil War' (first published in 1923, the year he was awarded the Nobel prize) how in the turbulent yet heroic past 'some powerful man /Called architect and artist in' to 'rear in stone /The sweetness that all longed for night and day'.

A writer in *The Catholic Bulletin* (a journal of Irish Ireland polemic whose editor was influential with advanced nationalist opinion of the day) in the same year offered a different perspective on the Yeatsian ideal of eighteenth-century achievement. He noted how 'the big house..., set stockily on one side of the landscape, with its bleak white walls, its rows of blank windows, a lumpy mass of ugliness' was 'utterly out of keeping with the spacious realms of God's work into which it obtruded'. For this aroused nationalist the big house of the Irish countryside

> matches with the men who built it: they and their works had and have nothing in common with the country they dominated over... the big house abides today; like its owners, it is now a sorry emblem of what they did and failed to do...

And because the Georgian town houses of Dublin were built by the same overweening caste, they too were symbols of an Ascendancy which had 'lost the war'. And the Ascendancy overlords 'were literally the architects of their own ruin'.

In the absence of a secure sense of an appropriate national style, architecture as a public art form languished in newly independent Ireland. In 1926 one commentator noted in *The Irish Statesman*, in an article entitled 'Nationality in Architecture', how Irish building offered merely a provincial version of mediocre English practice,

> ...because a popular knowledge and appreciation of architecture... is as moribund in Ireland as it is in England... The average educated Irishman is as completely ignorant of the elements of architectural quality as is the Englishman.

And in 1929, despite much reconstruction, which the violent birth of the new state had necessitated (the Office of Public Works was responsible for the rebuilding of the GPO, the Four Courts and the Custom House in Dublin), another commentator lamented in the same periodical (in an article on 'The Importance of Architecture to Ireland') that

During the last twenty years there has been throughout the entire world a vast revival of architectural taste... To this great movement Ireland has given no attention worth speaking of. An improvement in the average style of building; the visits and addresses of a few prominent architects show that she has begun to yawn and shake herself; but as yet she has produced nothing national or characteristic, on a scale sufficient to attract notice.

So grim indeed was the architectural prospect in the new state that R M Butler, Professor of Architecture in University College, Dublin, in the official handbook of Saorstát Éireann, issued in 1932, assessing the country's architectural heritage, was forced to conclude lamely:

...few buildings, ecclesiastical or secular, have been erected in more recent years in Ireland, a remarkable falling off from the high traditions of the eighteenth and early nineteenth centuries.

The architectural imagination of the country was in fact calibrated at this stage of Irish history on a domestic not a public scale, which further inhibited discussion and implementation of large-scale public projects. This limitation of focus is evidenced in the Saorstát Éireann publication, which was a handsomely illustrated volume with reproductions of paintings and with sketches and woodcuts amplifying the sense of social and cultural success it wished to generate in its prose entries. (The Department of Industry and Commerce commissioned the volume.) Yet, tellingly, there is only one illustration of a truly modern building in the book, that of the power station on the Shannon at Ardnacrusha, completed in 1929. By contrast with that construction's somewhat brutalist, functional façades, the volume offers repeated images of the Irish countryside in works by such as Paul Henry and Maurice MacGonigal, in which white-washed cottages nestle in their landscapes, in touch with nature, but offering the intimacies of a close-knit rural community to protect against her more cruel moods.

It was, after all, a period in which Daniel Corkery in a widely read book of 1925, *The Hidden Ireland*, had declared that everywhere literature was 'creeping back to the national hearth'.

And when Éamon de Valera took over the Free State's government in 1932/3 it was with the avowed, if impracticable, aim of settling thousands of new families on the land upon which the majority of citizens already depended for their living. It was no time for anything but slum clearance in the capital city and for the construction of modest domestic dwelling houses in a country already predominantly rural in social complexion. Fianna Fáil's bucolic Utopianism struck a chord in a society that considered urban life an essentially alien intrusion on Irish civilisation and this militated against architectural innovation in the cities.

Throughout the nineteenth century, the Board of Public Works had been responsible for a wide variety of public architectural projects. Indeed, when the Free State government took over part of Leinster House (the property in Kildare Street, Dublin, of the Royal Dublin Society) in September 1922, to use for meetings of the Dáil, it was surrounded by the Board's last great Victorian achievements – the National Museum and the National Library – while in the first decades of the twentieth century the Board had added the adjacent Merrion Street complex of Government Buildings and the College of Science (completed just before the transfer of power to the new administration).

The Board of Works continued its work under the new dispensation as the Office of Public Works, even if its ambitions were reined in by a government made intently cost-conscious by the straitened economic conditions of the 1920s and '30s. All over the country there were Garda stations, post offices and schools to be built. The latter of these drew on the simple nineteenth-century model of the national school building. For the rest, the Office of Public Works supplied the nation with sturdy, serviceable and durable public buildings that settled inconspicuously into their surroundings. In a cultural climate that was generally uninterested in architectural matters (literary and linguistic concerns were the staples of cultural debate in the period) and where overstated references to past styles could easily carry ambiguous political messages, such modest employment of means to meet practical purpose was well judged. The OPW earned the trust of official and public Ireland alike and went about its business with an unemphatic classicism as a characteristic idiom.

Two projects stand out from this period of sensible discretion. At the end of 1938 work began on the construction, under the direction of the Office of Public Works, of a new building to house the department of Industry and Commerce in Kildare Street. This building boldly echoed the austere, monumental classicism that had been adopted by Fascist and democratic states alike in the 1930s to express both impressively functional modern power and proper respect for the past. Completed in 1942, it remains one of the Irish state's most fully-realised twentieth-century buildings.

A panel over the main entrance to that building depicts Lugh, mythological god of the sun, releasing a flight of aeroplanes from his left hand, and it was in fact aviation that released the OPW in the late 1930s from its customary conservatism, allowing it to throw caution to the winds. In what was then a green-field site (in which there was almost no built environment to inhibit invention) at Collinstown, Co Dublin, the OPW saluted the technological age with an airport building that was the Irish state's elegant tribute to international modernism. Now dwarfed by more recent buildings, it marks a moment in the nation's history when a public building first expressed unalloyed enthusiasm for the challenge of contemporary experience.

If the tradition of the OPW in independent Ireland has been one of civic pragmatism and responsible efficiency within strict financial limits, the economic advances the country has enjoyed since accession to the European Community in 1973 has meant that it has been called upon in the last two decades to undertake major tasks of conservation and reconstruction. The kinds of cultural and political sensitivities that might once have made some of these seem dubious enterprises no longer affect the public mood. Georgian and eighteenth-century Dublin is now understood to be just as much a testimony to the genius of Irish artisans and craft workers as a symbol of superseded power. The Royal Hospital, Kilmainham, with its British military associations, has been adapted to house a museum of modern art. Even so resonantly iconic an edifice as Dublin Castle has been magnificently restored by the OPW to act as a kind of palimpsest in stone of the Irish historical experience of conquest and rebellion and to serve as a notable official and public facility.

The OPW now does its work in a distinctly conservationist climate. And restoration and conservation involve existing buildings being put to imaginative new purposes (as, for example, Collins Barracks in Dublin to house the nation's repository of folk artifacts). For it is widely recognised in modern Ireland that when Yeats's 'violent' man 'called architect and artist in', the artist at least was almost certainly Irish. To conserve and use creatively what Irish craft and artistic skill have bequeathed to the nation is now taken for granted as legitimate, indeed vital, public policy. So Leopold Bloom, who mentions an official of the old Board of Public Works in the episode of *Ulysses* in which he inveighs against the architecture of Dublin at the beginning of the century, would surely have a good word to say for its successor body at the century's end, and for the built environment it has helped to restore, conserve and create.

The Architecture of State Buildings. OPW: Ireland 1900–2000

Part 1: Selected Major Works

Office of Public Works Head Office
51 St Stephen's Green, Dublin 1912

Towards the start of the twentieth century, the OPW converted number 51 St Stephen's Green into its new headquarters. The building, on the east side of the Green, occupies the site of the seventeenth-century residence of the Monck family. Having been purchased by the government in 1848, it became the Museum of Irish Industry — forty examples of Irish marble which line the walls of the foyer date to this period. The museum was later amalgamated with the Royal College of Science. In 1911, new accommodation for the college was completed at Upper Merrion Street, and the OPW adapted its former premises on St Stephen's Green for its own use.

Royal College of Science and Government Buildings

Upper Merrion Street, Dublin

1904–22 and 1990

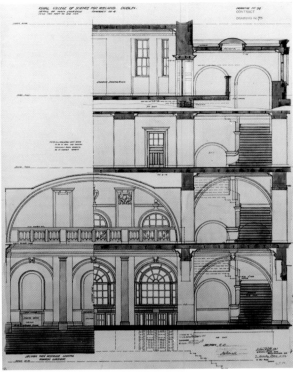

The imposing complex of the Royal College of Science and State Offices on Upper Merrion Street was the last major architectural scheme undertaken by the British administration in Ireland. It was designed for two new government departments, the Local Government Board, and the Department of Agriculture and Technical Instruction, as well as the Royal College of Science, then housed in 51 St Stephen's Green. Ironically, the complex was completed in March 1922, and was immediately occupied by the new Irish Free State government. In more recent times, the building has been converted and entirely refurbished to form modern accommodation for a number of departments, including the Department of the Taoiseach.

1904–22

John Howard Pentland, Principal Surveyor, had completed considerable groundwork by the time of the 1903 Act of Parliament sanctioning this project, and as a result, King Edward VII laid the foundation stone as early as April 1904, shortly after the renowned London architect Aston Webb was appointed project architect. Thomas Manly Deane, who had recently completed work at the National Gallery of Ireland, was appointed executant architect.

The dramatically 'Edwardian baroque' buildings are arranged around a square quadrangle. The college, inaugurated by King George V in 1911, occupied the western half of the site, where its lecture theatres and laboratories were furthest from the disruptive effects of street traffic. Architecturally, it is the centrepiece of the composition,

its colossal Ionic portico and dome visible through the columnar screen on the street elevation. The balancing north and south wings were completed in March 1922, following the demolition of numbers 1–13 Upper Merrion Street.

Public opinion impelled the architects to give an undertaking that four-fifths of all building materials would be of Irish origin, and Wicklow granite is employed externally, with superior Portland stone detailing. Allegorical sculptural figures above the parapet and portal screen were executed by Albert Power. The interior demonstrated the use of the latest advances in building technology. Steel and reinforced concrete were used in the construction, and electric power installed throughout, along with elevators, ventilation fans, and turf-fired central heating.

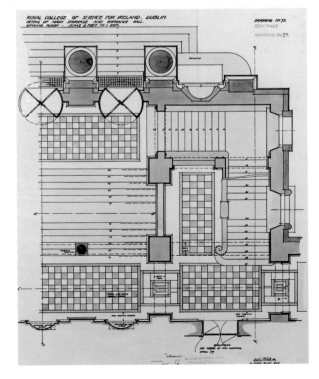

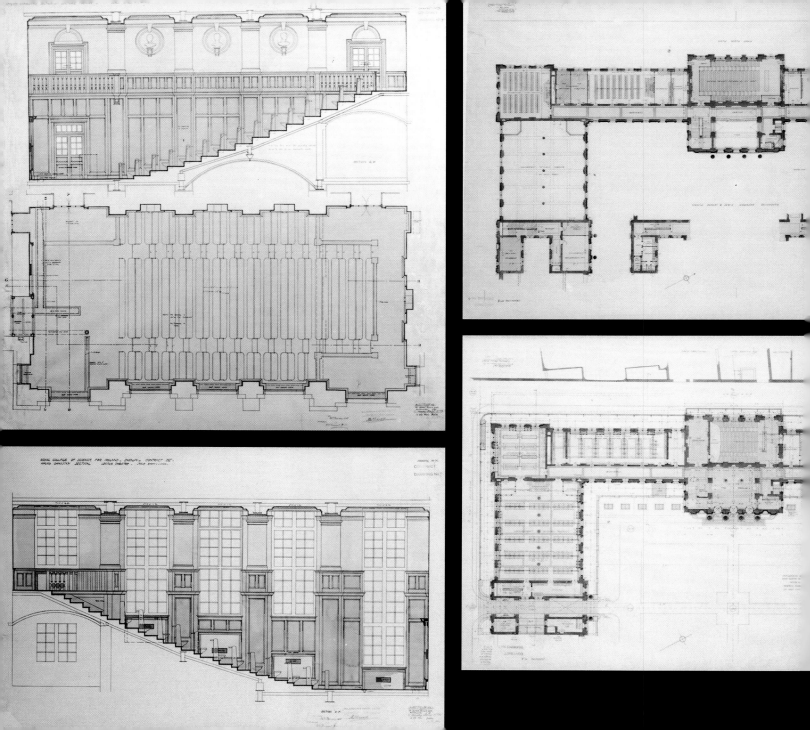

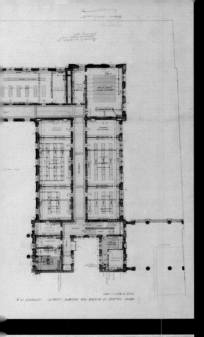

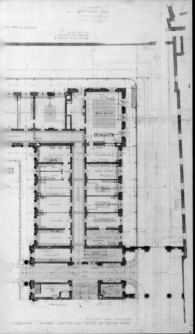

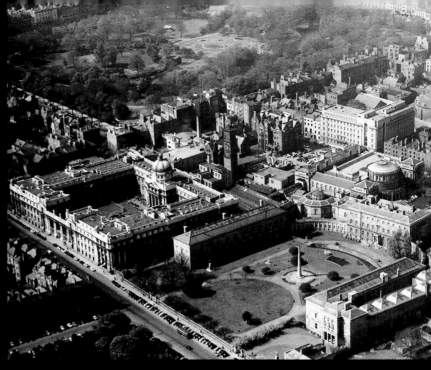

1990

The Royal College of Science (which had merged with UCD in the 1920s) transferred to new campus facilities at Belfield in 1989. Commencing immediately, and with a sensitivity of design and respect for the building's historic inheritance, the OPW converted the former laboratories and lecture theatres into offices suitable for the transaction of government business at the highest level, with state-of-the-art environmental conditioning, electronics, information technology and communications. The project was completed in 1990, and occupied by the Department of the Taoiseach.

Exterior treatment

Using techniques perfected at the Custom House project (see page 56), the external stonework was meticulously cleaned, revealing attractive bands of darker stone under the parapet. The courtyard was given a simple treatment, with salvaged tram-setts used to form the peripheral carriageway and car-parking bays, and the central area divided into four grassed lawns. A low-level water feature, in scale with the surroundings, is positioned at the intersection of the granite paths, and lime trees were planted to soften the landscape. The entrance steps were reshaped and carried forward, to create a more dignified entrance and a podium for receiving guests.

Staircase

The cool, bright entrance hall has been visually extended by breaking through the wall of the former principal lecture theatre beyond, and strengthening the floor to accommodate a ceremonial stairway. The focus of this warm, inner hall is the stained glass window by Evie Hone called 'My Four Green Fields'. It was originally commissioned by the Department of Industry and Commerce for the Irish government's pavilion at the 1939 New York World Trade Fair. It depicts the four provinces of Ireland, and, though the composition is primarily abstract, emblems and symbols can be clearly distinguished. Its luminous colours are reflected in the warm beechwood balustrading and panelling, and vibrant carpet commissioned from artist Mary FitzGerald.

The first floor houses the offices of the Taoiseach and his advisors, conference rooms and the government secretariat. Here, the architectural intention was to interpret the feeling of the strong external façades, to maintain the sense of expectancy from outside to inside, and to provide spaces and rooms of dignity, commensurate with the status of the occupants and their guests. Plastered panelled walls and coffered ceilings, panelled doors and heavy architraves and chair-rails (carrying the electrics and communications) combine to give a sense of scale and texture to the rooms. Materials used throughout the building are in the main of Irish manufacture, and specially designed and manufactured furniture was commissioned, using native Irish timber. Contemporary art works supplied by the OPW and the Arts Council enhance the walls of all the rooms and corridors.

The remaining two storeys accommodate cellular offices. A principal feature of the basement is the specially created press centre, fully equipped with sound enhancement, recording facilities, television broadcasting, simultaneous interpretation, autocue, and slide projection.

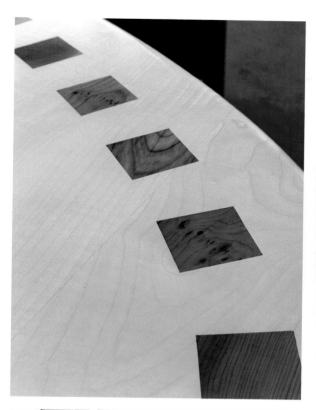

Awards

Government Buildings has won a number of awards commending the project and its improved access for the disabled, including the RIAI Silver Medal for Conservation for the period 1987–92. The citation commented that 'the re-use of this existing building of acknowledged quality for this new, and entirely fitting purpose, has created a special identity for Government, and has contributed considerably to Dublin's status as a European capital.'

National Gallery of Ireland
Merrion Square, Dublin

The National Gallery of Ireland was founded partly to commemorate the significant contribution of William Dargan to the success of the Dublin Exhibition of 1853. When formalised by an Act of Parliament in 1854, the site chosen was that of the exhibition: Leinster Lawn, overlooking Merrion Square. The building was designed by Captain Francis Fowke RE in 1858, who reworked earlier designs by Charles Lanyon.

The elevations echoed those of Frederick Clarendon's Natural History Museum (1857) on the south side of the Lawn, with the addition of a one-storey entrance hall on the east elevation. It incorporated two principal exhibition spaces – the Sculpture Hall and Queen's Gallery – and four small galleries for cabinet pictures. Fowke's experience of working on the design of the South Kensington Museum (the V&A) in London shows in his advanced treatment of ventilation, heating, gas lighting and floor construction in the National Gallery of Ireland.

The gallery was officially opened by the Lord Lieutenant in January 1864.

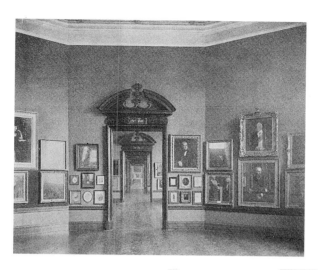

The 1968 wing

By the early 1960s, the gallery was home to over 6000 paintings and 2000 prints. Extension plans were drawn up in 1962 and the so-called 1968 wing (because the work was completed in that year), a reinforced concrete structure extending from the Merrion Square façade of the existing building to Clare Lane, added approximately 45,000 square feet to the gallery, increasing the display area by 50%. It incorporated an art library, conservation workshops, an auditorium, cloakrooms, lavatories and a restaurant, which opened onto an outdoor sculpture court. The wide helical staircase at the northeast corner of the building is possibly the most striking feature of the new wing. It was designed with spacious landings arranged for the display of paintings and sculpture at successive levels, so that it forms in itself a display area and an interesting progression from gallery to gallery.

The Milltown wing

The Milltown wing, completed in 1903, effectively doubled the available exhibition space. It was designed primarily to accommodate a gift by the Countess of Milltown of over two hundred family paintings and pieces of furniture from Russborough House. Designed by Sir Thomas Deane and his son, the new section is parallel to the original Dargan wing, extending westwards from the entrance hall. The extension added a new portico and entrance hall, office accommodation, and the Milltown Rooms, which comprise the suite of six handsome octagonal galleries on the ground floor and corresponding square galleries on the floor above.

A comprehensive OPW review of the gallery in 1984 highlighted deficiencies in the environmental conditions, disabled access, and the security and safety of the building for staff, visitors and art works. A master plan was drawn up as a result, detailing an extensive refurbishment of the premises, which was realised between 1985 and 1996.

The interior of the 1968 wing, renamed the north wing, was entirely remodelled, greatly increasing its hanging space. On the ground level, the area has been divided into five bays along an arcade, while a series of differently sized rooms were created on the first floor to accommodate the Spanish, Dutch and Flemish works. The galleries in the 1864 and 1903 wings were also refurbished in line with regulations regarding, lighting, security and fire, while respecting the way they had been designed by their original architects.

The former outdoor sculpture courtyard was glazed over to form an atrium, designed as a street space for the public with its different scales and different elements, and as a focus for social events and receptions. The atrium links two of the wings with the restaurant, gallery shop and print gallery and creates a series of successful circulation routes for the visitor.

Two Georgian terrace houses on Merrion Square have been integrated into the new gallery network for use as admininstrative offices, and the private rear garden was landscaped by David Lambert. The basement contains a new library, fully accessible by the disabled through an underground tunnel from the main building. The installation of a hydraulically operated lift in the well of the oval staircase has permitted disabled visitors to access all floors of the gallery.

Opened in 1999, the Yeats Room occupies a space in the Dargan wing which was initially intended for Marsh's Library, before their eighteenth-century premises in St Patrick's Close were restored. On display here are paintings and sketches by members of the Yeats family, as well as archival material donated to the gallery by Anne Yeats.

The Millennium wing

The UK practice of Benson & Forsyth was selected, in a restricted competition, to design a major new wing on Clare Street (below). It consists of three main levels over basement to provide additional gallery space reserved for international travelling exhibitions and the gallery's own in-house shows, a suite of new rooms to facilitate the display of pictures from the gallery's permanent collection, improved visitor facilities and conservation services. Other public facilities included are an audiovisual room, bookshop and a winter garden restaurant. Additional floorspace will total some 4000 square metres.

Housing for Ex-Servicemen
1919

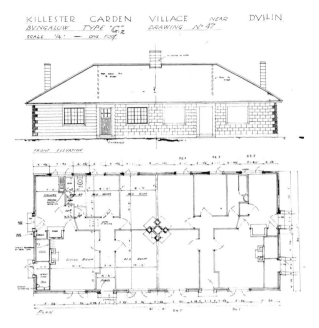

The Irish Land (Provision for Sailors and Soldiers) Act of December 1919 aimed to provide housing for some of the 80,000 Irish World War I veterans as part of a broader demobilisation programme. Similar schemes were initiated in Britain, but the government believed the Act would have a particularly beneficial effect in Ireland, where it was believed it could help to dissuade ex-soldiers from joining the IRA.

The Irish Local Government Board, which administered the scheme, proposed to establish small 'colonies' of loyal ex-servicemen scattered throughout rural Ireland, each family owning a modest plot of land and a home of an unprecedentedly high standard in comparison with that allowed under all previous public housing acts. The OPW was entrusted with their design and construction.

Initially intended to encourage rural revitalisation, the provisions of the Act were extended to urban areas in August 1920, which precipitated many thousands of extra applications. The preferential treatment extended to ex-servicemen, at a time of widespread housing problems and shortages, was inevitably a controversial policy among Irish nationalists, who likened the scheme to a second 'plantation'. Consequently, the new Irish Free State government refused to accept financial responsibility for the continuation of the programme.

The Irish Soldiers and Sailors Land Trust was formed in January 1924 to this end, by which time the OPW had completed almost 2000 homes. Over the next decade, the trust saw this number double as they continued to build, but to modified architectural designs.

Killester

The largest example of the developments reserved for ex-servicemen is at Killester in north County Dublin. The scheme comprised 247 houses embodying the latest principles of garden suburb design. The layout was engineered by Frank C Mears, the Scottish town planner, respecting many of the site's existing landscape features. Three distinct neighbourhoods were formed: the Demesne contains mainly five-room houses of just over 1000 square feet, aimed at commissioned officers; and the Middle Third and Abbeyfield were on a smaller scale, for men of other ranks.

All the houses are single-storeyed, mostly semi-detached with hipped roofs and gardens front and rear.

In the initial stages, the construction was the subject of a relief scheme employing war veterans under the supervision of a retired royal engineer, and each house cost £1500 – well above the estimated average of £900. Late in 1920, the OPW took direct control of the project, deciding to adopt the relatively novel concrete block system of construction, and entered negotiations with building contractors. The Killester estate was completed in August 1923.

Dún Laoghaire

The twenty-four houses on Library Road, Dún Laoghaire (1923) sought to emulate a decorative device that had recently been employed by Liverpool Corporation. The concrete blocks were cast with differently coloured facings in shades of light red, white, blue, blue-black and grey, and finished by hand after removal from the mould, to add texture. *The Irish Times* (of 20 September 1923) remarked that 'this is a distinct departure in concrete construction in Ireland, and gives a colour effect at once pleasing and unique'. A dramatic roof line and red roof tiles completed the effect. The design was reused at other sites, such as Sandymount Road, Co Dublin, and Nenagh, Co Tipperary.

Palmerstown

Robin Villas in Palmerstown, Co Dublin, is a more typical example of the OPW's housing for ex-servicemen built in the period 1920–3. The simple semi-detached plan accommodates three bedrooms, a living room and a scullery in a lean-to on the gable end. This type was repeated in many rural areas, such as Roscrea, Co Tipperary, Crosshaven, Co Mayo, Randalstown, Co Antrim, and Whiteabbey in Belfast.

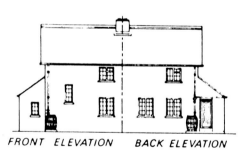

FRONT ELEVATION   BACK ELEVATION

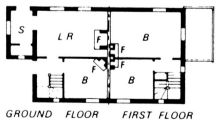

GROUND FLOOR   FIRST FLOOR

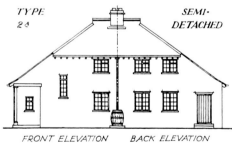

TYPE 24   SEMI-DETACHED

FRONT ELEVATION   BACK ELEVATION

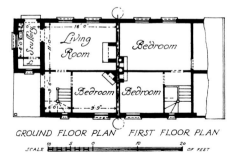

GROUND FLOOR PLAN   FIRST FLOOR PLAN

SCALE ▮▮▮▮▮ OF FEET

NORTHERN IRELAND AND THE IRISH FREE STATE.

Sup. area 722 ft.

Leinster House
Kildare Street, Dublin

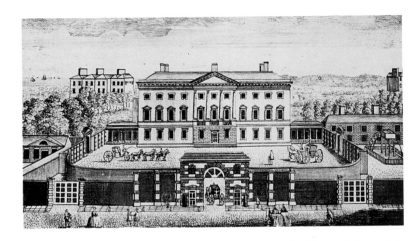

Dáil Éireann (the Irish parliament), together with Seanad Éireann (the Senate) and the President of Ireland, makes up the Oireachtas, which is the Irish legislature. There are 166 *teachtaí dála* or Dáil deputies and 60 senators. Both houses of the Oireachtas are accommodated in Leinster House.

Leinster House was originally the town residence of James FitzGerald, Earl of Kildare, and was known as Kildare House until his elevation to the Dukedom of Leinster in the 1760s. Constructed between 1745 and *c* 1748, Leinster House is the work of Richard Cassells, who had extensively remodelled Carton House, the FitzGeralds' country mansion in Kildare, in the 1730s. Towards the end of the eighteenth century, Leinster House was described as 'the most stately private edifice in the city, pleasantly situated at the south-east extremity of the town…enjoying in the tumult of a noisy metropolis, all the retirement of the country' (James Malton, *A Picturesque and Descriptive View of the City of Dublin*, London, 1794)

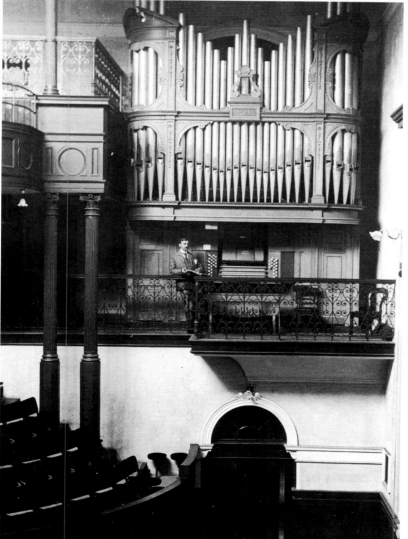

RDS theatre

The third duke sold the house to the [Royal] Dublin Society in 1815. During its occupancy, the RDS constructed a 700-seat lecture theatre linked to the southern façade of the house. Opened in 1897, it was well equipped, with electric lighting, an organ, a laboratory bench for practical demonstrations, and cinematic projector.

Oireachtas conversion

The Minister for Finance, Michael Collins, took the decision to establish Dáil Éireann in the lecture theatre of the RDS headquarters in 1922. Simultaneously, the Senate convened in part of the National Museum, other areas of which were adapted for temporary use as offices and committee rooms for the Oireachtas staff. The unsatisfactory nature of this arrangement prompted the OPW to prepare alternative plans for the conversion of the Royal Hospital, Kilmainham (see page 114).

However, in the summer of 1924, the OPW negotiated the acquisition of the whole of Leinster House for the sum of £68,000. The alterations carried out to accommodate the Oireachtas between 1924 and 1926 involved few structural interventions, and the house retains virtually all its original layout and character. Other minor works were effected over the next few years, including the addition of a restaurant (1929), reconstruction of the Dáil public gallery (1931) and an extension towards Kildare Place (1932).

Senate

The Senate meets in the former salon or picture gallery on the *piano nobile*, or first floor. It extends the full depth of the house (24ft) and is situated at the north end with a generous bow window to maximise the available daylight. The walls are plain, in keeping with its original function, but the FitzGerald collection of Old Master paintings were not part of the sale in 1815. The fine stucco ceiling, the most ornate in the house, is attributed to James Wyatt, and designed in the Adams style, which is characterised by precise symmetry and the use of classical motifs.

The senators are seated in semi-circular rows on axis with the window recess, in which is placed the Cathaoirleach's chair. Galleries at either end of the room are provided for visitors, and the media.

Structural investigations in the Senate chamber in 1985 revealed serious distortion in the supporting framework, which was threatening the delicate stucco work. A major reconstruction of much of the north wing of the building was necessary, followed by plasterwork restoration and redecoration. This work was completed in 1989.

The Dáil chamber

The Victorian lecture theatre still houses the Dáil chamber. During the conversion project, the capacity of the octagonal chamber was reduced to less than 200 and the floor level was raised. Five rows of seats descend in tiers to the floor, accessed by a corridor which encircles the whole chamber. Along the back wall is gallery seating for the media and political correspondents, in front of which is the Ceann Comhairle's dais. The government occupies seats to the left of the chair, and the main opposition party is seated to the right. The mahogany furnishings were made by the craftsman James Hicks to OPW designs.

Cenotaph on Leinster Lawn

The granite obelisk on Leinster Lawn (1950) replaces an earlier timber-and-plaster cenotaph which paid homage to Michael Collins and Arthur Griffith. The 65-foot tall obelisk surmounted by a gilt bronze flame acknowledges its formal architectural environment and harmonises with the stonework of Leinster House. Incorporated into the circular plinth are bronze portrait plaques of Collins, Griffith and O'Higgins by Laurence Campbell. The architect simultaneously reworked the surrounding lawn, designing a still pool with a shell-shaped fountain basin, and granite benches.

Alterations 1962–8

An office and restaurant block south of the Dáil chamber, visible from Kildare Place, was built between 1962 and 1968 to meet pressing needs for accommodation. The reinforced concrete-framed building is six storeys high over a basement, connected at ground and first floor levels to the older structures of Leinster House. It incorporates extensive new dining areas, as well as offices.

In the mid-1990s, the members' and visitors' restaurants and bar facilities in the Leinster House extension block were completely refurbished, providing upgrading of services, full wheelchair access and an improved ambience for both diners and catering staff. The self-service restaurant was replanned with three separate servery counters, screened from the dining area by a timber and glass screen. Banquette and other styles of seating cater for the lone diner as well as for larger groups.

The members' restaurant caters for both houses of the Oireachtas. The design objective was to provide a bright airy environment with the optimum of natural light and pleasant views, with the ability to transform into a more relaxed and subtly lit space for evening functions. Large, ceremonial-style doors lead into a marble-floored lobby and cloakroom, providing a sense of arrival and welcome. The window wall was subdivided into three large windows by dummy polished plaster columns. The opposite wall features a mural by Tom Curtin depicting the mythical tale of Fionn and Sadhbh.

New Oireachtas building
In November 1997, the government approved a proposal to construct a new Oireachtas building as a result of a significant number of new functions and requirements, particularly the expanding committee system. It had been apparent for several years that the Oireachtas was in need of additional modern accommodation and facilities if it was to fulfil its brief as a democratic parliament in the new millennium. The chosen site is between Leinster House, the National Library and the National Gallery, formerly occupied by the National College of Art and Design. The OPW was asked to implement this decision, and substantive works began on site in 1998.

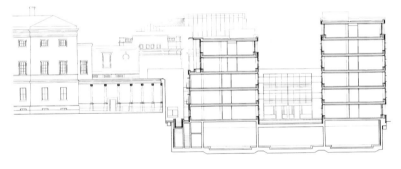

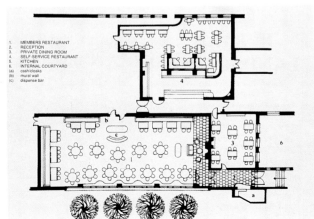

1. MEMBERS RESTAURANT
2. RECEPTION
3. PRIVATE DINING ROOM
4. SELF-SERVICE RESTAURANT
5. KITCHEN
6. INTERNAL COURTYARD
(a) cash/cloaks
(b) mural wall
(c) dispense bar

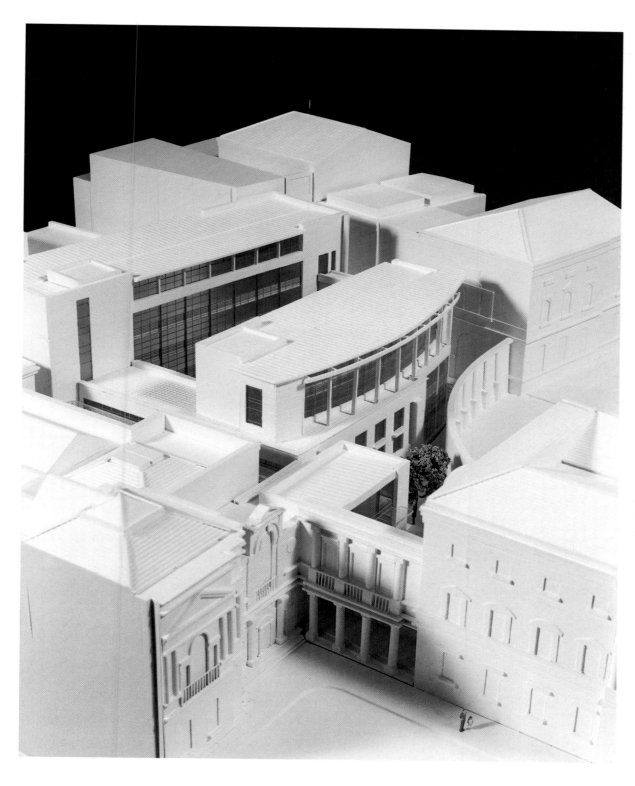

The new complex consists of two interlinked blocks laid out around a central garden and landscaped courtyard. The main public entrance will be from Kildare Street, through a new double-height classical-style screen. This addition will mirror the existing façade, which links Leinster House with the National Museum, and will complete the symmetry of this historic enclosure.

The scale of the 'front' block facing south towards Leinster Lawn has been carefully evaluated so as to avoid dominating its rich architectural milieu. This block of five storeys over basement will be substantially screened by the existing wall which links the house with the National Gallery, so only the top two floors will be visible from Merrion Square. Its receding curved profile is designed to act as a visual counterbalance to the older curved wall, and the elevation will be finished in stone to complement its surroundings. In all, the new developments will provide the Oireachtas with an extra 9000 square metres of accommodation.

GPO and Other Post Offices

The Irish postal system has operated since the sixteenth century, but was formally established in 1784. In the early nineteenth century, its service was greatly facilitated by a combination of the railroads and mail coaches, ensuring rapid and reliable communication between the capital city and rural towns. From 1856, the OPW was responsible for the erection and maintenance of post offices, and later telephone exchanges. The main functions of the Department of Posts and Telegraphs were taken over by two new semi-state bodies, An Post and Telecom Éireann respectively, in 1984, marking the end of OPW involvement.

For much of the nineteenth century, post offices were established in existing shops or houses, and therefore involved little architectural input (above left). However, a major building programme around the turn of the century aimed to provide many of the larger towns with adequate, purpose-built facilities.

The designs which date from these productive years borrowed style motifs from many periods: the Queen Anne (Birr, Co Offaly, 1903, centre left); the neo-Georgian (Sligo town, 1902); and the contemporary Arts and Crafts movement (Clonmel, Co Tipperary, 1902). Characteristically they are of terracotta bricks with contrasting limestone or moulded brick dressings and a remarkably high standard of interior finish. The eye-catching example in Castlebar, Co Mayo (left), was completed in 1902.

General Post Office

Francis Johnson, architect to the Board of Works, completed the General Post Office in Sackville (later O'Connell) Street in 1818, at which stage the GPO transferred from its previous premises on College Green. The new building was symmetrical in plan, ordered around a quadrangle, constructed of granite and Portland stone. It was three storeys high with a projecting portico of six fluted Ionic columns supporting an entablature and pediment. Above the Royal Arms carved in the tympanum are the figures of Mercury and Fidelity flanking Hibernia. The whole was finished with a balustrade above the cornice.

GPO 1904–16

By the start of the twentieth century, repeated alterations and additions had caused a certain degree of inconvenience, which was addressed in a major scheme commenced in 1904. In that year, Ball's Bank on Henry Street, adjoining the GPO premises, was acquired and adapted for use as office space for postal staff. Further property was purchased on

Prince's Street in 1910 and demolished to allow for the erection of a 21,000-square-foot, four-storey wing, accommodating sorting offices, registry, kitchens etc. Only after these two phases were completed in 1912, without interruption of the postal or public business, was the original block improved. The most significant change was the re-instatement of the public entrance under the portico, which had been closed since 1870. This gave onto a 'large, well lighted, and architecturally imposing' new public office (*The Irish Builder and Engineer*, March 1916) (right) in sympathy with the external character of the building. The 40ft width of the office was spanned by a reinforced segmental ceiling, with a pediment, carried by four Tuscan columns and two pilasters, finishing each end. Fittings and furniture were of Burmese teak and the floor of vitreous mosaic.

The final phase of works had been completed just weeks before the building was stormed, on Easter Monday 1916, and held for six days through constant bombardment.

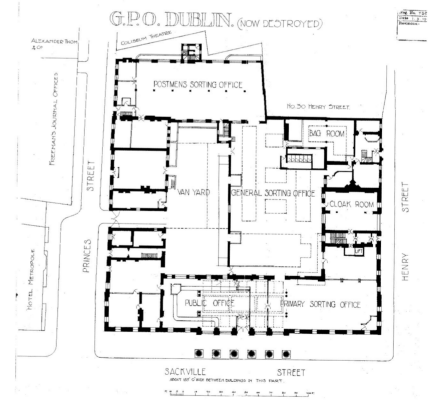

G.P.O. DUBLIN. (NOW DESTROYED)

Despite the destruction of the building, the principal façade was relatively uninjured – a fact which contributed to the decision in 1924 to reconstruct the GPO rather than clear the site. The first element of the new scheme to be completed was the northern elevation, to Henry Street. A row of thirteen shops was incorporated into the design at ground-floor level, with four further storeys for postal staff (left). A new steel-framed building on Prince's Street was linked to Henry Street by means of a covered arcade, also lined with commercial outlets.

The original central block was rebuilt to a new design behind Johnson's façade. The centrepiece of the building was naturally the public office and, at 6400 square feet, was larger even than that of 1916. The front portion was a double height space with a richly coffered ceiling. The walls were faced in Irish sandstone with marble pilasters. A counter some 126 feet long snaked around the large room, and was surmounted by a bronze iron grille. Little of this interior layout has been altered since the office was declared open by President Cosgrave in July 1929. The whole reconstruction programme was completed in 1932. A major refurbishment of the building was carried out in 1986 under the aegis of An Post.

General Post Office, Dublin.—Proposed new facade to Henry Street.   Architect—T. J. Byrne, A.R.I.B.A., F.R.I.A.I.

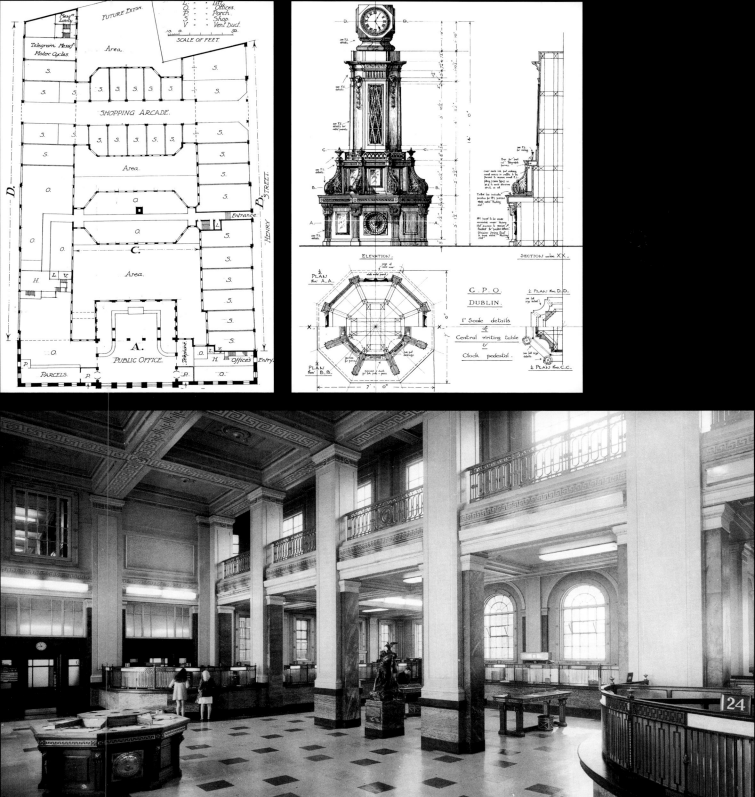

24

Rathmines PO 1934

The overall austerity of Rathmines post office and telephone exchange (1934) is relieved by a wealth of decorative details, from the grille over the main entrance, to the glazed screen between the public office and sorting office.

Tipperary PO 1978

When a competition for a new post office in Tipperary town was held in 1973, the winning submission was by Henry J Lyons & Partners of Dublin. Basically U-shaped in plan, the roofscape culminates in a glazed monopitch over the public office, signalling its importance in the overall design.

St Andrew's Street PO Dublin 1940s

The post office on St Andrew's Street was designed in 1947. The stone façade contains five castings depicting the role of the building. The tradition of high-quality detailing established in the past is maintained at St Andrew's Street, despite the economic situation of post-war Ireland.

Priory Park telephone exchange

The programme of telephone exchanges was accelerated and expanded in the 1970s to meet the demands of the Department of Posts and Telegraphs. Their design was determined mainly by engineering considerations, with fixed inter-relationship between rooms of various functions.

Priory Park in Stillorgan, Co Dublin (1984) supplemented an adjoining exchange completed in 1952. The building's bulk is reduced by a strong horizontal division separating the formally treated first floor with its continuous strip window, from the recessed ground floor with its changes in fenestration and profile.

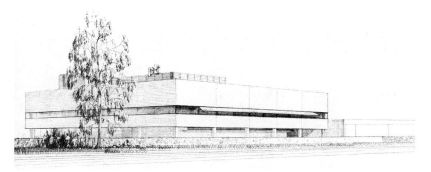

The Custom House

Dublin

In the 1770s, a revenue commissioner by the name of John Beresford lobbied for the construction of a new custom house, since the existing custom house, on Wellington Quay, had fallen into a dilapidated condition. Beresford proposed that the new custom house should be built downstream of the existing one, but this was strongly and violently opposed by the Corporation and the bulk of the city's merchants and brewers, who feared the devaluation of property in the older quarter of the city.

Nevertheless, the project was sanctioned by the Irish Parliament, and Beresford engaged the services of the London architect, James Gandon (1742–1823). The foundation stone was laid in August 1781 and building was completed in 1791.

The chosen location for the new building was a swampy, isolated wasteland, calling for innovative draining and foundation techniques, which partly accounts for the ten-year construction programme and final cost of over £200,000.

A former pupil of Sir William Chambers (see page 68), Gandon employed the language of the classical Tuscan order. He designed a free-standing building enclosed by a crescent of houses at Beresford Place and opening to the Liffey quays to the south. The focus of the southern elevation, overlooking the river, is a tetra-style portico supporting a neat pediment, and surmounted by a cupola. The seeming imbalance between the tall drum and the long, low river front is resolved when seen from a raking angle, from the river. The rusticated, open arcades on the south front led into public offices and the centrally located Long Room (right), while the entrance on the north elevation afforded access to more private administrative areas and the personal apartments of Beresford, the Chief Commissioner.

The architectural coherence of the large-scale complex is dependent on a number of consistent elements – the four uniform corner pavilions; virtually continuous cornice and dentil course; and the remarkable sculpture programme by the Irishman Edward Smyth.

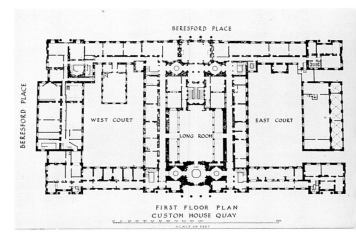

FIRST FLOOR PLAN
CUSTOM HOUSE QUAY
SCALE OF FEET

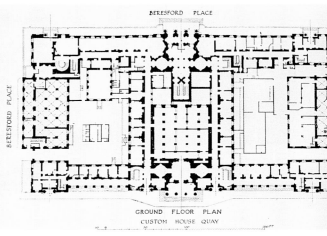

GROUND FLOOR PLAN
CUSTOM HOUSE QUAY

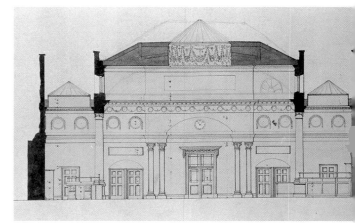

1921 fire

On 25 May 1921, the Custom House (which was seen as a manifestation of British power in Ireland) was seized by the Dublin Brigade of the IRA, in an attack sanctioned by Dáil Éireann. The raiding party was swiftly arrested, but not before it had set the building alight. The fire burned for five full days, destroying virtually the whole interior.

South-easterly winds steered the worst of the blaze away from the river façade, and the landward side was most badly damaged. Little survived of the interior, with the exception of a system of lobbies under the dome. The profusion of timber lintels, beams, partitions and furniture, combined with masses of paper records and documents, resulted in a blaze which reduced even brass fittings to a molten mass, indicating temperatures of at least 1850ºF. Cracks in the stonework were further exaggerated by contraction and settlement which took place during the cooling down process, which took several months.

In the immediate aftermath of the destruction of the Custom House, the OPW was concerned with rehousing those departments formerly based there. Serious consideration was given to the idea of razing the site and re-erecting the building to the original plan. However, the less radical approach of restoration proved more feasible.

The exterior was altered as little as possible. Broken bricks and stones among the debris were crushed to produce an aggregate for concrete used in the reconstruction, and some 230,000 whole bricks were gathered for re-use. The crowning balustrade was found to be dangerously defective, but the cost of its renewal in natural stone would have been prohibitive. Instead, castings of suitably faced artificial stone were made and set in place. All the window openings on the north front had suffered severely, and in most cases were beyond even partial repair. New stone dressings worked on the site were inserted and bonded to the old brickwork. The copper dome, having melted during the fire, was reinstated in every external detail. However, its new stonework was carried out in native Ardbraccan limestone, as opposed to Gandon's Portland stone from Dorset. The stone has since darkened in sharp contrast to the surviving white Portland. The scheme of rehabilitation was completed by 1930.

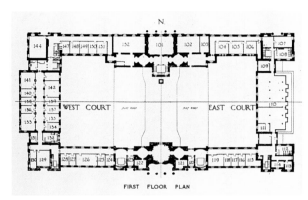

FIRST FLOOR PLAN

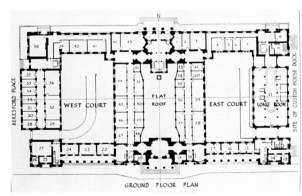

GROUND FLOOR PLAN

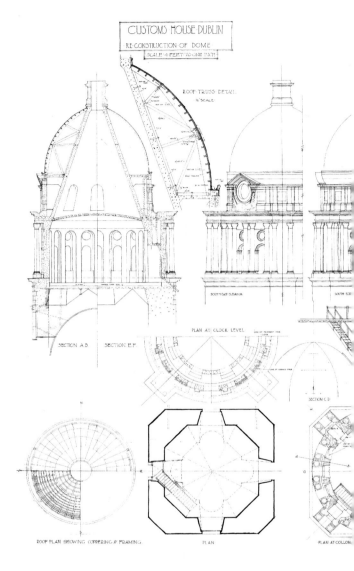

Restoration 1926–9

The restoration programme of 1926–9 did not attempt to recreate Gandon's interior layout, and the opportunity was taken to rationalise the accommodation to suit modern requirements. The new plan replaced the former central block with two parallel structures bridged by a glazed light-well over a basement boiler house. The old cellers were transformed into well-lighted lower ground floor rooms by excavating the two central courtyards. The Long Room was repositioned in the east block, with special teak joinery and fittings. Elsewhere, a simplified plan was evolved, incorporating fire-resistant structural materials, electric lighting, central heating and modern sanitary facilities.

Restoration 1984–91

Following a fall of stone in 1979, a detailed survey of the fabric of the Custom House was carried out, and it was found that the stone facings were in a precarious condition. The expansion and corrosion of iron armatures and ties inside the heart of the stone, mostly as a result of a fire in 1833 and another in 1921, had caused severe cracking and destabilisation. The full extent of other defects came to light, such as pollution, unsatisfactory repairs from the period 1926–30 and, surprisingly, some structural defects in the original design. The conservation philosophy from the outset was one of total respect for the existing fabric and, as far as possible, involved repair rather than replacement.

Restoration 1984–91

Gandon's sophisticated method of metal ties was no doubt learnt from Chambers. A major challenge for the conservation team was to find a non-destructive way of pin-pointing the hidden ferrous metal. Ultrasonic testing proved useful in mapping stone fractures.

A variety of repair methods was evolved to deal with the complex issue of substituting the iron where it was removed. In the case of the defective cornice, its cantilever of almost one metre was found to rely on the counterbalance of the balustrade for its stability, and a cast concrete ring beam concealed behind the stone now supports the weight. Other works involved the rebuilding of the attic storeys, repairing damaged sections of the pediments, frieze and string course, and replacing the balustrade which had been restored in concrete in the 1920s. Where replacement was necessary, offcuts of original stone were used, failing which similar Portland stone was sourced in England.

Numerous cleaning systems were tested. A poultice technique was developed, which was applied to the surface for up to twenty-four hours, with repeated applications as needed. A water-repellent silicone treatment was then applied to minimise atmospheric damage, and facilitate future cleaning.

The heraldic arms of Ireland, riverine heads, friezes and other statuary were painstakingly restored by skilled craftsmen and carvers. The four allegorical figures above the south portico, which had lain in fragments in the grounds of the Custom House since the 1940s, have now been reinstated.

Custom House conference suite 1993

The conference room in the centre of the north elevation was designed as the boardroom of the Revenue Commissioners. It was rebuilt in the 1920s, with a totally remodelled interior. By 1991, the room was in need of redecoration, and additional facilities were required.

Interventions were kept to a minimum, being restricted to the re-opening of the fireplace and flanking doors, and the consequent alterations to the wall panelling and plasterwork. The ceiling has a new plaster centrepiece cast from an eighteenth-century example in Rathfarnham Castle, with a large crystal chandelier. Air-conditioning was accommodated within the ceiling, interspaced with downlighters. In addition, a second conference room was created close by, which incorporates some very fine late neo-classical stucco-work from the library of the now-demolished Hilltown House, Bellewstown, Co Meath.

Custom House visitor centre 1997

The Custom House visitor centre is situated in the south hall and vestibule, directly behind the massive river-front portico. Its primary function is to allow public access to the only significant eighteenth-century interior space in the building to have survived the fire and remodelling earlier this century. The main structural alteration consisted of the re-insertion of the octagonal well beneath the dome, lost in the 1920s, modelled on Gandon's original design. A lift was installed to provide access to all areas of the two-storey exhibition.

The Four Courts
Dublin

James Gandon inherited the commission for the new Public Records Office and King's Inns following the death of Thomas Cooley, Clerk and Inspector of Public Buildings, in 1784. It was at this stage that the Irish Parliament enacted the decision to include accommodation for the courts of justice in the general scheme then taking shape on Inns Quay. Immediately, Gandon submitted new plans for the complex, which nonetheless respected Cooley's contribution to date. In 1796, the Irish courts transferred from their previous decrepit premises close to Christ Church cathedral to the new Four Courts north of the river.

A tall copper dome surmounts the classical temple-front of the main building. Roofline statuary above the balustrade by Edward Smyth personifies Moses, Justice, Mercy, Authority and Wisdom. To east and west are courtyards housing law offices whose elevations were designed by Cooley, and are screened from the street by Gandon's rusticated arcades. The eponymous four courtrooms lead directly from the immense rotunda at the heart of the building, dominated by twenty-five-foot piers. The coffered inner dome culminated in a circular opening, through which documents could be lowered by rope and pulley from the storeroom above. The extent of Smyth's interior stucco-work was virtually confined to this hallway, and is of a strongly didactic nature – above the door of each court was an historical panel, one of whose subjects was the abolition of the gaelic 'brehon' law by King James I.

OPW's nineteenth-century building works
Throughout the nineteenth century, the OPW was responsible for numerous additions and alterations in the Four Courts precinct according to the needs of the bar. These included the Law Library extension with two adjoining courts by Jacob Owen (1838), Encumbered Estates courts (1858), a new Law Library by consultant architect Thomas Drew (1897) as well as the Public Records Office.

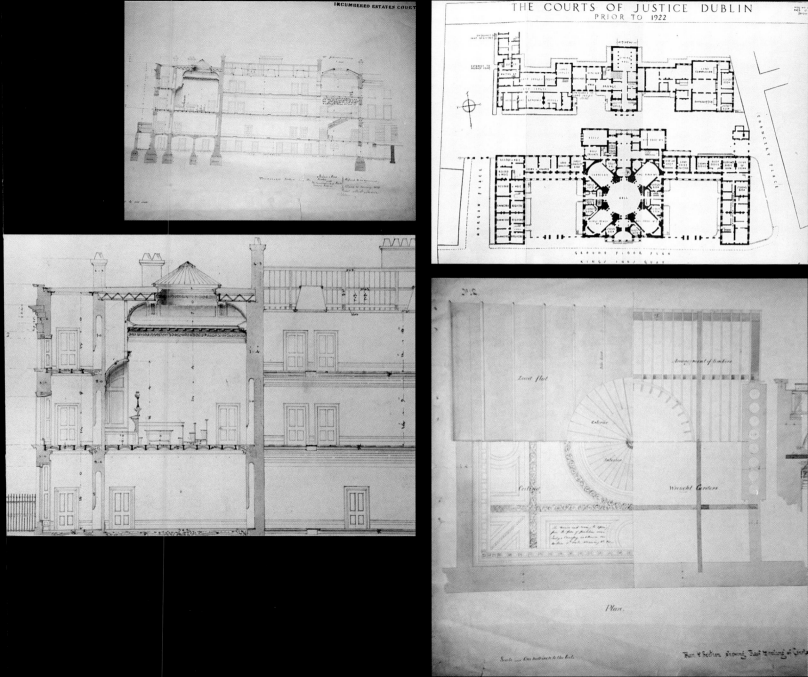

THE COURTS OF JUSTICE DUBLIN
PRIOR TO 1922

GROUND FLOOR PLAN

KINGS INNS QUAY

Plan.

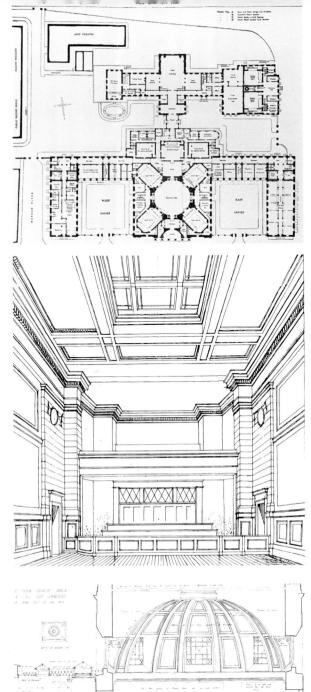

1922

On 29 June 1922, government troops on the south quays attacked the Four Courts with field artillery, in a bid to rout the anti-Treaty garrison who had been in possession of the building for the past two months. The battle, which signalled the start of the Civil War, raged for two and a half days, after which the rebels surrendered. In that short time, the building was reduced to a ruin, and a massive explosion of gelignite obliterated the Public Records Office,, destroying a priceless archive of manuscripts documenting the political, legal and social history of Ireland from the twelfth century onwards.

Reconstruction 1924–31

The task of clearing the debris commenced at the Inns Quay site in 1924, followed by an initial structural survey that revealed the effects of high explosives; some structures had literally 'jumped' their foundations. The idea of reconstructing the buildings to house the Oireachtas was considered, before it was decided to re-establish the courts of justice, their offices, the bench, the bar and the solicitors on the old site. The hollow shell was internally remodelled along simple lines, incorporating up-to-date methods of lighting, heating and sanitation. An internal system of steel framing was adopted, which braces the external walls and carries reinforced concrete floors. The four central courtrooms were reinstated in line with the original concept, with the addition of roof lighting, and a new Supreme Court room on axis with the portico designed (right). Externally, the river façade and screens were restored with local granite and Portland stone, the only obvious alteration being the decision to rebuild the end pavilions twelve feet further back from the river, making them almost flush with the arcade screens.

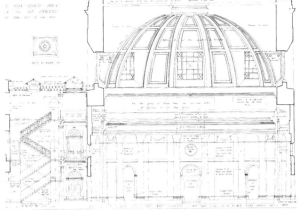

Reconstruction of the rotunda

The reinstatement of the cupola and drum presented a considerable challenge. The peristyle of the dome consists of twenty-four Corinthian columns about an inner wall with alternating windows and niches. Scaffolding supported the architrave while the columns were repaired or replaced by Portland stone copies; a task described by the architect as 'bristling with difficulties'. As most of the capitals were damaged to some degree, it was possible to rotate them so that the damaged sides faced inwards. After repairs to the architrave, frieze and cornice, the dome itself was cast in six-inch concrete embedded with steel, to its former profile. The unusual operation was performed by twenty men, working for thirty hours with only a short interval. The dome was then clad with sheets of copper in the manner of the original. As no accurate records of Smyth's stucco-work existed, the ceiling of the rotunda was reconstructed with simple plaster mouldings. Towards ground level, the eight colossal piers surrounding the hall are composed of rubble masonry faced in granite. As most exhibited signs of cracking, it was necessary to cut out the damaged facings and replace with newly carved sections. The new floor of the hall was lined with sandstone from Kerry.

Refurbishment 1994–7

Between 1994 and 1997 the central block and wings were the subject of a major re-organisation and refurbishment to bring the building into line with modern requirements, including compliance with current safety regulations. Previously the administrative area, the west wing was replanned to provide an extra five courtrooms together with judges' chambers, while additional accommodation for the Supreme Court included conference rooms for judges. In the rotunda, the stonework was cleaned and the decorative treatment was simplified. The stone floor had been covered with rubber since the 1930s, and for technical reasons it was not possible to reinstate the older material. A floor covering with an intricate pattern and border was designed. The bulk of the refurbishment programme was completed in time for the bicentenary celebrations in 1996.

The Casino, Marino
Dublin

This and all other National Monuments are managed by the Department of Arts, Heritage, Gaeltacht and the Islands

James Caulfield, First Earl of Charlemont, had a deep admiration for the classical world, its scholarship and aesthetics. At the age of 18 he embarked on the customary grand tour of Europe, the Mediterranean and the Greek islands, culminating in Rome, the great cultural centre of the eighteenth century. His devotion to Ireland enticed him home nine years later.

His stepfather, Thomas Adderley, presented Charlemont with an estate house and demesne at Donnycarney, three miles north of Dublin city, 'suitable to house your growing collection of antiquities'. Charlemont renamed his new home, with views across Dublin Bay, 'Marino', and embarked on a major programme of remodelling.

At the same time that Matthew Peters was re-landscaping the 200-acre demesne in the style inspired by the Italianate landscapes of Claude and Poussin, the Scotsman William Chambers was designing a garden villa or 'casino' to grace this arcadia. What he and his patron created was to be one of the finest exercises in neo-classical architecture of its day. The Casino (1759–c 77) at Marino displays such a wealth of subtlety, craftsmanship and innovation, in an architectural idiom so perfectly in tune with contemporary taste, that it ranks among only a handful of buildings of international significance in Ireland.

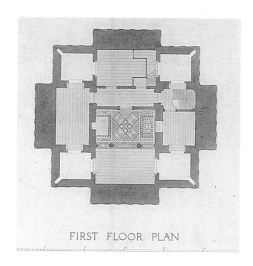

FIRST FLOOR PLAN

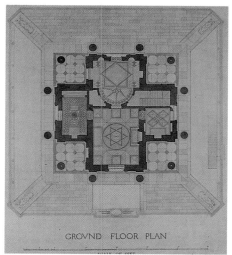

GROVND FLOOR PLAN

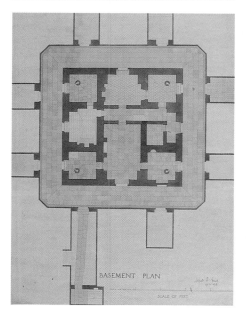

BASEMENT PLAN

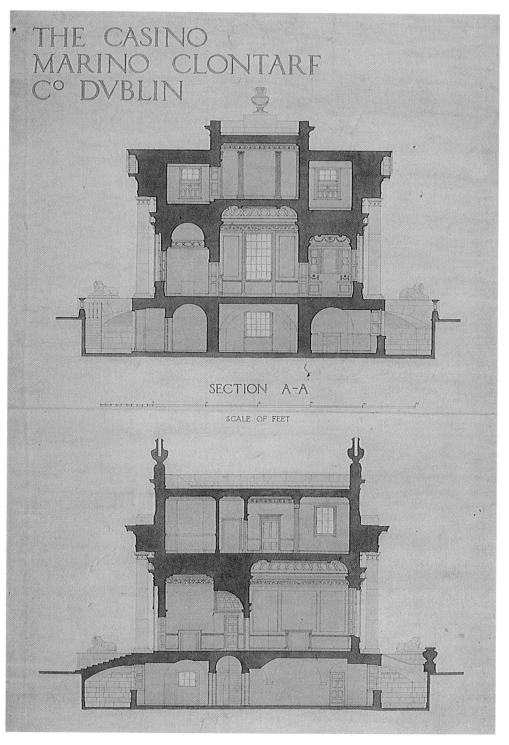

THE CASINO
MARINO CLONTARF
Cº DVBLIN

SECTION A-A

SCALE OF FEET

Designed with a mastery of proportions as a venue for parties and entertainments, the pavilion contains no less than sixteen rooms across three storeys, including reception rooms, bedrooms, kitchen and servants' quarters.

A richly carved entablature is supported by a dozen Roman doric columns, in a Greek cross plan. The northern timber doorway is barely distinguished from the Portland stone, while the enlarged windows to east and west contain small panes of convex glass, which prevent the visitor from seeing into the interior. A number of talented artists whom Charlemont befriended in Rome – Joseph Wilton, Giovanni Battista Cipriani, and Simon Vierpyl – collaborated on the sculptural ornament. Vierpyl also supervised the whole building project. No expense was spared in its construction and furnishing: Charlemont spent over £20,000 and never recovered financially.

The National Monuments Act of 1930 was specially worded to allow for the essential preservation of the Casino at Marino. By that time, the building was the property of the Irish Christian Brothers, and had suffered years of neglect and pilferage. The Inspector of National Monuments, Dr Harold G Leask, made this report in 1933:

The original roof was found to be on the verge of collapse owing to the ravages of dry-rot consequent upon long-standing leakages. The rot had extended downwards and had affected much of the internal woodwork, particularly that of the floor of the State Bedroom over the Saloon and the wall linings and cornice supports of the ceiling in this fine room.... Only the minimum of restoration was attempted, sufficient to heal the most obvious scars.

The OPW's intervention in the early 1930s rescued the basic structure of the Casino, and small-scale work of this nature continued until 1974, when the building was threatened by wet rot on the ground floor and ownership was transferred to the state. A major programme of restoration commenced, headed by consultant architects O'Neill Flanagan & Partners.

A careful inspection was made of the stonework, followed by cleaning and consolidation. The interior had fared worse. Not only were innumerable repairs necessary to the stucco ceilings, the parquet floors, the joinery and other elements of the building fabric, but in spite of exhaustive documentary research, little evidence survived as to the furnishing and decorative schemes of the Casino. All paintings, sculpture, fireplaces and furnishings had been sold or lost without trace in the nineteenth century. Pooling information gleaned from archival sources (including the Charlemont/Chambers correspondence), scientific examination of extant paint and cloth particles, Chambers's 'A Treatise on Civil Architecture' (1759), and knowledge of similar interior decoration of the 1770s, the Casino has been returned, as authentically as possible, to its appearance on completion in the eighteenth century. A minimum of furniture has been provided, pending the possible discovery of more accurate details or recovery of original items.

The extraordinary ten-year restoration project was acknowledged by the first RIAI medal for restoration. The citation reads: 'The Casino... has been restored with care and restraint, and in its present form it complies perfectly with the objectives and aspirations of the RIAI in founding the Restoration Medal.'

Dublin Airport
Collinstown, Co Dublin, 1942

In 1936, the government announced plans to develop the site of a derelict World War I Royal Flying Corps training base at Collinstown, north of Dublin, as Ireland's first civil airport. The OPW took on the task of developing the 700-acre site and designing the buildings and the contract was placed in late 1938, the cost of the whole airport project being shared by the state, Dublin Corporation, and Dublin County Council. Though the OPW handed over the site to the Department of Industry and Commerce in January 1940, the terminal building was not completed until the spring of 1942 as a result of wartime shortages.

Dublin Airport terminal building, designed in 1937 by a young and enthusiastic team, marked a new departure in Irish architecture. It is Ireland's most significant exercise in the contemporary International style, a unique and pioneering design inspired by the trends then prevalent in European architecture.

Wartime censorship meant that no descriptive accounts, photographs, sketches or plans of the airport were made public until 1945, and so the airport building did not achieve international recognition at the time. However, the Irish architectural community became aware of its importance, and it was

awarded the prestigious RIAI Triennial Gold Medal in 1943.

The curved plan of the terminal building was primarily a practical device to maximise the number of aircraft which can be served along its outer perimeter. Repeated bands of horizontal glazing characterise this style of architecture, and form the dominating character of the western façade, overlooking the airfield. Cantilevered terraces and promenades on several levels provide further opportunities to enjoy the spectacle of flight. Intending passengers entered from the concave 'landward' façade, directly entering the double-height space of the main concourse.

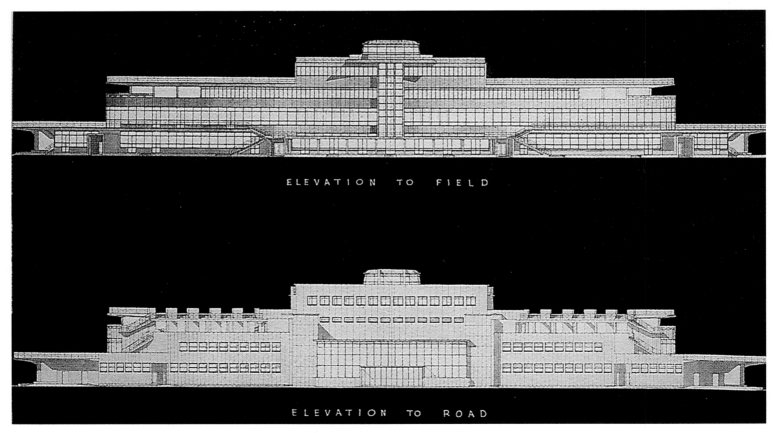

ELEVATION TO FIELD

ELEVATION TO ROAD

Booking desks, finished in walnut and sycamore, were located opposite the entrance, beyond a row of columns supporting the first floor. The customs hall, administrative offices, bank, post office, lounge and bar were also found on the ground floor, in a plan which was especially praised for its considered circulation routes. Staircases of travertine marble with bronze balustrades and wooden handrails at either end of the 80-foot long concourse led to the first floor (below left), which accommodated management offices and the restaurant, with its circular maple dance floor (left), overlooking the airfield. At the opposite end of this storey 'is a conference room, which is a rather luxurious-looking apartment with comfortable chairs, a built in circular carpet and a circular recess above carrying concealed lights as in the restaurant' (*The Irish Builder and Engineer*, 28 July 1945). The airport became a fashionable venue for all sorts of social gatherings.

The terminal building is an example of 'total design', whereby every detail of the interior, from the carpets and furniture to the menu cards, is conceived as part of the overall design. The remaining three floors, each of diminishing size, housed meteorological and radio services, pilots' and crews' rest rooms and the control room which formed the pinnacle of the building, and was glazed on all sides. The original terminal and surroundings have been significantly altered since the 1940s.

Baldonnel Aerodrome
Co Dublin

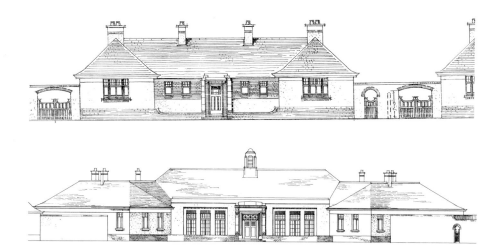

Baldonnel Aerodrome, formerly the headquarters of the Irish branch of the Royal Flying Corps (later the RAF), was occupied by the Irish Air Service in April 1922. Renamed Casement Aerodrome in 1965, Baldonnel has continued to be the main operational base for the Irish Air Corps.

The officers' mess was built between 1929 and 1931, at the request of the Department of Defence, in conjunction with an accommodation block. The comfortable suburban ambience of this area known as the 'Lower Camp' is created by the domestic scale of the buildings and attractive design details. The OPW designed a further accommodation scheme, which was built in the late 1930s and early 1940s. It is seen to best advantage from the air.

The Roman Catholic church at Baldonnel was built in wartime (1943–4) when materials were expensive and difficult to obtain.

The design of the gymnasium (1946) was similarly constrained by a shortage of materials, and after experiment, a special kind of concrete roof was developed with parabolic units cast on fibrous plaster formwork. All window frames are of concrete, and the army obtained sufficient seasoned timber for the flooring. Adjoining the principal hall is a block of changing rooms and an external staircase gives access to separate projection and rewind rooms, allowing the hall to be used as a cinema.

Department of Industry and Commerce
Kildare Street, Dublin, 1939–42

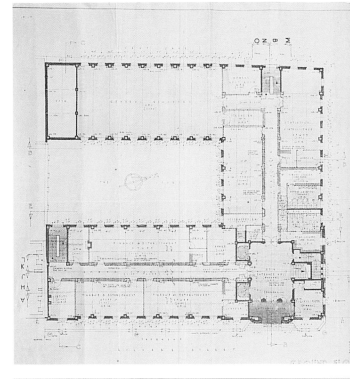

The Department of Industry and Commerce was created in 1924 from an amalgamation of earlier ministries including Transport, Employment and Labour. Eleven years later a decision was made to overcome the inconvenience of having the departmental offices scattered throughout Dublin, and an architectural competition for the design of a new headquarters was announced. The reaction of the OPW to the idea of a competition was as follows: *[W]hile it is improbable that Architects in private practice will be found in any degree better qualified than the Board's Architectural staff for designing and carrying out a building of the size* contemplated here, we agree *that, generally speaking, competitions of this kind often produce building schemes both attractive, novel and economical and afford opportunities to young Architects to make their talent known, and attract, as well, eminent Architects whose experience in private practice may be of particular value.*

The site was that of the former Maples Hotel, on the corner of Kildare Street and Schoolhouse Lane, in close proximity to the Oireachtas, and Government Buildings. It was the first, and for many years the only, purpose-built government office commissioned since independence (1922).

Of thirty-six entries, J R Boyd Barrett's submission became the winning design. Boyd Barrett, who had served as architectural assistant at the OPW between 1924 and 1926, had a healthy practice in the south and west, based in Cork.

The competition results were published in December 1935, followed by two years of preparation at the drawing board. The contract for construction was won by the Cork-based John Sisk & Co and was one of their first commissions in the capital. Smith & Peterson built the 'backbone of 1,040 tons of steel' supporting the structure. Six hundred personnel of the Department of Industry and Commerce and the Department of Supplies occupied the building in 1942.

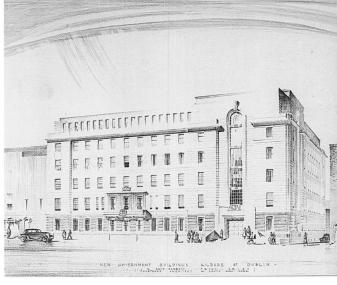

The building displays an unusually successful blend of classical and contemporary art deco characteristics. The screened basement, heavily rusticated ground floor and window proportions echo the neighbouring terrace. Limestone cornices also help to ease the visual discrepancy of a six-storey building in a street of four-storey Georgian townhouses. On the main façades, narrow sheets of glazing soar through five floors, their steel frames patterned with zigzags and chevrons. The careful layering of planes, especially evident on the Kildare Street elevation, progresses to form an emphatic doorcase – another classic motif of the period. Overall, the cleanly defined articulation and bold stylisation are reminiscent of New York's inter-war architecture.

Gabriel Hayes designed and executed the external sculptural ornament. Her themes were those of Irish trade and commerce – the relief over the Kildare Street lintel depicts Lugh, Celtic God of Light, animating a fleet of aeroplanes, particularly pertinent since Ireland's first commercial airport at Collinstown was under construction at the time. The ministerial balcony has relief representations of the tobacco, milling, iron, shoemaking and cement industries, as well as the Shannon hydro-electric power station of the 1920s. Above the entrances, Éire and St Brendan the Navigator grace the keystones, which were carved in situ. They form an artistic link with Edward Smyth's famous riverine heads on the façade of Dublin's Custom House. Hayes's delight in bold form and pattern neatly complements the dynamic architectural mood.

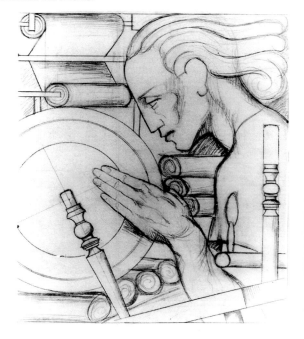

In spite of the difficulties in obtaining certain materials in wartime, the interior spaces display an impressive degree of craftsmanship and finish. The foyer on each level is identically panelled and glazed, a Ruboleum-lined floor reflecting the deeply coffered ceiling. Wide doorways with curved jambs line the axial corridors, similar to those seen in contemporary hospitals. The resulting thick walls provide built-in storage and electrical services.

The ministerial suite includes conference rooms and secretarial space. The private office (above) looks on to Kildare Street and is identified by the sole projecting balcony.

Abbotstown Estate

Blanchardstown, Co Dublin

Facilities on Abbotstown Estate

Abbotstown House

AI Centre

Central Meat Control Laboratory

Experimental Animal Farm

Fisheries Research Laboratory

Foundation Stock Farm

Infectious Diseases Unit

Pathology Unit

State Laboratory

Veterinary Diagnostic Laboratories

Veterinary Field Station

Veterinary Research Laboratory

Abbotstown House was purchased by the Department of Agriculture in 1950, with over 400 acres, at a cost of £40,000, to accommodate the Veterinary Research Laboratory and state farm.

The early-nineteenth-century house and farm buildings remain the focal point of the estate, and several farming and scientific facilities have been gradually added, some of which are under the aegis of other government departments. The OPW is responsible for numerous works of construction, adaptation and maintenance at Abbotstown, including regular modernisation of facilities.

Two of the latest additions to the estate are a dairy science laboratory and major new storage facilities, both of which were under construction in 1999.

Foundation Stock Farm 1958–65

Desmond FitzGerald, who was responsible for the adaptation of the house and overall development plan for the estate, was engaged as a consultant architect to design the proposed Foundation Stock Farm in 1955. The phased work involved the construction of an implements store and accommodation for cattle and pigs. A yardman's house and associated office space were also incorporated into the small complex, which was completed in stages between 1958 and 1965.

Artificial Insemination Centre 1961

A VRL research unit was completed in 1961 to provide facilities for study and experiment in the field of artificial insemination. The unit consists of a laboratory and office block joined by a large bull shed, with a block of isolation boxes, a hay barn and a stockman's cottage grouped around three sides of a concrete paved courtyard.

Veterinary Field Station 1965 (above)

The accommodation consists of a central two-storey block with offices, cafeteria and kitchen on the ground floor and laboratories on the first floor. Flanking it on one side are lecture halls and a library, and on the other side are classrooms, storerooms and a kennel area. The building is constructed in reinforced concrete with concrete brick facings externally.

The OPW undertook the adaptation of the field station for the Seed Testing and Pesticide Control Service in 1990.

The State Laboratory 1982

Accession to the EEC in 1973 brought about a vast increase in demand for services from the State Laboratory, leading to the requirement for new modern facilities at Abbotstown.

Among the design considerations was the important aspect of creating a structural form housing 3250 square metres of analytical chemical laboratories, to be sited harmoniously in a rural farmland setting, without denying its expression of function and stature as an important state institution. The solution is a broad, low, single-storey building with occasional raised elements and stacks protruding into the skyline. The plan form is square, with a large central courtyard which has been landscaped and planted. Laboratories and offices are loaded each side of a corridor spine, and special rooms and ancillary areas are removed to the outside corners of the square. The project was completed in July 1982, at a cost of £2.25m. An extension providing conference and library facilities was commenced in 1999.

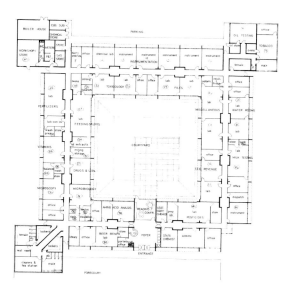

Veterinary Diagnostic Laboratories 1984

The Veterinary Diagnostic Laboratories (1984, left) were designed as high-security units for the rapid diagnosis of rabies, classic swine fever and Newcastle disease. The small L-shaped building forms two self-contained wings, each consisting of a suite of laboratories, and associated facilities, showers and sterilisation areas. Ventilation is predominantly by mechanical extraction, with extensive filtering through the roof at high level, most of the plant being contained within the roof space.

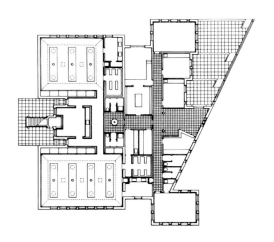

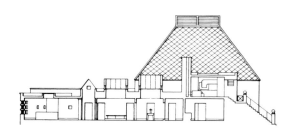

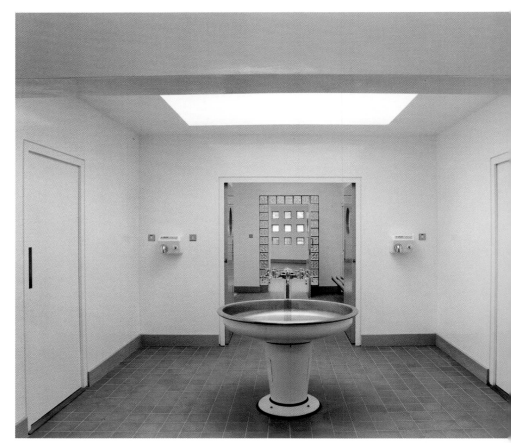

Central Meat Control Laboratory 1985

In designing the central Meat Control Lab, the brief requirement for extracted fumes to be discharged at high level promoted associations with the roof forms of maltings and mill buildings, and inspired the distinctive large-hipped roofs. In general, the building is composed of several discrete volumes brought together in an arrangement that is reminiscent of the economic layout characteristic of Irish rural industrial and agricultural settlements of the eighteenth century. The south wall and palisade is 'hinged open', emphasising the entrance route, and, while contradicting the symmetry of the general layout, aligns with the meandering service road through Abbotstown estate. On entering the building, the axis is re-established, marked by a series of nine small square windows. Between the offices and the segregated suite of laboratory rooms runs a glass-roofed internal street.

Interior finishes fulfil the client brief for clean laboratory space with coved floor skirtings, jointless floors and wash-down walls. Detailed workings of the services are suppressed in favour of a clutter-free interior with certain incidents such as entrance, circulation and washing emphasised. The building was designed in 1981 and completed in 1985.

Garrison Church of St Brigid
Curragh Camp, Co Kildare, 1959

In 1944, the Department of Defence requested the OPW to proceed with plans to replace the Roman Catholic church at the Curragh Camp, the chief and largest military base in the country, which then accommodated approximately 5000 military personnel and 1000 civilians. The old church dated to 1855, the year the camp was established, and, like much of the original architecture, was constructed of American white fir timber and red pine (above right).

The 1944 design was deferred until after the Emergency. When the project was revived, a completely new set of plans was presented in August 1948. During subsequent meetings with church representatives, the head chaplain at the Department of Defence objected that '...the new Catholic Church, the plans of which were now under discussion, was not in conformity with existing religious architecture in the diocese'. The OPW maintained

that the September 1944 plan was considered to be more representative of the 'village' type church, and having regard to the importance of the location it was felt that a radical departure from the conventional style church was justified.

Following some reworking, which incorporated a belfry, and external brick finish 'so as to tone with the Camp buildings in general,' the proposal was approved in April 1950.

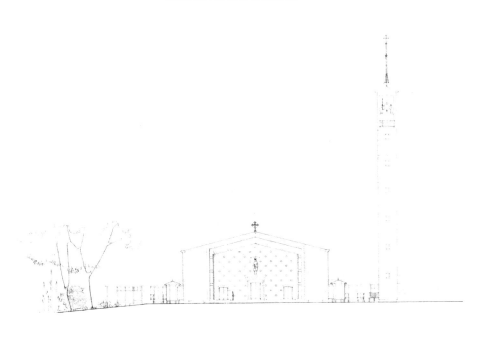

The principal, west façade of the church reflects the forms of the interior steel framework, the uniform red brick relieved by a pattern of indented stars. Oisín Kelly carved the teak sculpture over the main portal, depicting St Brigid, special patroness of the diocese, to whom the church is dedicated. Inside, the exposed deep green framework affords uninterrupted views of the soaring timber panelling behind the altar, continued on the ceiling, entrance porch and choir balcony. R E Meates & Son built a new organ, which is framed by a ribbon of stained glass by John Murphy on the subject of the Lamb of God, and the River and Tree of Life. Broad bands of fenestration on the north and south elevations are dappled with occasional panes of richly coloured glass. Most of the altar furniture was commissioned from the monks of Glenstal Abbey, Co Limerick, and Patrick Pye designed the large altar crucifix suspended over the baldacchino.

Valentia Observatory

Cahirciveen, Co Kerry, 1948–62

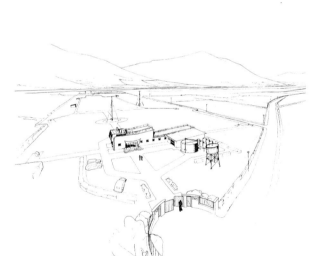

Valentia Observatory moved from Valentia Island to Westwood House on the mainland in 1892. On behalf of the Irish Meteorological Service the Department of Industry & Commerce approached the OPW with a view to having changes made for technical reasons.

The OPW's 1948 scheme was executed by 1962, and numerous minor alterations suggested in the early 1950s were incorporated, ensuring that the observatory could meet the needs of a modern transatlantic meteorological service.

The principal new building (above) is undoubtedly influenced by the contemporary modern movement in Europe. It was designed to facilitate the proper handling of radar-observed *radiosonde* balloons. These balloons carry a small transmitter, which gives readings of temperature, pressure and humidity as the balloons rise and drift down-wind.

Irish Meteorological Service Headquarters

Glasnevin, Dublin, 1978

The Meteorological Office in Glasnevin accommodates the headquarters staff of the Irish Meteorological Service together with the range of computer equipment necessary for modern weather forecasting. The form of the building was determined by two requirements: the building should not overshadow nearby houses and the Central Analytical and Forecast Office (CAFO) had to have a maximum sky view.

The laboratories, workshops, library, printing shop and all heavy floor loads were accommodated on the ground floor, with CAFO and its computers on the top level, where floor-to-ceiling glazing opens onto balconies giving magnificent views over the city. It was natural to group back-up services on the two intermediate floors, and so a truncated pyramid was the form chosen.

The building, which is square in plan, is constructed of reinforced concrete, and the external walls, which slope inwards at an angle of 23 degrees off vertical, were originally clad in Ballinasloe limestone, later to be replaced by aluminium cladding.

Kilkenny Castle

The Parade, Kilkenny

Phase I: 1969–76; Phase II: 1990–4; Phase III: 1998–9

This and other Historic Properties are managed by the
Department of Arts, Heritage, Gaeltacht and the Islands

1171	Anglo-Norman Walter family arrive in Ireland
1172	Strongbow erects first timber fortification on site of present castle
1185	Theobald Walter changes the family name to Butler
*c***1195**	William Marshall builds stone castle
1392	James Butler purchases Kilkenny Castle
1650	Oliver Cromwell attacks Kilkenny, destroying the south wall of the castle
1684	First Duke of Ormonde remodels castle
1826	Rebuilding programme commenced
1854	Long gallery completed
1922	Castle briefly in hands of Republicans
1935	Contents of the castle sold at auction
1969	Kilkenny Castle is handed into state care

Restoration: Phase I 1969–76

The entire contents of Kilkenny Castle, except for the family paintings and tapestries, were sold off in 1935 by the Butler family. In the 1960s, a local initiative created the Kilkenny Design Centre and workshops in the former stables. A local committee acquired the castle and carried out emergency repairs. Ownership of the building was transferred to the state in 1969, with the intention that it should be used as a centre for cultural and artistic activities. After the fabric was treated for dry rot and wet rot, a phased programme of restoration started.

The centrepiece of the Victorian alterations is the 120ft-long east wing, which was rebuilt in the 1850s by Deane and Woodward (far right opposite and overleaf). It was also the focus of the first phase of restoration. It was designed to house the Butlers' extensive collection of family paintings and portraits, and still maintains this role. The timber hammerbeam ceiling is similar to that in the nearby thirteenth-century St Canice's Cathedral, and was painted by John Hungerford Pollen in a colourful quasi-medieval manner. Charles W Harrison carved the sandstone corbel of each beam with beautifully articulated birds, animals, plants and fruits. He also collaborated with Woodward on the Moorish staircase (right opposite), the well of which is a winter garden.

Between 1969 and 1976, when this section of the castle opened to the public, the wing was reroofed and painting stabilised. The ground floor was adapted for the use of the Butler Gallery, a commercial art gallery operating independently of the castle, and the dining room in the north tower was adapted for small recitals and meetings. Also at this time, the surrounding parkland, comprising the original private demesne, was replanted and landscaped.

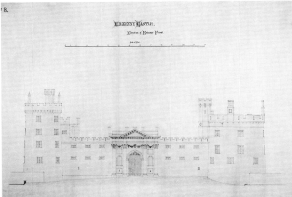

BUILDING FOR GOVERNMENT

The library/drawing room

The first floor of this block consists of the principal reception rooms. In the 1830s, William Robertson, a local architect, converted them into a central library flanked by an anteroom and family drawing room, and it is this period of its history to which it has been restored.

Following the basic reconstruction of the internal partitions, the salvaged material was carefully reinstated. Where the originals were missing or beyond resuscitation, faithful reproduction of high quality has ensured a consistent aesthetic. Fragments of the Irish silk poplin wallcovering were found behind skirting boards and, with the aid of nineteenth-century photography, identical new fabric was woven in Lyons, France. The carpets were specially made to historic designs by the original manufacturer; the window pelmets were modelled, cast and gilded after original photographs; and the fine mahogany bookcases were replicated locally using one original as a model. The building is fitted with sophisticated security, fire and environmental monitoring systems, discreetly housed within the historic interiors. The rooms have been furnished with as much original or suitable Victorian furniture, paintings and effects as possible, recreating the air of the comfortable 'big house'.

Restoration: Phase II 1990–94

Phase II of the restoration programme commenced in 1990, concentrating on the central block of the castle, and repair of all remaining roofs. After extensive surveys, it was agreed that the structural condition of much of the roof, walls, floors and ceilings had deteriorated to the point where selective demolition and reconstruction was the only viable option. Doors, windows, architraves, fireplaces, panelling and all other salvageable materials were tagged and stored off-site for later re-use, while the stonework was consolidated and made watertight. At this stage the block was one large empty space from basement level to roof.

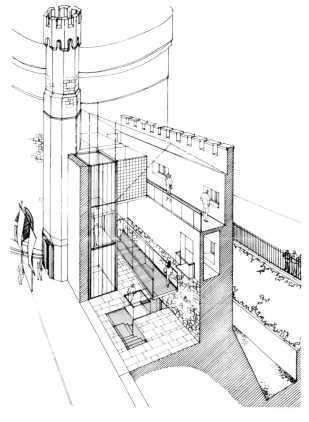

Restoration: Phase II: The breakfast room

The breakfast room is situated on the ground floor of the central block, adjacent to the former billiard room. The handpainted wallpaper was imported from China *c* 1760–80, but was badly damaged by the widespread rot and ingress of rainwater earlier this century. The Chinese wallpaper in one of the bedrooms on the second floor was in a similar state. The project architect chose a different approach when considering the restoration of each. In the breakfast room (above), surviving patches were replaced in their original position after conservation. From old photography, the remainder of the oriental garden and wildlife design was painted in as a 'ghost image', retaining the cohesiveness of the room while clearly defining the original paper from the modern. In the Chinese bedroom, twenty-six new rolls of handpainted paper were commissioned from China, to the original design. The other former bedrooms on this floor, off the striking 'blue corridor', have been adapted to exhibition space, and host many local and travelling exhibitions.

Restoration: Phase III 1998–9

The third and current phase of work focuses on the restoration, conservation and adaptation of the parade wing. The principal feature will be a multi-functional space in the medieval south tower, suitable for lectures, exhibitions, dramatic performances and concerts, with a retractable stage to accommodate banquets. The remarkable pine-trussed roof, dating to the 1820s is being restored, complementing the new Irish oak floor. This double-height space, accommodating up to 250 people, is accessible to wheelchairs at second-floor and third-floor balcony level, as is every part of this wing. During functions, the hall will be serviced by bar, kitchen and toilet facilites in the parade wing.

At a lower level, the tower has been designed to have environmental conditions suitable to house archival material relating to the Butlers of Ormond and other local families, together with a reading room and exhibition space. A function room has also been provided for the use of the Butler Society. Archaeological excavation has revealed many details of the medieval castle, including two postern gates and steps leading from the curtain wall to the dry moat, and a rare wattle-and-daub ceiling in the west tower. The subterranean excavation of the central wing will be accessible to the public in a manner similar to that at the undercroft in Dublin Castle (see page 98), while a section of the moat to the entrance front will remain on permanent exhibition.

National Concert Hall
Earlsfort Terrace, Dublin, 1981

THE DUBLIN WINTER GARDEN PALACE.

Dublin's music community had long been agitating for a concert hall in the city, and in fact plans were drawn up for various sites, but on each occasion the idea was shelved, for one reason or another.

The National Concert Hall finally threw open its doors in September 1981. It comprised a converted section of University College Dublin on Earlsfort Terrace. More correctly, the new hall was a work of restoration, for the building was erected initially to accommodate the Dublin International Exhibition of 1865 (left), and was retained as 'a structure where the citizens might enjoy national recreation combined with the elevating influence of the Arts'.

Only twenty years later, the 'exhibition palace' was acquired by the Royal University of Ireland, involving major works of alteration, including a new façade in 1914–19. But for lack of funds, the surviving remnant of the 1860s building would have been demolished to make way for the expanding institution.

In the 1970s the various faculties began to vacate Earlsfort Terrace in favour of the new Belfield campus, and the university's 'great hall', used for conferring ceremonies, debates, exams and dances (above), and sculpture gallery was made available to the State. The Minister for Finance, Richie Ryan, announced the proposed conversion of Earlsfort Terrace in May 1974, arguing that 'the Great Hall will provide a reasonable solution to the pressing problem of providing a base for the RTÉ Symphony Orchestra'.

Being almost a perfect double cube, the space was acoustically very promising, and all intervention to adapt it for the National Concert Hall was with a view to reaching its maximum potential in this area. Dr V L Jordan of Denmark, whose previous work included acoustic design for the Sydney Opera House and the Metropolitan Opera in New York, acted as consultant.

A new sloping floor was added, and a balcony with curved profile surrounds the hall on all sides, that part above the stage designated for a choir of 200.

In all, seating is provided for over 1200. Above the stage are suspended sixteen mobile discs, which, along with acoustic absorbers set in panels lining the walls, can be tuned to various frequencies, depending on the desired sound

balance. The roof was replaced by a lightweight structure, reminiscent of the original exposed beam ceiling, designed to eliminate external noise. The existing masonry and decorative plasterwork were carefully repaired and restored.

The National Concert Hall has played host to such talents as Yehudi Menuhin, Bernadette Greevy, the Russian State Ballet Company, and the

Chieftans, among many others, as well as being the official home of the National Symphony Orchestra.

The refurbishment of the foyer and the John Field Room in 1995 improved the accommodation for small-scale recitals, and provided good opportunities for the display of contemporary Irish art works.

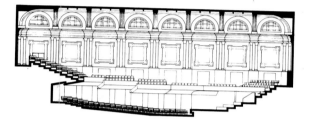

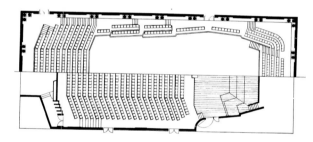

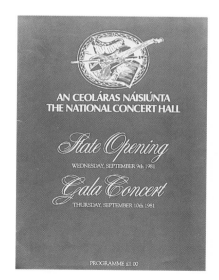

AN CEOLÁRAS NÁISIÚNTA
THE NATIONAL CONCERT HALL

State Opening

WEDNESDAY, SEPTEMBER 9th 1981

Gala Concert

THURSDAY, SEPTEMBER 10th 1981

PROGRAMME £1.00

Dublin Castle

For seven hundred years after its construction in 1228 on the orders of King John of England, as a military fortification (the only obvious remnant of which is the Record Tower), Dublin Castle was at the heart of the city, politically, militarily and socially, as well as geographically.

In the twentieth century, the castle has made the transition from bastion of British authority in Ireland to a place of civic prestige, and remains the focus for many of the Republic's most important ceremonies. The architectural challenge has been to expose and give protection to the full historical evidence, commensurate with providing government accommodation to contemporary standards, and effecting a transformation to an environment commanding the respect and enjoyment of the occupants and visiting public.

George's Hall

In anticipation of the visit of King George V and Queen Mary in July 1911, a large supper room adjoining the State Apartments was built. The construction of George's Hall presented some difficulties, as it covers the space once occupied by the moat. In addition, the living accommodation in the State Apartments was updated with adequate electrical supply and sanitary facilities for the royal guests and their entourage.

World War I

Between 1915 and 1919, the State Apartments and official residences in the Upper Yard were altered for use as a Red Cross military hospital during the war. James Connolly, one of the captured leaders of the 1916 Easter rebellion, was treated for his wounds, and court martialled, in the castle hospital shortly before his execution.

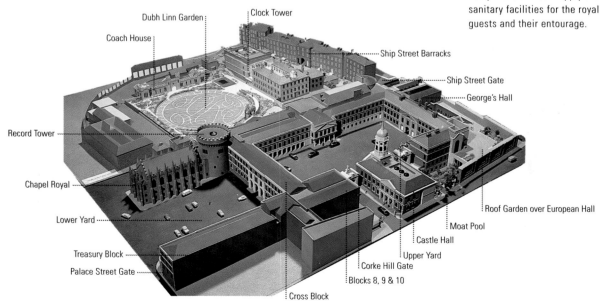

Labels: Dubh Linn Garden · Clock Tower · Coach House · Ship Street Barracks · Ship Street Gate · George's Hall · Record Tower · Chapel Royal · Lower Yard · Roof Garden over European Hall · Moat Pool · Castle Hall · Treasury Block · Upper Yard · Palace Street Gate · Corke Hill Gate · Blocks 8, 9 & 10 · Cross Block

State Apartments

Sir William Robinson redesigned the first-floor State Apartments in their current form in the 1680s, following a fire which obliterated much of the medieval character of the castle. Remodelling continued sporadically until approx. 1761. One of the architects involved was Joseph Jarratt, deputy Surveyor-General, to whom the garden façade of the State Apartment block (above) and the top-lit State Corridor have been attributed. The role and general layout of this south range was unchanged, however, and the bedrooms, Throne Room (above) and St Patrick's Hall (left) still occupy the site of their medieval equivalents.

Immediately after the devastating fire of 1941 (above), a temporary roof was erected over the damaged eastern half of the State Apartments. A structural survey was conducted in 1956 which revealed serious foundation failures, rampant dry rot, and external walls so out of plumb line that they were in danger of collapse. The best course of action was to demolish and rebuild the interior partitions while retaining the façades. Commenced in 1958, this work took ten years to complete, and involved not only this half of the State Apartments, but the entire Cross Block between the Upper and Lower Yards which was found to be in a similar condition.

The vibrant peacock blue, wine and gold decorative scheme of the State Drawing Room (above right) is seen to best effect at night, when the room is lit by the Waterford glass chandeliers. The internal plasterwork and joinery was reconstructed from samples that survived the fire. Much of the surviving furniture was restored, and new oak and mahogany parquetry floors were designed. Carpets were designed by Raymond McGrath and hand-tufted by Donegal Carpets Ltd (right).

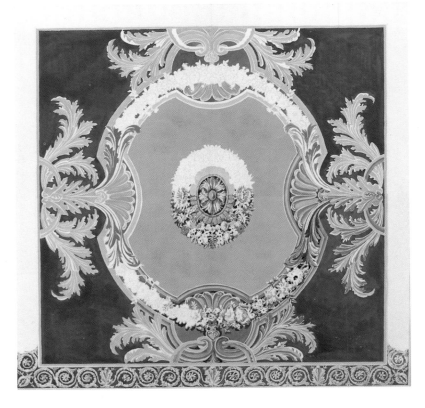

With similar attention to detail, the sumptuous rooms including the Wedgwood Room (above) comprising the rest of the State Apartments were rebuilt and restored using a wealth of specialised craft skills. Off the State Corridor, a panelled room from the former Tracton House was incorporated. Its superb stucco ceiling of *c* 1745 depicts the sun-god Apollo and the signs of the zodiac. In St Patrick's Hall, the ceiling paintings by Vincenzo Valdré (1783) were removed, cleaned and restored. The OPW won the RIAI 1946–76 Silver Medal for Architectural Conservation for this project.

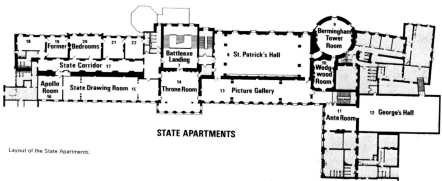

STATE APARTMENTS

Layout of the State Apartments.

1946 development plan

For over thirty years after its symbolic hand-over in 1922, there was little architectural intervention at Dublin Castle except minimal maintenance. However, an accidental fire originating in the State Apartments in January 1941 was the impetus for a contentious debate over the future role of the historic complex.

In seeking to accommodate those civil servants made homeless by the fire, the OPW concluded that a large-scale rationalisation of government accommodation in the castle precinct was essential. In 1946, the OPW presented a development plan which proposed the demolition of the agglomerate of early nineteenth-century infantry barracks, coach houses and other outbuildings in the Lower Yard and castle garden. In their stead, a crescent of buildings would reach from the Palace Street gate to Ship Street, with the ability to house 4000 civil servants from a variety of departments. The OPW estimated that the scheme would take twenty years to realise.

Government approval, though granted in 1946, was reviewed on several occasions in the wake of public and media comments. In particular, the *Irish Independent* and *The Irish Times* strongly objected to the proposal in editorials, arguing that the centralisation of personnel was inadvisable in view of the already seriously congested traffic situation. *The Irish Times* went so far as to suggest that a possible alternative use of the five-acre space would be 'a badly-needed central car park' (18 October 1948).

Stage I (new Revenue offices) was approved in 1955 and the remainder was shelved, as the conservation of the Castle's building fabric became an over-riding concern in the late 1950s.

Revenue offices 1974

The new Revenue offices (opposite) in the Lower Yard of the castle completed a courtyard bounded by the Treasury Block (1714), the Cross Block which was rebuilt in the 1960s (opposite), and the early nineteenth-century Chapel Royal. The project represented Stage I of the 1946 plan which was approved in 1955.

The planning stages were prolonged by the expanding requirements of the department, especially the Stamping Branch, and commenced on site in 1969. The four-storey office block, known as the Stamping Branch, extends southwards from the Palace Street gate, and screens the former printing works and ancillary accommodation.

Along with a two-storey block on Dame Lane and a basement for storage, the complex provides 100,000 square feet. The main block is of reinforced concrete, the structural elements of which are exposed, with large windows between the piers on the principal elevation. The height of the building was restricted to the height of the parapets in the Lower Yard, and projecting balconies at each of the upper floor levels allow for easy external maintenance and the control of solar gain.

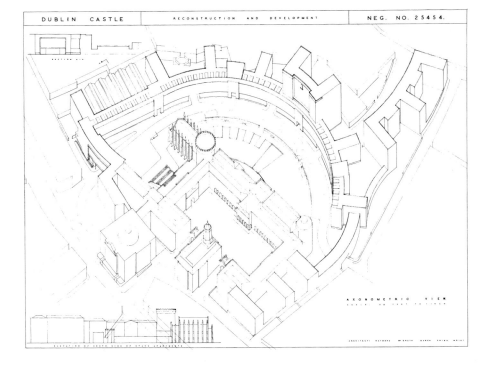

DUBLIN CASTLE — RECONSTRUCTION AND DEVELOPMENT — NEG. NO. 25454.

AXONOMETRIC VIEW

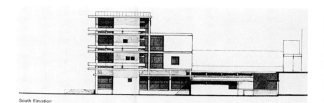

South Elevation

Elevation to Lower Castle Yard

Castle Hall and conference centre 1989

Between 1987 and 1989, the demolition of various dilapidated annexes and structures in the Upper Yard enabled the development of quality office space and three independent conference centres, while re-establishing the original Georgian appearance of the Upper Yard. The centrally located Bedford Tower, c 1760, formerly served as the headquarters of the Irish Linen Board and subsequently the Irish Genealogical Office. It received external and internal conservation and, along with a modern extension to the rear, it now forms the multi-purpose Castle Hall. The dining areas overlook the symbolic moat pool, reminiscent of the original castle moat. In the older structures, finishes are in the Georgian tradition – painted plasterwork and joinery, and ornate fireplaces, while in the new areas similar materials are used but in a contemporary manner.

A large purpose-built meeting room known as the European Hall is built at basement/moat level so that the form of the Upper Yard is maintained. This building was inaugurated in 1990 by conferences associated with Ireland's Presidency of the EC. The new two-storey structure is clad with alternate bands of Wicklow granite and Carlow limestone slabs. The screen windows in its south wall are evocative of medieval tracery, and look out onto the base of the Corke Tower. Also accommodated behind the west range are new kitchens, press corps facilities, and a roof garden.

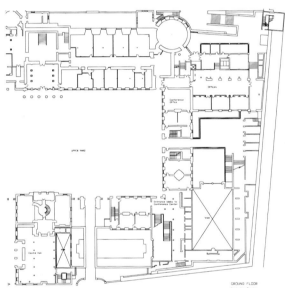

GROUND FLOOR
Not to Scale

The problems raised by the absence of controlled development, fabric deterioration and inefficient use of space in the castle estate, were considered in the early 1980s. Central to the philosophy was the need to retain and enhance the integrity of the historical complex, while redefining the future role of the castle. This would be effected through adaptation and new structures, which would be both complementary and contemporary, and in doing so transform the popular image from that of a centre of repression to a centre of enjoyment.

Blocks 8, 9 and 10 and the undercroft 1989

In the process of stabilising and restoring the buildings knows as blocks 8, 9 and 10 in the north range of the Upper Yard, archaeologists uncovered the magnificent stone base of the thirteenth-century Powder Tower; a section of the city walls, and remains of a Viking embankment. The tower is bounded on two sides by the original moat which is filled with water, the level being dictated by tidal movement. These structures are of great significance archaeologically, and almost 100,000 artefacts were discovered in the course of the excavation. Visitor access to the 'undercroft' was facilitated by the installation of lighting and walkways.

Major alterations to the proposed structural system of blocks 8–10 was necessary to avoid damage to the undercroft. The Upper Yard façade of the subsiding building was retained, while the rebuilding above basement level followed along the lines of the original Georgian structures, from which every attempt was made to salvage materials for re-use in the reconstruction.

Van Nost sculptures

The symmetry of the north range was completed by rebuilding the previously 'blind' Gate of Fortitude and thus providing another access point to the Upper Yard from Castle Street. The lead statues of 'Justice' and 'Fortitude' crowning the pediment of each gateway were executed by Jan Van Nost the Younger in 1753. In conjunction with the work in this area of the castle, they were removed for painstaking repair and conservation, part of which involved working on tiny areas at a time, using dental equipment, in order to retain the original level of detailing. Before their reinstatement, the statues were painted in Portland stone colour, which matched the original paint layer discovered on analysis.

The Treasury Block 1992

The treasury wing dates to *c* 1714, making it Dublin's oldest surviving purpose-built office building. The architect was Thomas Burgh, Surveyor-General, who raised the block on a level podium, keeping the doorways well above the sloping Lower Yard which was then dominated by stables. By the 1980s, it was in a structurally defective condition, and it was decided to initiate a restoration programme to provide office accommodation to modern standards and visitor facilities in the barrel-vaulted basement. The project was completed in 1992.

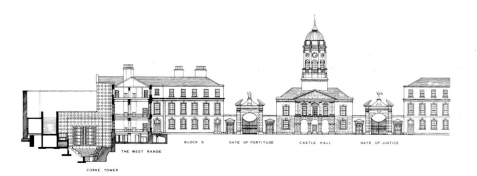

CORKE TOWER | THE WEST RANGE | BLOCK 5 | GATE OF FORTITUDE | CASTLE HALL | GATE OF JUSTICE

Chapel Royal 1989

The Chapel Royal was constructed between 1807 and 1814 to the design of Francis Johnson, who engaged some of Ireland's premier craftsmen such as Edward and John Smyth (stone and plaster sculptors), Michael Stapleton (stuccodore), and Richard Stewart (wood carver).

During the recent restoration project, it was found that structural movement over the years had resulted in severe cracking in the walls and floor vaults. Consolidation of the building was carried out by stitching and grouting, followed by stonework repairs and cleaning, with minimal interference to the natural ageing of the stone. With the help of a watercolour by George Petrie (above right), the timber and plaster vaulted interior has been restored to its authentic appearance. The original simulated effect of ashlar stonework was recreated, the original buff tones having been identified through scientific analysis. The project also involved the installation of underfloor electric heating and cleaning of carved oak-panelled balconies and sanctuary.

Coach House 1995

The castellated Coach House was built in the nineteenth century by Jacob Owen, to provide a more pleasant view from the lodgings in the State Apartments in advance of a visit by Queen Victoria. It was restored in 1995 and used as a press centre during the EU presidency the next year. Beyond structural and stonework repairs, a policy of minimal intervention was followed, to allow the existing materials and spaces to speak for themselves.

Dubh Linn Garden 1995

Topographical evidence indicates that the black pool or 'linn dubh', which it is said gives its name to Dublin (Dubhlinn), at the mouth of the River Poddle, existed on the site of the later castle gardens. The garden is therefore at the nucleus of the city. The pool was reclaimed in the seventeenth century, and the Poddle now flows underground.

In conjunction with the coach house, the castle garden has been redefined. The requirement for a helicopter landing-pad dictated the open circular area 50 metres in diameter, and occupying most of the available space. An interlocking Celtic pattern was used for the design. The six lines, formed of brick paviers set in a compact lawn, have serpents' heads with glass eyes, which are part of the system of guiding lights for approaching helicopters. This area sets up an axis between the gothic-revival elevation of the coach house, and Jarratt's façade of the State Apartments. The four distinct corner gardens each have a water feature by contemporary Irish artists. Finally, the historic route linking the State Apartments with the garden via a bridge has been reopened and extended.

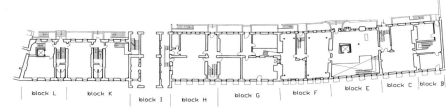

GREAT SHIP STREET BARRACKS REFURBISHMENT

Ship Street Barracks 1995

The Great Ship Street buildings originally served as soldiers' barracks from the eighteenth century, and were allocated to the various branches of the military. They comprised nine houses externally similar to the basic domestic terrace units that formed the streets and squares of Georgian Dublin. In the early 1920s, the buildings became redundant as barracks, and have since served a variety of purposes.

The architectural approach was to strip the buildings of all layers of plaster and paint to expose the structural brickwork, and so to prepare the shell for new use. All the houses, or blocks, were interconnected, with independent entrances and stairs, so the brief requirement for flexibility of use by various government departments was possible. The buildings had suffered from widespread cracking, unstable chimney stacks, dry rot and settlement. In order to compensate for the poor structural condition, steel-framed construction was selected to avoid the dead load which reinforced concrete would have imposed on the suspect walls. Stairs of light steel were incorporated into each block, allowing a diffused light to penetrate deep into the well, and serve to emphasise the contrast of contemporary architectural elements in an historic framework.

Block E was opened up from basement to roof level to form a 16-metre-high atrium, which is the focus of the complex and incorporates the main entrance and reception. The pendant sculpture in the atrium is by Vivienne Roche, and is called 'Plumbline'.

Clock Tower 1995

The Clock Tower building dates from the eighteenth century. It was remodelled in the early nineteenth century, probably by Francis Johnson, and has recently been extended to house the Chester Beatty Library collection of international art and manuscripts. The project comprised the construction of a modern purpose-built exhibition area linked by a glazed concourse to the U-shaped Clock Tower, which was restored. The two-storey extension includes exhibition space, an audio-visual theatre, storage and a roof garden, and will satisfy all the environmental requirements for the preservation and display of the unique collection.

The eponymous timber clock tower and mechanism were repaired, and a new weather vane was commissioned.

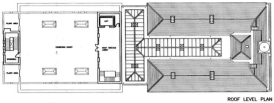

ROOF LEVEL PLAN

SECOND FLOOR PLAN

FIRST FLOOR PLAN

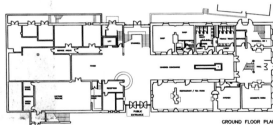

GROUND FLOOR PLAN

Skellig Michael
Co Kerry

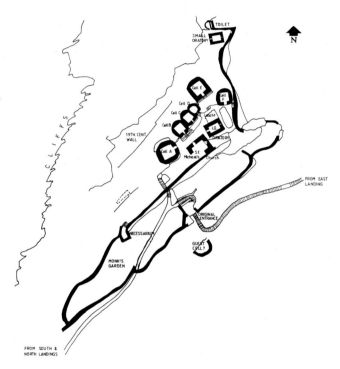

A Christian monastery was established here by the seventh century, and a spectacular hermitage was subsequently constructed on the South Peak. The monks continued to inhabit the island until the twelfth or thirteenth century, by which time they had established a monastery at Ballinskelligs on the mainland.

The current programme of works to preserve this spectacular and unique monastic settlement began in the summer of 1978 and has continued each season since then. Access to the island is limited to the summer months – a period of about fifteen weeks each year.

The site comprises six drystone beehive huts, two drystone oratories, St Michael's Church, a cemetery and two large enclosed terraces which were possibly used as gardens. The abandoned monastery was inhabited briefly in the early nineteenth century by the lighthouse builders, who undertook works to make the site more usable and to conceal their debris. This intervention was fully documented before its removal to reveal most of the original monastic construction. The site was fully paved throughout, which gave the enclosure a very urban quality.

The conservation and consolidation of Skellig Michael has been an interdisciplinary project involving archaeological, architectural, engineering, mountaineering, surveying and other allied skills. The works have been carried out by a skilled and dedicated workforce with the necessary safety expertise. These works will continue into the next century.

In 1996, Skellig Michael was designated a World Heritage Site by UNESCO. This is the ultimate international acknowledgement of the importance of this monument and the approach taken to its conservation and management, and elevates the site to the status of the Pyramids of Egypt, Stonehenge and Machu Pichu among others. The only other Irish site so classified is the archaeological complex of the Boyne Valley.

Royal Hospital, Kilmainham

The Royal Hospital at Kilmainham was built in the grounds of a ruined twelfth-century priory and hospice of the Knights Hospitallers, itself occupying the site of an early Christian monastery (Kilmainham means 'Maignenn's church').

The driving force behind the Royal Hospital, undoubtedly inspired by l'Hôtel des Invalides in Paris (below left, completed 1676), was James Butler, first Duke of Ormonde, who spent several years in exile in France with the future King Charles II (see Kilkenny Castle page 88). The concept was outlined in the Kilmainham charter of 1679: *that such of the....Army, as hath faithfully served....in the Strength and Vigour of their Youth, may in the Weakness, and Disasters, that their Old Age, Wounds or other Misfortunes may bring*

them into, find a comfortable Retreat and a competent Maintenance therein.

The architect was William Robinson, Surveyor-General and designer of Marsh's Library in Dublin and Charlesfort in Kinsale, Co Cork. Ormonde, who was also Lord Lieutenant, laid the first stone in April 1680, and the first residents moved in four years later.

The Royal Hospital is ranged around an almost square courtyard, reputedly once planted with lime trees, which were believed to have medicinal benefits. The north range is taken up by the centrally located Great Hall, chapel and master's quarters, the balance providing accommodation for approx-imately 250 invalids and pensioners. The separate infirmary, with adjoining physic garden, was designed in

1730 west of the main building by Thomas Burgh, successor to Robinson, and now accommodates Kilmainham Garda Station.

The Royal Hospital holds a unique place in the architectural history of this country, being, as Edward McParland puts it, 'the most important seventeenth-century building in Ireland, and the earliest full-scale exercise of architectural Classicism in the country'.

The Royal Hospital was transferred to the new Irish Free State army in December 1922 by the master of the hospital, who was also by tradition the commander-in-chief of the army. At this time, virtually all the veterans and contents of the hospital were removed to Chelsea Hospital, London (a similar institution opened in 1692).

A limited programme of conservation began in 1957, which focused on urgent treatment of dry rot and woodworm in the chapel, Great Hall, master's quarters and tower (an addition dated 1701), structural work and reroofing.

The newly restored baroque chapel in the Royal Hospital was dedicated to the late King Charles I in January 1687. The warm oak panelling was carved under the direction of the Huguenot James Tabary with outstanding skill, while the stained glass mostly dates to the Victorian period and features the heraldry of various masters. Unknown stuccodores created the remarkable ceiling, with clusters of vegetables, fruits and flowers bordering the deep coffers. Almost from the start, this sculptural masterpiece caused anxieties, as the virtually free-standing plasterwork placed unexpected pressures on the roof structure.

The OPW annual report of 1901 reports that 'in the early part of 1900 new signs of weakness presented themselves, and as they involved risk to worshippers, it was found necessary to close the Chapel in May of that year'. Members of the architectural division inspected its condition, calling in the advice of Sir Thomas Drew who proposed the erection of 'a new ceiling on similar lines, and of improved architectural character'. Fortunately, the decision was made to engage the London firm of Messrs Jackson to construct a facsimile ceiling made of the lighter material, papier maché.

The more recent (1980s) programme included timber conservation, restoration of the sandstone window tracery, and rebuilding of the Master's Gallery.

The ongoing restoration of the formal garden to the north of the principal building began in 1987, after initial work in the 1970s.

Little evidence as to the original appearance and nature of the garden was available, so extensive research into Rocque's map of 1756 and contemporary garden plans has informed the design, which is being created in the spirit of the late seventeenth century, rather than being a historical reconstruction. It comprises a parterre of planted lawn, bordered by pathways and a wooded 'wilderness' to enclose the parterre. Suitable statuary and urns have been acquired for the parterre, and the central fountain has been restored. Future phases of this project include the completion of the historical planting and restoration of the small garden pavilion attributed to Edward Lovett Pearce.

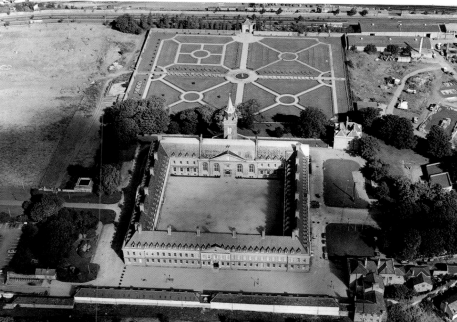

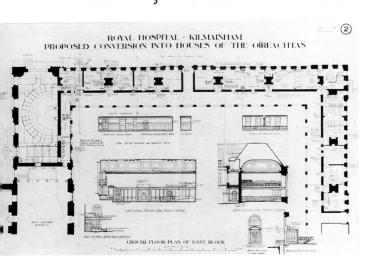

ROYAL KILMAINHAM HOSPITAL · DUBLIN ·

ROYAL HOSPITAL · KILMAINHAM
PROPOSED CONVERSION INTO HOUSES OF THE OÍREACHTAS

GROUND FLOOR PLAN OF EAST BLOCK

In 1923, the OPW prepared detailed drawings for the proposed conversion of the Great Hall and chapel to house the Dáil and Senate respectively. When this scheme was superseded by a more suitable location, the RHK became Garda Síochána headquarters from 1931 to 1950, by which time the building was suffering from many symptoms of old age.

Restoration work and maintenance continued throughout the 1960s, with the aim of transferring the folklife division of the National Museum, which used the buildings for storage at this time.

A major programme of restoration commenced in 1980. This project restored the main building to its appearance after Francis Johnson's alterations at the start of the nineteenth century, which had included reducing two storeys of dormer windows to one, and extension of the master's quarters. The challenging programme of work covered the whole building, its structure and finishes, including the panelled Great Hall, once the dining and recreation space for the veterans. On completion in 1984, the RHK opened to the public as the National Centre for Culture and the Arts, accommodating international cultural events and exhibitions.

The project won a Europa Nostra Medal 'for its contribution to the conservation of Europe's architectural heritage'.

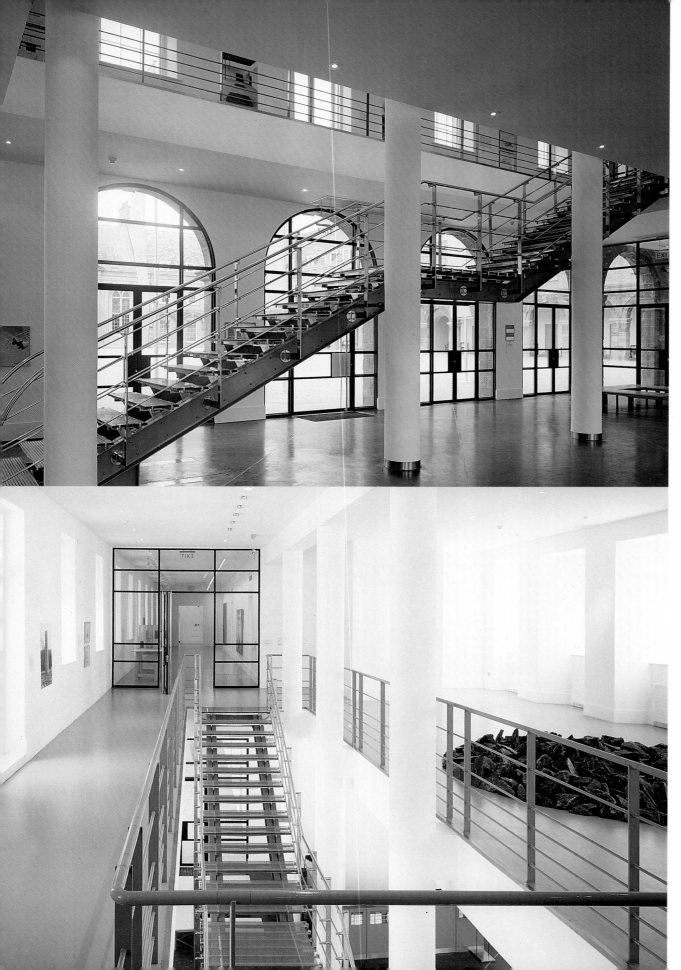

IMMA

Between 1989 and 1991, the east, south and west ranges of the Royal Hospital were converted to house the Irish Museum of Modern Art.

The ground floor rooms lead directly onto an open loggia which continues along the three ranges. Five central bays on the southern range were glazed in to form a new entrance to the museum, axially related to the Great Hall. A prominent new staircase of glass and steel leads from the new hall to the first floor and provides a strong spatial connection to the primary gallery spaces at the upper level. There, the individual rooms are accessed by a wide corridor, formerly used by the veterans for exercises in inclement weather.

The courtyard, acts as the first 'room' of the museum the visitor enters. It hosts special events as well as installation art works.

As part of a wide-ranging OPW plan for the regeneration of the Royal Hospital complex, the mid-nineteenth-century stable block and coach houses to the south of the main building were adapted to provide accommodation for artists' studios, workshops and stores for visiting artists and curators to IMMA. Half of the range had been demolished in the later Victorian period, and the surviving portion was in a dilapidated condition. The architectural challenge was to restore these ancillary buildings while adapting them sympathetically to modern uses.

Maximum light penetration was naturally an important consideration, and significant roof glazing was incorporated into the design. Existing semi-circular relieving arches located over the large doors were opened up to give additional light and ventilation. Internally, finishes were kept to a minimum, with painted rough stonework, exposed timber roof, metal stairs and galleries. The recovery of a number of original double-boarded doors influenced the design of the new block, which repeats some key external features and finishes of the original half.

The Deputy Master's House stands on the site of the north-east flanker building, one of four symmetrical flankers which were built in the 1680s as site offices and stores during the original construction. The present house dates from 1763 (extended in 1797), and acted as lodgings for the deputy master and his family.

Much of the original room layouts and character of the house survive, and the current programme for its adaptation allows for the preservation of the interior and exterior fabric. A major restoration project was completed in 1999, providing high quality interior spaces with appropriate environmental control for the display of delicate material. The basement accommodates a further gallery, conservation laboratories and secure storage.

Glebe House and Gallery
Churchill, Co Donegal, 1983

In 1953, Derek Hill, the English-born painter, stage designer, curator and avid collector, while staying at Glenveagh Castle in Donegal, heard that a nearby house was for sale: *It was an old rectory, a glebe as the Irish call it. For years it had been a fishing hotel on the Lake of Gartan... I immediately fell in love: it was on a lake, it faced south and the ground fell away from it: it was just the right size and charming architecturally, exactly the sort of house I'd always wanted to live in and the countryside about it was miraculous...* – Derek Hill, from *Derek Hill - An Appreciation* by Grey Gowrie, Quartet Books, London 1987

Hill bought the house and made his home there until 1981, when he generously presented it, together with its magnificent 22-acre garden and his collection of art works to the Irish state.

Hill transformed the rust-red glebe house with the help of his brother John, who was director of the interior design firm of Green & Abbott in London. Furniture, paintings, prints and china, often gifts from friends or mementoes of his extensive travels, form a personal history of Derek Hill's life at St Columb's.

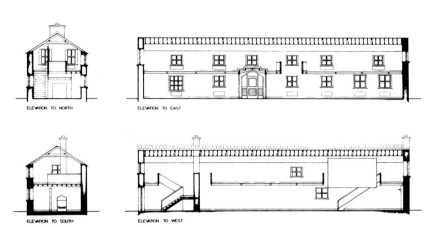

ELEVATION TO NORTH   ELEVATION TO EAST

ELEVATION TO SOUTH   ELEVATION TO WEST

The Derek Hill collection includes works by Constable, Degas, Picasso, Landseer and Le Brocquy; Scottish Wemyss ware; Chinese wood-blocks; Islamic pottery; and a number of the artist's own paintings. To house these, and accommodate touring exhibitions, the housekeeper's cottage, a low two-storey building near St Columb's, was adapted as a modern art gallery. The project was part-financed by EU cross-border funding.

The building had suffered the ravages of wet rot, dry rot, woodworm and leaking roofs. It was replanned internally to allow for easy circulation and access to exhibits. Stairs were arranged at both ends of the gallery, and the floors were opened up to form double-height spaces and lightwells. Surviving fireplaces, one of which is free-standing, were restored as focal points. Two separate flanking buildings were constructed, accommodating a caretaker's lodge, store, toilet block and kitchen, creating a three-sided courtyard.

To date, the Glebe Gallery has hosted numerous exhibitions, including 'Tory Island Painters' (1984), 'A Study in Pattern: The Art of Islam & William Morris' (1985) and the annual OPW 'Art of the State' exhibitions.

Killykeen Forest Park
Co Cavan, 1986

Killykeen Forest Park was the site of a research and development project, designed to discover and demonstrate the potential of Irish timber in construction, while simultaneously providing a series of holiday chalets in an economically underdeveloped border region rich in natural beauty. The self-catering holiday home complex was the first proposed by the Forest and Wildlife Service, responsible for the management of state forestry and wildlife conservation. Situated in rolling drumlin country, on the shores of Lough Oughter, Co Cavan, the complex draws families, groups and anglers attracted by the outstanding woodland setting, leisure and sporting amenities and renowned fishing. Killykeen Forest Park is managed by Coillte the Irish Forestry Board.

Twenty two- and three-bedroomed chalets, one of which is adapted for disabled access, along with a caretaker's home, recreation centre and ancillary services building (laundrette, shop), form the largest-scale use of native timber ever in this country. Previously, Irish timber resources suffered from a poor image, generally confined to the low-value end of the market such as fencing. Consequently, Killykeen was an experiment of major importance. Seven native species were employed, including Douglas fir for external cladding and oak flooring. New quality standards were established in terms of sawing, drying, stress grading, preservation and fire precautions, which were adopted by the Irish timber industry.

Each structure sits on concrete and steel columns which keep the building out of contact with the ground, and preserves the existing sloped ground profile. The compact interiors demonstrate an imaginative manipulation of a limited space, making particularly successful use of glazing to maximise sunlight, natural heat gain and spectacular views.

Parke's Castle
Co Leitrim, 1989

Parke's Castle is a valuable surviving example of a type of fortified manor constructed by Plantation settlers in areas of strong Gaelic support, such as Fermanagh, Leitrim and Sligo.

Some 1000 acres on the shores of Lough Gill was mortgaged from the O'Rourke clan by Captain Robert Parke in the 1620s. Parke levelled his predecessors' tower house at Newtowne, and over the next twenty to thirty years built the castle on the same site. The encompassing bawn defends the compact, self-contained domestic unit of residence, gate house, stables, blacksmith's forge, dovecote and stores.

Like many of the Planters themselves, the builders of such fortified manors were often of Scottish origin, and this is evident in the case of Parke's Castle. Architectural features such as the four bawn corner turrets reflect the contemporary Jacobean vernacular style in Scotland.

Robert Parke's only surviving child, Anne, married Sir Francis Gore of Ardtarmon, Co Sligo, ancestor of the Gore-Booth family of Lissadell, who thus inherited the castle at Newtowne. It is believed to have been uninhabited since the 1690s.

The first stage of restoration involved a complete archaeological excavation, which revealed the foundations of the O'Rourkes' towerhouse, and outbuildings. Also uncovered, just outside the bawn wall, was a seventeenth-century 'sweathouse' or sauna, used as a health cure, especially for rheumatism.

The manor house was reroofed and restored, the enclosing wall and parapet walk repaired, the blacksmith's forge rebuilt and equipped, and the stable block reconstructed for café use. Temporary and permanent exhibitions are housed in the manor and gate lodge, illustrating the history not only of Parke's, but also of the other historical attractions in the region.

Crucial to the success of the Parke's Castle project was the fact that the OPW architects could tap into a wealth of local vernacular building skills. Craftsmen reconstructed the timber flooring, roofing and the masterful Irish oak spiral staircase, carved the limestone for window mullions and thatched the new forge. Among its other roles, Parke's Castle is a showcase for their versatility and knowledge.

Newmills

Co Donegal, 1994

A watermill was first recorded at Newmills, near Letterkenny in Co Donegal in 1683, and since the start of the nineteenth century both a corn and flax mill have been in operation – a characteristic of many early industrial complexes in Ulster. Newmills played an important role in the regional economy, processing the oats, barley and flax purchased from local farmers. A brief revival in demand during World War II was followed by a sharp decline in production, until the complex closed in 1982. Four years later, the OPW acquired the site from the Gallagher family, and an eight-year major restoration project commenced.

The upper mill originally scutched flax, which is the first stage in the spinning of linen, and the lower mill ground corn. A timber chute connects the two buildings, channelling water from the River Swilly to power the water wheels attached to the mills.

The corn-mill wheel measures 7.63 metres in diameter. It operated the stone quern, which grinds kernels into oatmeal. The other stages in production – kiln-drying, cleaning, winnowing, sieving and packaging – were also accommodated in the corn mill.

The restoration of both mills involved extensive structural repairs to the buildings and reconstruction of the machinery and mill furniture throughout. A former storehouse has been converted into an exhibition space and visitor facility.

National Library of Ireland
Kildare Street, Dublin

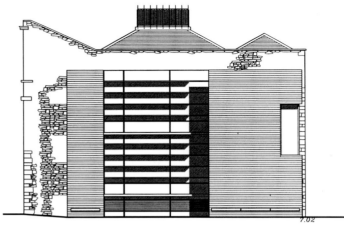

Though not formally established until the 1870s, the core of the National Library's collection dates back as far as 1731. In that year the [Royal] Dublin Society was founded to promote 'the improvement of husbandry, manufactures and other useful arts and sciences,' and these broad interests were reflected in the library it gradually amassed.

In 1877, the government purchased virtually the entire library at a cost of £10,000 and the collection has continued to expand with the aim of assembling and preserving items of Irish interest in the various media of printed books, newspapers, original manuscripts, photographs, prints and drawings. An increasing number of readers visit the library annually, to consult the wealth of material gathered there, which dates from the twelfth century to the present day.

An architectural competition announced by the OPW in 1883 sought designs for a twin National Library and Museum of Art and Science flanking the forecourt of Leinster House. Thomas Newenham Deane and his son (who, with their late business partner, Benjamin Woodward, had been responsible for the Museum building at Trinity College Dublin (1857) and the alterations to Kilkenny Castle (begun 1859)) submitted the winning proposal.

Two colonnaded rotundas frame the classical façade of Leinster House, the elevations inspired by Sansovino's Library of St Mark in Venice (begun 1537). The buildings were faced in ashlar granite from Ballyknocken, Co Wicklow; door and window details were from a newly tapped sandstone quarry at Mountcharles, Co Donegal, which was used in preference to Portland stone. However, the sandstone began to deteriorate at an alarming rate, and soon needed replacement.

The interior also reflects the Deanes' and the OPW's concern to utilise the best and most varied of Irish materials and craftsmanship, where it was available. The stone staircase with its Connemara marble balustrade leads from the entrance vestibule, rich in mosaic and stained glass, to the domed and airy D-shaped reading room. The oak screens, bookcases, fireplaces and doors are a tribute to the outstanding skills of Carlo Cambi of Sienna, and the Dublin carver Mulligan.

Twentieth-century works

The east wing of the library remained unfinished until 1925/6, when the government made available the funding to complete the building. However, the Victorian scheme did not allow for the increasing volume of material and additional services necessary in a modern national library, and throughout the twentieth century space has been at a premium. In the mid-1960s, plans were in hand to include a new library building in the John F Kennedy concert hall and cultural complex at Beggar's Bush barracks, before funding issues caused the ambitious project to be shelved.

A major programme of redevelopment commenced in 1995 with the aim of ensuring the safety and accessibility of the library material, the comfort of staff and facilities for readers. Essential repairs to the roof of the historic building and extensive restoration of the interior began, along with safety and security works. The racquet hall of the former Kildare Street Club has been adapted for use as a technical services building (1997), accommodating a modern conservation unit, a book bindery and a newspaper microfilming unit. Also housed in parts of the former Kildare Street Club are the current manuscripts reading room and the Genealogical Office, which became a branch of the library in 1943.

Another addition to the library complex is the attractive National College of Art and Design building (established as the Dublin Society Schools, opposite), constructed adjacent to Leinster House in 1823. Having been vacated in 1997, it is being refurbished for the storage and consultation of original manuscripts.

A master plan for the future of the library was developed by the National Library Council of Trustees in 1999, and approved by the Minister for the Department of Arts, Heritage, Gaeltacht and the Islands (below).

National Museum of Ireland
Kildare Street and Collins Barracks, Dublin

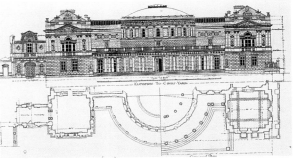

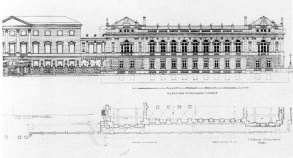

Kildare Street

The National Museum in Kildare Street shares many architectural similarities with its twin, the National Library. It is furnished with richly ornate mosaic floors, interior carvings by Charles Harrison, marble inlays, decorative wrought-iron columns and majolica door frames.

The Lord Lieutenant declared the Museum and Library open to the public on 29 August 1890, and simultaneously conferred a knighthood on the architect, Thomas Newenham Deane. The core of the museum originates in the collections of the Royal Irish Academy, the Museum of Irish Industry and the Royal Dublin Society. The scope of the collection broadened rapidly, and since the acquisition of all the collections by the government in 1877, the National Museum has been responsible for the state's collection of antiquities, decorative arts, historical industry and folklife artefacts and zoological and geological specimens.

As with the National Library, the OPW has been responsible for the provision and maintenance of the property of the National Museum since 1890. This has involved an ongoing maintenance programme, including the re-roofing of the majority of the museum and the renovation of the central court in the late 1980s.

In addition, exhibition displays are designed and executed by the OPW. One of the permanent exhibitions called 'Ór – Ireland's Gold' (1992) was designed for the sunken court specifically to highlight the outstanding collection of prehistoric gold in the care of the museum, while 'Ancient Egypt' (1997) creates a sepulchral atmosphere in which to display the often enigmatic artefacts of that civilisation. 'Viking Ships' (October 1998–September 1999), devised jointly by the Viking Ship Museum in Roskilde, the National Museum of Denmark, and the National Museum of Ireland, was ranged around the gallery of the central court. It explored the archaeological evidence for ships and shipbuilding during the Viking Age (approximately ninth century to twelfth century). During the course of the exhibition, shipbuilders from Roskilde built a replica of a small boat from the Roskilde find, while other craftsmen demonstrated rope making.

Serious erosion of the Mountcharles sandstone on the National Museum and Library façades was addressed in the early 1990s. Detailed surveys and examinations were undertaken to identify the extent of the problem and the most suitable method of treatment. Following a period of comparative research and testing, a mortar was developed to meet the specific needs of this project.

When the damaged stone surface is removed to a suitable depth, the newly exposed face is keyed, and the mortar, which incorporates a degree of sandstone to retain the original texture and ochre colouring, is applied. Plasterwork experts from the OPW's Building Maintenance Service are currently executing the painstaking project. The project began on site in May 1995, starting with the museum façade on Kildare Place, moving clockwise around the building. On its completion, work will commence on the Library.

THE BARRACKS

Collins Barracks

The Royal Barracks was designed by Colonel Thomas Burgh, Chief Engineer and Surveyor General, whose other projects include the library at Trinity College Dublin, Dr Steevens' Hospital and the original Custom House on Burgh Quay. It was first occupied in 1704 and marked a new development in the approach taken to the housing of soldiers. Situated on twenty acres on the north banks of the Liffey, at Oxmantown Green, it has remained the longest continuously occupied military barracks in Europe. In the 1920s it was renamed in memory of Michael Collins, late Commander-in-Chief of the national army.

As part of the Department of Defence's rationalisation programme, the decision was made to close Collins Barracks, and it was offered for sale in 1988. Five years later, an OPW study ascertained its suitability as accommodation for sections of the National Museum, which had long been hampered by lack of space in its Kildare Street headquarters. A number of alternative sites had been considered for the expansion of the museum, including the Royal Hospital, Kilmainham before its conversion for the Irish Museum of Modern Art. The report concluded that the buildings forming Clarke Square were particularly appropriate for exhibition use, and that those in the remainder of the complex were suitable to house the many support functions particular to a national museum. The government approved the proposal in September 1993, and site works commenced the following summer.

Collins Barracks was originally
laid out as four squares.
The central Collins Square is
flanked to the west by Connolly
Square, and to the east by
Clarke Square and Pearse
Square. Towards the end of
the nineteenth century, during
a serious outbreak of fever, all
the buildings forming Collins
Square and the corners of
Clarke Square were demolished
with a view to improving the
air circulation.

Phase I of development
(1994) involved extensive
stonework conservation and
re-roofing of the buildings
on Clarke Square, surface
treatment of the square, and
hard and soft landscaping to
Pearse Square. The main
façade of Pearse Square was
rejoined to east and west
by glazed link buildings
accommodating staircases
and lifts.

The suitability of the
barracks for exhibition space
meant that few structural
interventions in the historic
fabric were necessary. The long
rooms, which had previously
accommodated two rows
of beds with a central
corridor, now have the outer
fenestration blanked out, the
remaining windows overlooking
the square act as a constant
orientation reference. The
alternating spaces through
the principal new galleries
provide a circulation route
for the visitor.

The National Museum's art and industry division is now located at Collins Barracks. The inaugural exhibition in the west wing, which opened in September 1997, provides a narrative insight into the operation of a museum. 'Curator's Choice' comprises twenty-five items chosen by the curators, illustrating the diverse character of the museum's collections. The double-height 'Out of Storage' exhibition provides a view of the museum's artefacts in storage, each explained by multimedia computers, while 'The Museum at Work' explains the essential process of research and restoration. In the south block, new exhibition approaches are employed to display some of the museum's major collections, such as the Irish silver gallery (right), scientific instruments and Irish country furniture.

National Folklife Museum

In 1996, the government decided to accommodate the folklife division of the National Museum at Turlough Park House and demesne near Castlebar, Co Mayo. The house is a medium-sized domestic house built around 1865, by Thomas Newenham Deane. New structures adjacent to it are under construction (left). Carefully designed to assimilate with the character of the demesne, these will provide approximately 1500 square metres of exhibition space, and 2000 square metres of storage. The house is undergoing extensive restoration and adaptation to visitor facilities and museum administration, while the beautifully landscaped gardens are being restored by Great Gardens of Ireland in association with Bord Fáilte. Mayo County Council is co-funding the entire project.

Natural History Museum

The Natural History Museum was the first purpose-built museum in the RDS cultural complex surrounding Leinster House which included the National Gallery, National Museum and National Library. Containing thousands of native and exotic zoological and geological specimens, it was inaugurated in 1857 by Dr David Livingstone.

The OPW has undertaken basic maintenance works in the museum, but the Victorian mode of display is unchanged, reminiscent of the popular eighteenth-century 'cabinets of curiosities'.

Collins Barracks – phase II

The second phase of works is in progress, and allows for a new centrally located building to accommodate large visitor numbers and provide the type of flexible, quality space necessary for visiting international exhibitions. The eighteenth-century riding school will be adapted to special exhibition use, and the west range of the relatively modern Transport Square will accommodate conservation laboratories. Site development works (see page 136) and the probable inclusion of a station for Dublin's light rail system will complete this phase.

1798 memorial

The 1798 Bicentenary Commemorative Park (above) is located in the open space known as the esplanade or the Croppies' Acre, which connects Collins Barracks and the quays. This site was reputedly part of a mass grave for 'croppy boys' who were executed in the aftermath of the 1798 rebellion. The large unmarked granite slabs are symbolic gravestones. Connected to this area by a meandering path is the Area of Contemplation – two ascending walls forming split circles, on whose flanks are inscribed the names of those known to be buried near-by. The overall landscaping has been designed to re-establish the visual and historical connection between the Barracks and the Croppies' Acre.

Royal Irish Academy

Dawson Street, Dublin, 1996

The Royal Irish Academy was founded in 1785 for 'promoting the study of science, polite literature and antiquities'. Under its first president, Lord Charlemont, the Academy immediately began publishing scholarly papers, forming a unique collection of manuscripts and archaeological treasures, and taking various innovative steps in the field of scientific research. The Academy transferred its artefacts, including the Tara Brooch and Ardagh Chalice, to the National Museum when the latter opened in 1890.

Today, the RIA is renowned for the quality of its library, which is home to many priceless manuscripts such as the *Cathach*, or Psalter of St Columba, which is the oldest surviving Irish manuscript, believed to date to the sixth century. Many special collections have been donated by members and friends over the centuries, focused mainly on the subjects of Irish language, history and culture. The eighteenth-century Northland House on Dawson Street was purchased by the state for the RIA in 1851, and adapted by Frederick Villiers Clarendon of the OPW. The principal spaces created are the library (above) and meeting room (right). Extensive refurbishment work completed in 1996 involved renovating the entire premises; upgrading for fire and building regulations and improving storage facilities, office space and disabled access.

The Zoological Society of Ireland
Dublin, 1994–

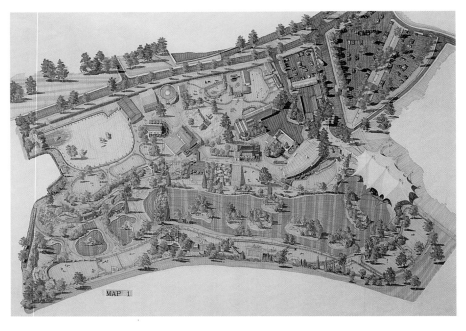

MAP 1

The *Plan for the Future of Dublin Zoo* (above) was published in April 1994 by the Zoological Society of Ireland and the OPW. This plan detailed the ways in which Dublin Zoo would achieve the highest calibre of animal welfare and fulfil its role as a centre for research in conjunction with Ireland's third-level colleges, while ensuring its commercial viability. Implementation of the plan was approved by the government, and the OPW, as agents for Dublin Zoo, was directed to put in place the approved capital works.

OPW's approach
The zoo's guiding principle behind the remodelling design was the concept of a 'zoo without bars', where each animal would enjoy an environment that, as far as possible, allows it to display much of its innate natural behaviour. From this grew the proposal to create 'themed' areas, which allows the animals to be understood in a broader context. The vision was of a place of lush vegetation where animal groups enjoy landscaped open spaces, while it is the visitor who is confined to narrow paths.

A general upgrading of the zoo's infrastructure (electrical and gas supply and drainage system) has been implemented. Other works include a temporary paddock for the rhinoceros, new enclosures for the tapirs and red pandas, refurbishment of the penguin pool, and a new filtration plant for the polar bears and sea-lion pools.

Since the zoo is one of Ireland's most popular heritage attractions, the improvement of visitor facilities is a significant element of the overall scheme, involving a new entrance building and shop (below left 1999), pedestrian walkways, and interactive play areas.

World of Primates 1996

This section of the zoo creates accommodation for each of six primate species, in natural surroundings which allow scope for behavioural enrichment as well as for animal husbandry.

The results are island habitats landscaped with extensive tropical planting and tall climbing structures. Land-based houses, connected to the islands by means of a rope and timber bridge, use native timber in structure and cladding, and contain heated enclosures and sleeping dens as well as keeper facilities. Each species is allowed to roam freely between their houses and islands, using the bridge.

The public is afforded a view into the houses, which are located just off the main path.

Fringes of the Arctic 1997–9

Phase 1 of this project (opposite left) provides a geographically themed area for polar bears, arctic foxes and snowy owls, who share a common habitat in the wild. The new bear enclosure is ten times the size of the old one, and affords views over much of the zoo. A range of stimulating natural elements is included, such as earth, rock, sand, grass and water. A second phase, which opened in spring 1999, incorporates areas for the Siberian tigers and Arctic wolves.

The study of the polar bears during the last 17 months has shown the improvement in their behaviour and quality of life since moving to their large new purpose-built enclosure. Pacing behaviour has disappeared in the male, and the level of repetitive swimming has greatly decreased in the female. This enclosure mimics the habitat found around the Hudson Bay area of North Canada during the summer and autumn months, where there is a large population of polar bears. The increased area, different substrates, deep pool and waterfall, observation platforms and natural vegetation has encouraged the bears to swim, dig, dive, graze, play, and rest at their leisure...

Observing such behaviours as these in captive bears is very encouraging as they are commonly recorded in studies of wild bears. (Extract from preliminary report of M Sc thesis by Elizabeth Barry, TCD, April 1999)

World of Cats 1998

This project (above) created a new habitat and dens for each of three species of big cats, namely lions, jaguars and snow leopards, on a 1.75 acre site. The job was complex and difficult, largely because of the requirement to minimise the visual impact of built elements.

Each enclosure provides appropriate natural surroundings of grassland, lush forest or rocky mountain terrain, with plenty of scope for behavioural enrichment. Features include climbing structures, timber shelters, pools, water features and a variety of ground substrates.

The 'World of Cats' was shortlisted for a Construction Industry Federation award in 1998.

African Plains project

This key element of the development plan will see the size of Dublin Zoo double as it acquires an extra thirty acres consisting of a large lake, pasture land and mature woodland, formerly part of the Áras an Uachtaráin demesne. Known as 'the African Plains', it will provide a home for many of the Zoo's African mammals such as giraffe, hippopotamus, rhinoceros and chimpanzee, and allow for the introduction of a number of smaller complementary species, some of which are endangered. All enclosures and paddocks will be integrated into the existing landscape. The project will be completed in the course of 2000.

Castletown House

Co Kildare 1994–

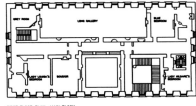

FIRST FLOOR PLAN MAIN BLOCK

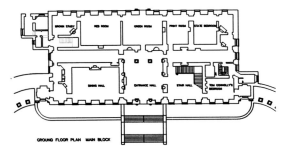

GROUND FLOOR PLAN MAIN BLOCK

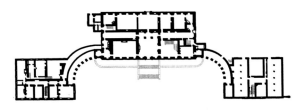

Ireland's grandest Palladian mansion, Castletown House, in Celbridge, Co Kildare, was built by William Conolly (1662–1729), Speaker of the Irish House of Commons. Speaker Conolly was then the wealthiest man in Ireland, and Castletown House was to be the ultimate symbol of his achievements.

Alessandro Galilei designed the façade of the main block *c* 1719, in the style of an Italian palazzo, but the actual construction began in 1722 under Sir Edward Lovett Pearce, who added the curved colonnades and terminating pavilions. The use of this classic Palladian scheme was widely imitated throughout Ireland.

The interior was unfinished at the time of Conolly's death in 1729, and it was only in 1758, after the marriage of his great-nephew Tom Conolly, who had inherited the Castletown estate, that this work commenced. His fifteen-year-old bride, Lady Louisa Lennox of Carton House, played a significant role in the development of the house and its decoration in the following years.

The Conolly family lived at Castletown until 1965, when the house, contents and 600 acres were sold to developers. Two years later, the Hon. Desmond Guinness purchased the abandoned house and some of the original demesne, which became the headquarters of the Irish Georgian Society, and commenced a programme of essential restoration. The Castletown Foundation was established in 1979 to take over the ownership and administration of Castletown House, and still acts in an advisory capacity in relation to the interior and its contents. Castletown House was formally taken into state care in January 1994.

The transfer to state care marked the launch of an extensive and on-going conservation programme. The initial stage focused on external fabric repairs to the main block, roof repairs and stonework (right and below, far right).

Phase II, completed in the autumn of 1998, sought to stabilise the internal environment through the renewal of the mechanical and electrical system, and upgrading of the security and fire alarm systems. A heating system was installed under the floor of the Dining Room, which had been enlarged by Lady Louisa Conolly in the 1760s to the designs of William Chambers (right).

The third phase of works on the main block has concentrated on structural issues and repair of internal finishes.

The ceiling of the famous Long Gallery (below), which measures 80 feet by 23 feet and dates to the 1720s (redecorated in the mid-1770s in the Pompeian manner then fashionable) was strengthened and the plaster-work was conserved. The three colourful glass chandeliers were made specifically for the room in Murano. Portraits of Tom and Louisa Conolly hang at either end of the room, which was furnished as a drawing room.

The house reopened to the public in the spring of 1999, and it is intended that it will remain open during future restoration work.

We then went to the house, which is the largest I ever was in, and reckoned the finest in the kingdom. It has been done up entirely by Lady Louisa, and with a very good taste; but what struck me most was a gallery, I daresay 150 feet long, furnished in the most delightful manner with fine glasses, books, musical instruments, billiard-table – in short,

everything that you can think of is in that room, and though so large it is so well filled that it is the warmest, most comfortable-looking place I ever saw; and they tell me they live in it quite in the winter, for the servants can bring dinner or supper at one end, without anybody hearing it at the other; in short, I never saw anything so delightful.
Lady Caroline Damer recounting a visit to Castletown in 1778, *The Georgian Society Records* volume 5 (1913) Dublin University Press

Further phases will include repairs to the collonades and entrance steps; work on the extensive grounds and parkland; and restoration of the Castletown Folly, gates and lodges. Conservation of the fabric of the wing blocks is also planned, and the location of visitor facilities in the east wing, formerly the stable block.

Future works will also include conservation of the embrittled mid-nineteenth-century silk damask wall hanging and carpet in the Red Drawing Room (above).

The Print Room dates to the 1760s, and is the only eighteenth-century room of this nature in Ireland to have survived intact. Lady Louisa and her companions enjoyed the fashionable pastime of pasting favourite engravings onto the walls, with elaborate borders and swags. One image is a print of 'Lady Sarah Bunbury Sacrificing to the Graces' (after a painting by Reynolds). The subject of the portrait was Lady Louisa's sister. The examination and conservation of this room will form part of future works.

Lady Louisa added the staircase to the east of the entrance hall in 1759–60. The cantilevered Portland stone staircase was built under the direction of Simon Vierpyl. The walls are decorated with plasterwork in the baroque manner by the famous Swiss-Italian stuccadores the Lafrancini brothers. 'The Boar Hunt' by Paul de Vos, one of the three original panel paintings which once hung here has been recovered. Careful structural examination and non-destructive testing of the cantilevered staircase has revealed serious problems which require delicate intervention to protect the wonderful plasterwork above and below the stairs.

Conservation priorities are being developed in line with available funding as a timescale of ten years is envisaged for completion of the main phases of the project.

Rathfarnham Castle

Rathfarnham, Co Dublin, 1987–

Rathfarnham Castle dates to 1583, when Adam Loftus of Yorkshire (later Archbishop of Dublin) constructed it in the form of a central residential block flanked by four corner towers. By the end of the sixteenth century, it was acknowledged as one of the finest castles in Ireland.

Speaker Conolly of Castletown purchased the building in 1725 for £62,000, but never lived here. A series of his tenants made slight alterations. The superb rococo plaster ceiling in the family drawing room dates from this period.

Rathfarnham experienced a renaissance under the patronage of Henry Loftus, Earl of Ely. Between 1769 and 1771 the interior was entirely modernised and became renowned for its collection of furniture and works of art.

Rathfarnham went into decline from 1783 when the earl died, but in the 1850s the Hon Francis Blackburne saved the building from its 'ruinous' state. The Society of Jesus, who occupied the castle from 1916, extended and adapted the building as a college and retreat house. Rathfarnham Castle was protected as a national monument in 1986, and purchased by the OPW the following year, when the current programme of conservation began.

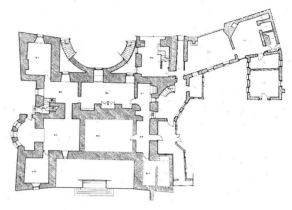

Restoration

Rathfarnham is presented to the visitor as a castle undergoing active conservation.

Ornamental stonework and other structural repairs have been completed. Minute examination revealed the makeup of the external eighteenth-century lime render, and the castle has now been re-rendered to the same aggregate size and appearance.

Extensive research into the interior, through the study both of surviving fabric and archival sources, is in progress. A number of rooms will be fully restored, as faithfully as possible; others will remain relatively untouched, revealing the methods, style and artistry of five centuries.

Drawing room

This room (1913 right) is attributed to the English architect James 'Athenian' Stuart (1713–88), one of the earliest architects to refer to Greek, as opposed to the popular Roman, architectural principles.

Ten painted panels, attributed to the Swiss artist Angelica Kauffmann, used to fit into the plaster ceiling, but were auctioned in 1913. Shortly after, they were replaced by scenes from the life of Christ by Patrick Tuohy. Kauffmann stayed at Rathfarnham during her visit to Dublin in 1771, and five panels in the breakfast-room ceiling are possibly after her designs.

This Castle is square, with a large square Tower at each Corner – on the South side in the Centre is a semicircular Tower. In its original State, it was embattled & had small Gothic Windows – these on Account of admitting but little light have been modernised & the Battlements taken off & a Coping of Mountain Stone substituted. ... The Gallery [probably the Drawing Room] is a beautiful room, at the far end is a curious Cabinet of Tortoise Shell and Brass containing some most extraordinary Work in Ivory. To describe this place particularly would fill a large Volume – suffice it to say – the Rooms are finished in a most superb manner, all profusely filled with elegant paintings, China, Vases, Urns etc etc [1781].
From *An Eighteenth-Century Antiquary: the sketches, notes and diaries of Austin Cooper 1759–1830*, edited by Liam Price, Falconer, Dublin 1942

National Botanic Gardens
Glasnevin, Dublin

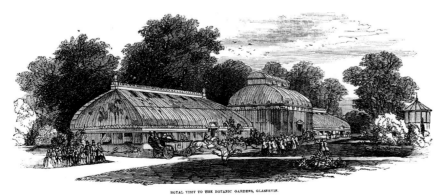

ROYAL VISIT TO THE BOTANIC GARDENS, GLASNEVIN.

Purchased and cultivated by the [Royal] Dublin Society, the Botanic Gardens at Glasnevin were funded by a grant from the Irish Parliament in 1795. The 19.5 hectare gardens (approximately 48 acres), situated just north of Dublin city centre, are now home to over 20,000 species of plants, trees and shrubs from every continent, some of which are extinct in the wild. Those not suited to the sandy lime-rich soil on the banks of the River Tolka are propagated in the Cactus House, Aquatic House, Fern House, Palm House or large artificial lake.

The purpose of the Botanic Gardens has always been to stimulate an interest in and appreciation of the plant kingdom among the visiting public. In addition, the gardens have earned an enviable reputation as a research, conservation and teaching institute, supplemented by an extensive herbarium of dried plant specimens, which plays a valuable role in the international arena of botanical and horticultural enquiry.

The OPW has advised the Botanic Gardens' managing bodies (the RDS up to 1877, and currently the Department of Arts, Heritage, Gaeltacht and the Islands) since 1842 on architectural matters.

Turner's 'Curvilinear Range'
The great Victorian Curvilinear Range of three interconnecting glasshouses, designed by Frederick Darley and the Dublin iron-master Richard Turner, replaced a number of early-nineteenth-century small timber-framed propagators. Richard Turner's output includes Dublin fanlights, domestic conservatories (for example that at Longueville House, Co Cork), the wings of the Palm House at Belfast Botanic Garden (1839) and the Great Palm House at Kew (1848).

The eastern wing was constructed inexpertly by William Clancy in 1843–4, and Turner's Hammersmith Iron Works in Ballsbridge subsequently fabricated and erected the remainder of the scheme between 1845 and 1869. Early on, Turner recognised the implications of recent changes in the manufacture of iron and glass, and high-quality wrought iron of immense tensile strength and flat, clear sheet glass facilitated his innovative curvilinear designs. Although built with the latest materials, the pilasters borrow an antique 'shorthand', with acanthus mouldings on the capitals, cornices and interior columns. However, ornament has been refined to express architectural junctions and so as not to detract from the overall lace-like quality of the buildings.

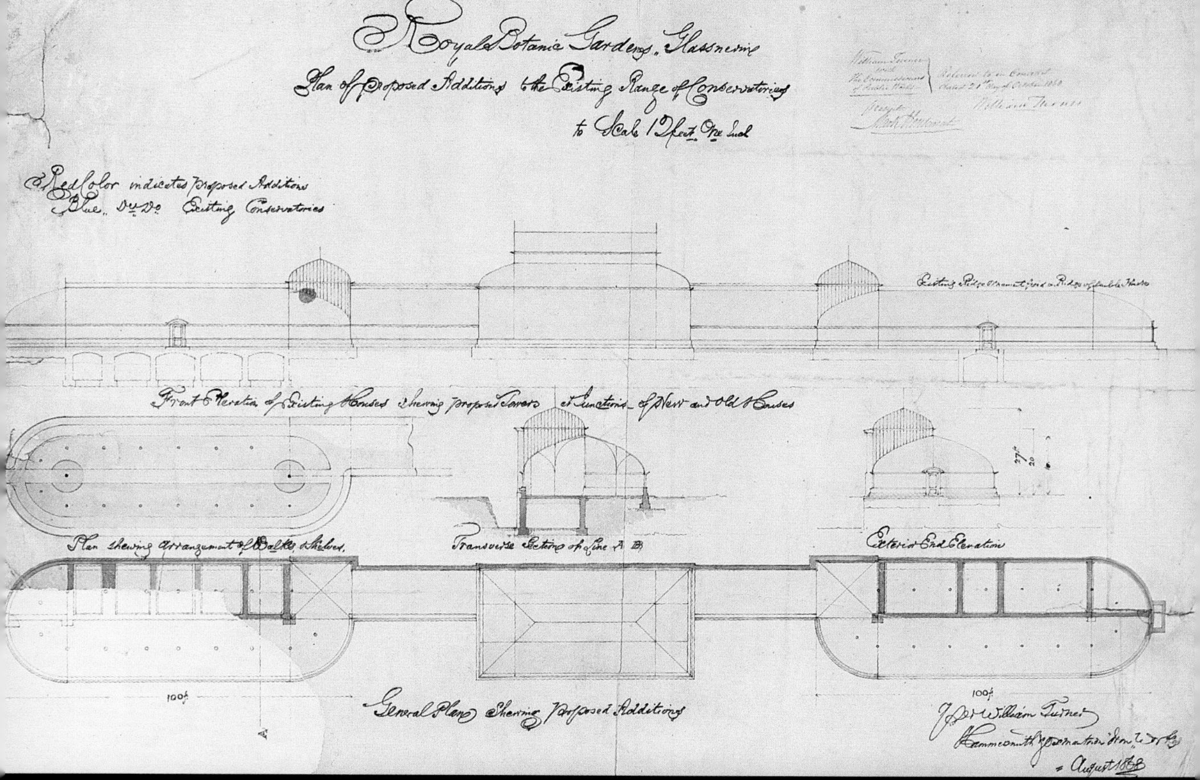

Royal Botanic Gardens, Glasnevin

Plan of Proposed Additions to the Existing Range of Conservatories

to Scale 12 Feet One Inch

Red Color indicates proposed Additions
Blue do do do Existing Conservatories

Existing Boiler Houses required to be Reduced to suitable Sheds

Front Elevation of Existing Houses shewing proposed Towers & Junctions of New and old Houses

Plan shewing arrangement of Boilers & Sheds.

Transverse Section of Line A B.

Exterior End Elevation

General Plan shewing Proposed Additions

100f

100f

Signed William Turner
Hammersmith Foundation Works Dublin
August 1868

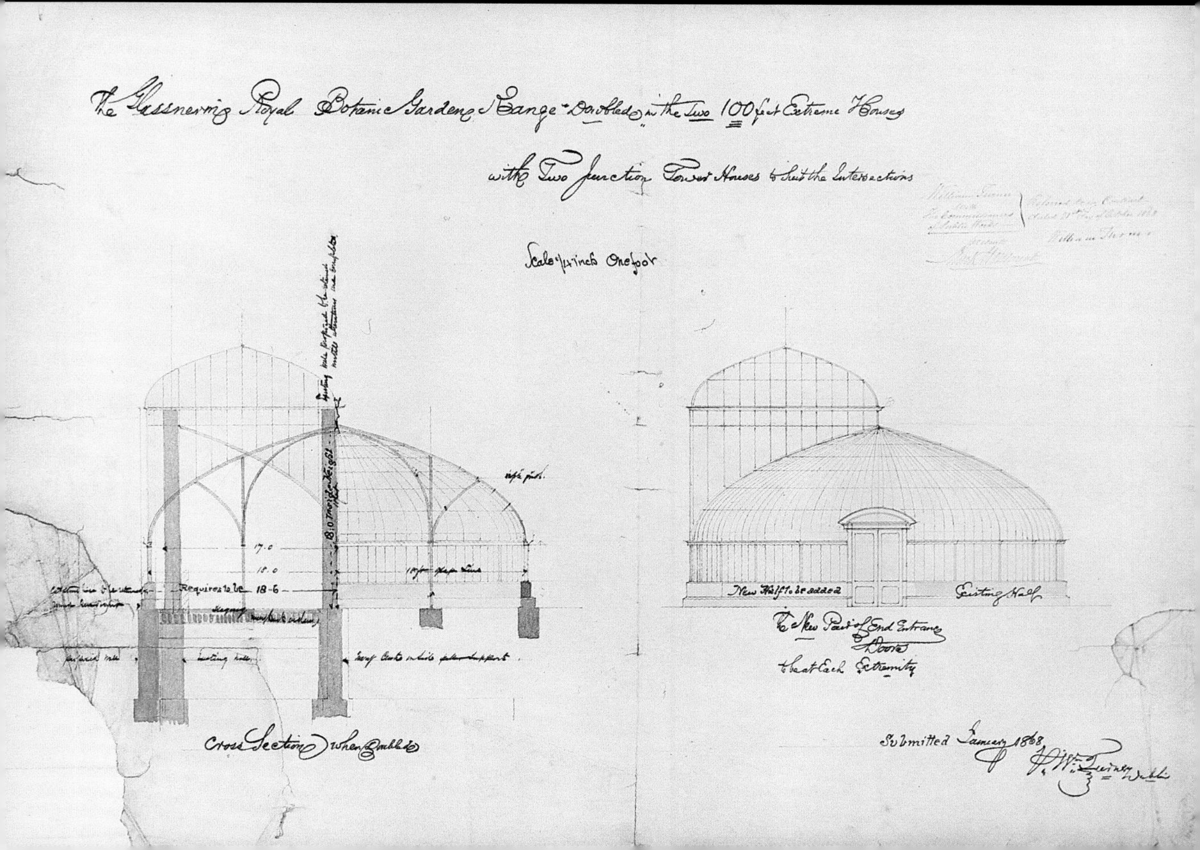

The Glasnevin Royal Botanic Gardens Range Doubled in the Two 100 feet Extreme Houses

with Two Junction Tower Houses to shut the Intersections

Scale ¼ inch = One Foot

Requires to be 18.6

17.0

10.0

Cross Section when Doubled

New Half to be added   Existing Half

To New Pair of End Entrance Towers
that each Extremity

Submitted January 1868
W. Turner

Restoration of Curvilinear Range

By the time the National Botanic Gardens were placed in the care of the OPW in 1992, the Curvilinear Range was virtually falling apart. Advanced metal corrosion, due to the tropical humidity inside, was manifest and other problems, such as defective foundations and inherent structural faults, became obvious.

The OPW architects entrusted with the task of restoration examined recent work on Turner's glasshouses in Belfast and Kew, both of which had been reconstituted by supplementing the original framework with modern steel glazing-bars, and fitting new glass. It was decided to investigate the practical and economic feasibility of a faithful restoration, maintaining the integrity of Turner's last surviving major project.

Even though no precedent existed for wrought and cast iron restoration and virtually none of Turner's original documents or drawings survived, the decision was made to proceed with the restoration, and so the Glasnevin Curvilinear Range for the second time became the medium for innovation in the field of wrought and cast iron architecture.

The existing ironwork was carefully tagged and dismantled and then cleaned, repaired and painted off-site. Only 13 per cent of the metalwork was beyond repair, and this was replaced by re-forged wrought iron of the 1840s from Turner's Kew Gardens, using a newly developed process called 'drop forging'. Replacement glass incorporated natural imperfections characteristic of the original panes. Using microscopic analysis, the original creamy white paint colour was discovered, though traditional lead-based paints were rejected in favour of a modern coating system of low permeability that would protect the underlying metal.

Planting, office facilities and a boiler house are provided to the rear of the building.

Three separate climatic conditions are maintained in the wings and central pavilion, monitored by computer-controlled temperature, ventilation and humidity sensors.

The restoration won the 1996 European Nostra Medal 'for the excellent and faithful restoration of one of the most important surviving nineteenth-century glasshouses in Europe, as an incentive for the development and research of wrought and cast iron restoration techniques'.

front elevation

National Botanic Gardens. 1795-1995

BUILDING FOR GOVERNMENT

Library

Formerly housed in a small students' hostel, the new research library and herbarium opened in autumn 1997. The unique site plan was inspired by the three styles of horticulture practised in the Botanic Gardens: the parallel furrows of agrarian cultivation; the arbitrary qualities of the 'picturesque'; and the classical geometry of formal garden design. Traditional terracotta brick makes visual reference to the director's house – the original demesne house, dating to the 1730s – while rich blue enamel tiles reflect a similar decorative feature on many Victorian terraces in Glasnevin.

Herbarium

The Irish National Herbarium on the ground floor contains some half-million pressed, dried and catalogued plant specimens, representing the entire botanical spectrum. These are stored in suitable environmental conditions in mobile cabinets. This invaluable archive is accompanied by offices, laboratories and a drying room. The first floor accommodates a unique library of 40,000 books, international journals, diaries, correspondence, watercolours, pressed-flower books and glass-plate negatives.

The interior fittings are fabricated in timber, in keeping with its research purpose. The shelving is of beech and cherry, and the doors are a patchwork of woods from around the globe. Wall-glazing presents spectacular views over the gardens and its other architectural elements. Natural lighting to the library is supplemented by three conical rooflights. Apart from the principal reference area, space has been provided for a librarian's office, a computer room, a conference room, and a rare books room with a controlled environment.

The restoration of the Curvilinear Range and new library/herbarium are only two of the projects recommended in the 1992 OPW Management Plan. Other completed projects include restoration of the director's house (1730s) and the chain tent pergola (1836) and the reinstatement of the old hydraulic pump and sluice gates for the artificial lake. Others are pending, such as the restoration of the great Palm House (1884), and a major new building incorporating lecture room facilities for audio-visual presentations and talks and a visitor centre.

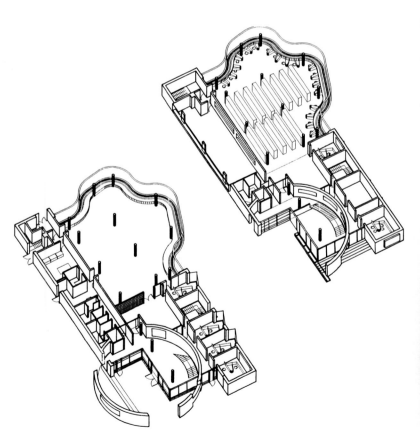

Barretstown Castle
Ballymore Eustace, Co Kildare, 1996

Though there has been a castle at Barretstown since the late twelfth century, the date of the present castle is uncertain. It was presented to the state in 1977, with a 500-acre demesne, and was used to accommodate official guests and to cater for conferences.

In the early 1990s, the Hole in the Wall Gang Camp in Ashford, Connecticut (a charity founded by Paul Newman to give seriously ill children and their families respite) mooted the adaptation of the Barretstown estate to create a similar camp for Europe. By 1993, a lease (at a nominal £1 per annum) had been negotiated and works funded by the Barretstown Gang Camp Fund Ltd commenced on site in the autumn of that year. The OPW are trustees of the estate, and the government donated all the necessary OPW architectural services to the fund. The camp was opened with a pilot programme in the summer of 1994. The camp is funded entirely through corporate, foundation and individual donations.

The architectural scheme involved the restoration and adaptation of an existing range of stable blocks, addition of new buildings and landscaping. The former stables (left) accommodate children's activity rooms including an arts and crafts centre and photographic room, and staff are accommodated on the first floor. Housed in an adjoining stone cottage is a fully equipped medical centre, which can provide treatment in a discreet and child-friendly environment.

BUILDING FOR GOVERNMENT

The dining hall and 280-seat theatre are new structures adjoining the stable courtyards, which employ the natural materials of uncut stone and timber.

Near by is the children's village, comprising nine cottages (three of which were erected in 1997 after the core building programme was completed). Each can accommodate eight children and four staff members, and incorporates a sitting room with an open fire.

The camp also has an adventure course, an archery range, a horse-riding area, a hilltop camp site with electricity and water supply, tennis and basketball courts, and the artificial lake is used for canoeing and fishing.

The Hunt Museum
Limerick, 1997

The Hunt Museum houses an internationally important collection of over 2000 original works of art and antiquities assembled over a lifetime by the late John and Gertrude Hunt. Among the works of art, dating from neolithic times to the twentieth century, is the personal seal of King Charles I (1625–49), a coin revered since the Middle Ages as being one of the 'thirty pieces of silver', and a small bronze horse by Leonardo da Vinci. The collection was donated to the nation in 1977, and in 1990, the remainder of the personal collection was presented by the Hunts' children, John Jr and Trudy.

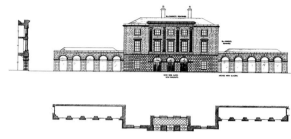

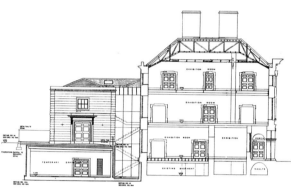

Limerick's custom house was completed in 1769, to a design by the Palladian architect Davis Ducart. It is situated on what was a busy Shannon quayside, but is now a quiet park. The main river façade is composed of a finely cut stone central block of five bays, with a rusticated ground floor, and flanked by loggias. It was used for customs and excise affairs until the early 1990s, when it was restored and adapted for the purpose of displaying and preserving the Hunt collection, incorporating a new gallery for visiting exhibitions and related visitor and staff facilities. The conversion project was partly funded by the European Regional Development Fund and Shannon Development.

Externally, this involved expert masonry repairs and the cleaning of the native Limerick limestone façades. Four chimney stacks were reinstated and supply fresh air to the air-conditioning plant.

The main entrance is located on Rutland Street, formerly to the rear of the waterfront building, in a new pavilion wing faced in Kilkenny cut limestone. Phase II proposes that a matching, balancing pavilion will provide symmetry and accommodate further educational and workshop spaces.

The Sacred Heart Oratory
Dún Laoghaire, Co Dublin, 1998

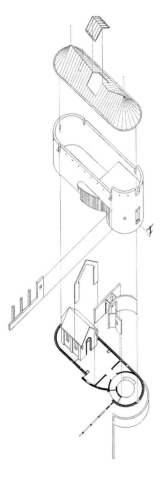

The Sacred Heart Oratory, the only remnant of the former Dominican Convent in Dún Laoghaire, was built in1919 as a gesture of thanksgiving for the armistice which signalled the end of World War I.

Between 1920 and 1936 a Dominican nun, Sr Concepta Lynch, devoted herself to painting the interior of this small free-standing building. Having trained as a manuscript illuminator, Sr Concepta combined stencil patterns and free-hand painting to create a jewel-like interior evoking the golden age of early Christian illumination.

Following the redevelopment of the convent estate in the early 1990s, the oratory was listed for preservation and became the property of Dún Laoghaire Rathdown County Council. By this time the art works had deteriorated. The OPW's conservation programme, completed in 1998, involved specialist cleaning and restoration of the paintings.

Meanwhile, the architectural team designed an encasing 'shell' for the oratory, to preserve the remarkable interior in a controlled and stable environment, and provide the space for an educational exhibition. The form of this outer building is sculptural, with references to ecclesiastical architecture, without being overtly religious. To ensure that the murals can be viewed as originally intended, the oratory is lit by simulated daylight through the stained glass windows (thought to be from the studio of Harry Clarke).

As part of the project, the surrounding garden was replanted, to help re-establish the oratory's original role as a place of contemplation and peace. This aspect of the project was undertaken by the County Council, which is responsible for the future management of the oratory.

Farmleigh

Entering the new millennium, the preparation of Farmleigh for use by the Irish government and visitors is one of the most significant projects entrusted to the OPW.

Farmleigh, the former Guinness estate next to the Phoenix Park, was acquired by the OPW, on behalf of the state, during 1999. The property comprises a Victorian mansion, dating to 1881; two gate lodges; numerous outbuildings; an extensive farm and well-tended formal gardens on approximately 78 acres.

Edward Cecil Guinness, the first Earl of Iveagh, bought the earlier, small house on the site in the 1870s, and extensively rebuilt it to form the present-day mansion. The remarkable ballroom, which spans the width of the building and gives onto the conservatory, is among six spacious reception rooms on the ground floor. The contents, including the library and many works of art, remain *in situ*, on loan from the Guinness family.

Farmleigh is to be used primarily for accommodating visiting heads of state and other dignitaries, for government meetings and other state or cultural purposes for the benefit of the people of Ireland. This includes a programme of public access to the house and various features in the estate.

The Architecture of State Buildings. OPW: Ireland 1900–2000

Part 2: Selected Other Works

RIC & Garda Síochána Stations

Prisons

Courthouses

Irish National War Memorial and Other Gardens

Government Offices

Schools

Embassies

Government Jet

Artworks

Social Welfare Local Offices

Visitor Centres

RIC & Garda Síochána Stations

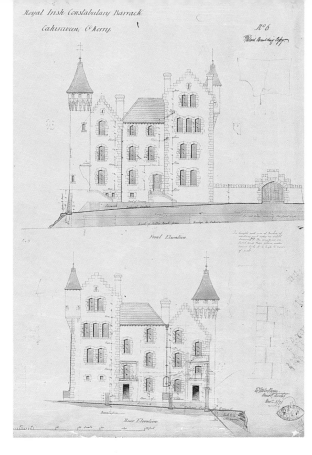

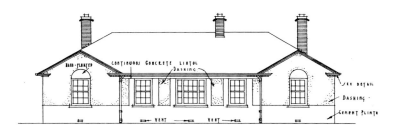

Reconstruction of the rural policing network following the troubled period 1919–21 was a crucial priority for the Irish Free State government. Considering the urgency of distributing the gardaí over the country, and the long-term question of housing, the OPW concluded that the restoration of damaged RIC barracks was in many instances the best option.

A type plan for an ordinary country station, to house a sergeant, sergeant's family and four guards, was employed in cases where wholly new stations were required. Four or five additional type plans were developed in the 1920s and 1930s (above). Each consciously made a break with the RIC past – the new stations were domestic in character and sympathetic additions to the rural village community, reflecting the Garda Síochána's role as an unarmed civilian police force.

In the 1950s, with the introduction of modern methods of communication and equipment and the necessity for increased accommodation for a new generation of recruits, it became evident that a considerable number of the older stations were inadequate and unsuitable. A programme for their replacement and the provision of new stations in population growth areas was prepared and new standard plans were designed (left). During the 1960s, fifty-eight new stations and eighty-seven houses were built, virtually completing the most urgent part of the programme, for which considerable funding was allotted.

By the late 1970s, the number of stations throughout the Republic had been reduced to its present level of 704, due to increasing mobility of the force. A major review of garda accommodation in 1982 revealed that 23% of all stations were more than one hundred years old.

Many older stations are now found to be too large in view of the trend towards a concentration of personnel in a number of centres. Larger stations designed in the late 1990s include cells, doctor's rooms, audio-visual room for filming suspects, rooms for illegal immigrants, as well as juvenile liaison and other administrative offices. Small 'basic units', such as that in Ballymahon, Co Longford, are meeting the needs of an increasingly mobile force. The character of these buildings is increasingly 'people-friendly', with a move to open-plan offices and areas for private consultation where required.

Cahirciveen

Cahirciveen RIC barracks in County Kerry was designed by Enoch Trevor Owen in 1871 (above). The surprisingly exotic style of this and the similar station in Dungannon, Co Tyrone, gave rise to the unconfirmed tale that these plans were destined for the Northwest Frontier Constabulary, while the Irish designs, through an oversight, were executed in the Khyber Pass.

Pearse Street Garda Station 1911–15

The Central DMP barracks was constructed between 1911 and 1915 on Great Brunswick Street, now Pearse Street. It replaced a three-storey terrace of Georgian houses and shop fronts, which had earlier been adapted. It employs a sober Scottish Baronial style popular in Ireland in the 1840s.

A phased modernisation programme was implemented between 1990 and 1997, creating an administrative headquarters capable of meeting the complex operational and functional requirements of a major central Garda station, and providing a pleasant and efficient workplace for members of the force. This essentially involved the cleaning and restoration of the finely detailed granite stonework, the excavation of a whole new basement floor, a major extension at the rear, and the upgrading of all remaining areas (detail page 171).

Donnybrook
This sober granite building in the heart of Donnybrook village was completed in 1931.

Roscommon

The prolonged deliberations at the planning stage of Roscommon Garda Divisional Headquarters were a symptom of the many developments taking place within the Garda Síochána in the middle of the century. In 1940, it was recognised that new, larger premises were necessary, when funding would allow. Six years later, the Department of Justice requested a sketch scheme which included living quarters for approximately seventeen single men. Eight married quarters were planned in separate houses close by. A revised plan (above right) was necessary in 1950, as it was proposed to incorporate many of the government staff in Roscommon in the station building. Finally, in November 1957, the Minister for Justice announced to the Dáil that 'the new barracks will be used for administrative purposes only',

while gardaí stationed there were entitled to a rent allowance. Working drawings were ready by mid-1959, providing for a station of 600 square metres, and two semi-detached married quarters, all of which was occupied in December 1961.

The gable ends of the main building reuse some of the limestone from the old gaol, the ruins of which were demolished to make way for the station.

In 1995, the original building was entirely refurbished and the office accommodation was upgraded to current standards. The project also involved the design of a new building – incorporating the new entrance, parade room, service facilities, dining and recreation space, offices, vehicle inspection bays and stores – which links the station with the married quarters.

Cork Garda Divisional HQ
1990

The site of 1.5 acres, formerly a depot for Cork Corporation, is on Anglesea Street adjacent to the City Hall and principal city fire station. Its formal composition complements the classical City Hall of the 1930s, and establishes it as an important public institution in the city. The entrance portico, which reduces in scale from three storeys, to two storeys to a single storey as one approaches the front door, makes the transition from the scale of the city to the scale of the individual building.

The plan is designed around a public reception hall, which is a rooflit, double-height cylinder with free-standing columns of highly polished limestone. The building provides 4400 square metres of accommodation, including reception areas for the five different operational sections within the Garda Síochána. An axial route leads from the entrance portico, through the vaulted entrance lobby to the reception hall cylinder, and continues through the lift lobby to the grand staircase with views over Cork city. The roof of the public office forms a courtyard at first-floor level, around which the upper three floors of office space are planned.

Tallaght

Tallaght Garda District Headquarters, completed in 1985 to replace a standard plan station of 1929, is located on the Belgard Road close to the Social Welfare Local Office and to the new town centre of this rapidly developing suburb. Walls are plastered externally and rusticated on the ground floor of the front elevation, painted pale blue and white, with navy blue doors and windows. The accommodation being essentially cellular in character, larger offices occupy the front of the two-storey element, facing south to the Dublin mountains, with smaller offices and ancillary accommodation in a single-storey section to the rear. Corridors in the two-storey section are interconnected and lit from above by banks of rooflights.

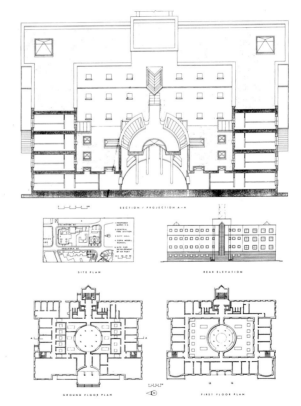

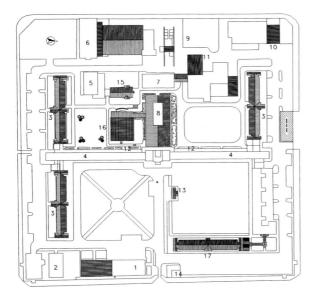

1 Garage
2 TV Studio
3 Residential
4 Offices/residential
5 Gymnasium
6 Physical Education
7 Recreation
8 Education
9 Tactical Training
10 Store
11 Restaurants
12 Glazed Link
13 Reviewing Stand
14 Security Control
15 Officers' Canteen
16 Education Block Extension
17 Residential Block

Templemore 1989–

The Garda Síochána Training College is situated in the nineteenth-century former military barracks at Templemore, Co Tipperary. The project was initiated in response to the Walshe Report on Garda training and its overall objective was to transform the barracks providing a 26-week elementary training course, into an up-to-date campus facilitating full third-level education for the Garda Síochána.

The main cross block, and one of the front square blocks were in a sufficiently sound condition to merit restoration, while the remaining three residential buildings replace derelict structures on the same sites. Other work on existing structures include the refurbishment of the driving school and gate lodge, while television studios and tactical training facilities were placed in the former barrack chapel and ball alleys respectively. The education building (below) is appropriately placed at the heart of the campus. It is approached via the new entrance hall, designed to recollect the tradition and dignity of the Garda Síochána, which leads to the light-filled atrium, from which all classrooms are visible and easily found. Further phases of work have provided a sports hall, squash courts and ancillary facilites. The college now caters for 550 students.

The construction of a 320-seat lecture theatre, and additional accommodation block commenced in the course of 1999.

Store Street 1998

Store street Garda Divisional Headquarters, in Dublin's north inner city, was completed in September 1998, and is the largest single Garda operational facility in the state. The new building closes off a vista looking north from the Custom House, while at the same time addressing the open space to the front at Store street. Two phases to the building contract allowed the gardaí to continue their day-to-day business almost uninterrupted, for the duration of the work, and many long-awaited Garda functions are now catered for at this city centre location. Façade treatment is symmetrical, with a curved entrance whose glazed feature acknowledges the nearby IFSC. Other materials include limestone cladding with glass blocks to the lower level, clay bricks to upper storeys with pitched slated roofs. The structure is designed to take a further storey extension upwards if the need arises for expansion.

Prisons

New prison programme

As part of the government's 'crime package' announced in July 1996, a programme was initiated to provide additional detention facilities. Prior to this, there was no specific, structured programme to provide new prison spaces. Such developments as were under-taken were concerned rather with providing new or improved facilities within existing prisons, such as the new training unit in Mountjoy Prison (1977). The exception is Wheatfield Prison in Clondalkin, Co Dublin, which opened in 1987 with accommodation for 230 prisoners.

The accelerated prison programme which commenced in mid-1996 focuses on the provision of completely new, modern, purpose-built facilities. The OPW handled the design, tendering and project management of the programme on behalf of Department of Justice Equality and Law Reform. Innovative fast-track design-and-build approaches were devised to deal with the demands of the programme. To the end of 1999, the OPW has created 1253 prison spaces.

Castlerea

The first project to be completed was a series of low-security units at Castlerea called the 'Village' (October 1996, above).

Women's prison

The state's first purpose-built women's prison with a capacity of 80 opened in 1999 next to Mountjoy Prison. The guiding principles in the brief were those of humane detention and preparation for return to normal society. To this end, the characteristic features of high-security institutions, such as barred gates, have been eliminated or disguised, and a fully-equipped 'personal development centre' with training, educational and physical education facilities is provided. The same philosophy is evident in the design of the residential area, where prisoners are accommodated in small groups similar to households, and the 'houses' in turn are grouped around open areas broadly similar to normal urban environments. Other elements of the prison are a health centre, oratory, library, laundry and an open visits area with play facilities for children.

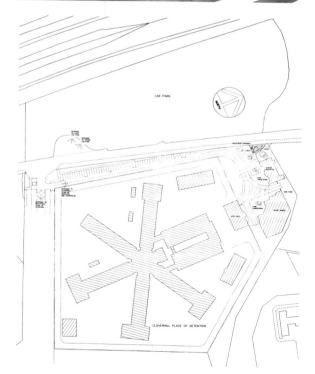

Cloverhill

Cloverhill Prison, Co. Dublin (left and above), the first dedicated remand facility in the state, was opened in 1999 with a capacity of 400. It is designed on the 'Pentonville' pattern, with cell blocks and offender facilities converging onto an operational hub. To allow for the segregation of different categories of prisoners, each cell block has its own classrooms, recreational areas, gymnasium and exercise yard. The main block also houses staff, catering and medical facilities, and a large visiting area. Within the prison wall are a separate administration block, store/laundry, and self-contained residence for certain prisoners. Directly outside the walls is a visitor reception, and a courthouse.

At Cloverhill, as at Castlerea, a new method of procurement was used for the first time. Called 'client-led design/build', it was devised by the OPW to meet the tight targets agreed with the customer, in the most advantageous way. It allows the OPW to design the building in outline, after which detailed working drawings are prepared by the contractor's team.

Midlands

The new Midlands Prison is situated adjacent to prison officers' housing, and the Portlaoise high-security prison compound. All construction phases will reach completion in the course of 2000, at which stage it will accommodate 515 long-term male offenders.

Four long cell blocks radiate from the centrally located medical unit, kitchen, training workshops, library and education facility; a 'bubble' at the outer end of each cell block provides indoor recreational space. An independent building will house forty additional prisoners, segregated for disruptive behaviour. Other ancillary features of the project include separate prisoner and visitor reception blocks, an administration block, five factory units and exercise yards. The entire scheme, incorporates a high level of modern technology in respect of security, safety and building management systems.

Courthouses

Historically, the provision of courthouses has been handled jointly by the Department of Justice, Equality and Law Reform and the various local authorities. Therefore, the OPW has had no continuing responsibility for a specific programme to provide new courts, but only for individual, standalone projects at the specific request of the department

Smithfield Courthouse, Dublin 1987

The Children's Courthouse was the first new courthouse commissioned by the Department of Justice since independence. Completed in 1987, it faces onto the seventeenth-century Smithfield market square, which had fallen into dereliction.

The three-storey corner building continues the parapet height and pattern of neighbouring houses. The external materials are smooth red brick, and alternating bands of unpolished, fossilised and plain limestone.

The client brief for the interior layout contained a stringent requirement for segregated circulation of public, witnesses, defendants and judges, with garda supervision at certain locations. Members of the public enter directly from Smithfield, and can proceed from the tiled hallway up the main staircase to the first floor waiting hall and two top-lit courtrooms.

Because of the specific needs of the juvenile court, it was decided that these rooms should not be traditional courtrooms, in which level changes reflect hierarchical status. Instead, specially designed oak furniture stands on a flat floor of timber blocks, under a vaulted daylight ceiling. Solicitors' offices and consultation rooms are ranged around the second-floor gallery.

Richmond Courts 1997

The new crime measures introduced by the government in 1996 required increased accommodation for the courts of justice. Between November 1996 and May 1997, the former Richmond Hospital in the inner city was adapted to provide five district courts. The U-shaped hospital was designed in 1879, to a plan first developed by Florence Nightingale, with two-storey pavilion wings accommodating large wards with a veranda at each end. All new works were designed to respect the existing detail and fabric of the building, many areas of which are listed for preservation. Remedying the poor acoustic qualities of the building dictated much of the design approach. Accordingly, great attention was paid to surface treatment and selection of materials.

Carrick-on-Shannon Courthouse, Co Leitrim 1997
The new courthouse at Carrick-on-Shannon, Co Leitrim, is located on an open site, close to the Garda station on the outskirts of the town. The building curves around an oval entrance courtyard – a sheltered space for gathering, waiting and conducting informal court business. The main entrance doorway itself is marked by an overhanging cedar-clad bay window. Three courtrooms and usual ancillary accommodation are provided at Carrick-on-Shannon, within a plan which utilises natural lighting to its full advantage.

Anglesea Street District Courthouse, Cork 1995
Cork Model National School was designed in 1862 by Enoch Trevor Owen to accommodate over 450 pupils. When the school finally closed in 1990, the needs of the Department of Justice for a separate district court in the city provided the opportunity to restore and reuse this important listed building, with minimal structural intervention.

The red brick and limestone structure consists of four main spaces, each with a gabled front on Anglesea street. Courtrooms at the south end of the building utilise two of the main spaces, whose main features are the roof trusses and Romanesque windows. The main public access is by the original entrance, indicated by the campanile. New waiting areas were provided along the spinal corridor in the form of light glazed extensions, clearly differentiated as new work. The northern half of the building is occupied by administrative offices, document storage and ancillary services. The Department of Justice took possession of the new district courthouse in 1995.

Irish National War Memorial

Islandbridge, Dublin, 1933–9; restored 1987–8

This and the other gardens illustrated, with the exception of Mount Congreve, are managed by the Department of Arts, Heritage, Gaeltacht and the Islands.

The work of Sir Edwin Lutyens (1869–1944) can be found in South Africa, India, Australia, the USA and throughout Europe. His phenomenal *oeuvre* ranges from the Viceregal Palace in Delhi to the Heywood Gardens in Ballinakill, Co Laois.

The Irish National War Memorial at Islandbridge came about from a need to somehow 'keep in remembrance the lustre, the glory and the valour of all those gallant Irish soldiers who endured all the undreamt of horrors of a war such as the world had never known before' ('The Irish National War Memorial – Its Meaning and Purpose', *British Legion Annual* 1941).

The Irish Memorial Committee, formed of veterans and the bereaved, gathered in July 1919. Within a year, it had collected £45,000 in public subscriptions to finance a memorial. The services of Sir Edwin Lutyens, architect of over one hundred Great War cemeteries and memorials, were engaged and construction to Lutyens's specifications commenced in 1931.

The labour force was made up of hundreds of unemployed ex-servicemen of the British and Irish armies. To create as much employment as possible, it was the policy of the Office of Public Works on this project to minimise mechanical intervention, and so the garden and its monuments were virtually handbuilt. To quote the British Legion Annual again:

A couple of hand winches, a few telegraph poles, an arrangement of pulley-blocks and a few hundred yards of flexible steel rope comprised all the tackle... [which] was rigged up by the men themselves, the unskilled workers.

The Irish National War Memorial is primarily a 20-acre garden on the southern slope of the Liffey valley. There is no cenotaph, regalia or triumphalist sculpture. Two circular-plan sunken rose gardens flank a large concourse. In the centre is Lutyens's altar-like Great War Stone (identical to stones found in dozens of other Imperial War Graves cemeteries), simply inscribed 'To the Memory of the 49,400 Irishmen who gave their lives in the Great War 1914–1918'. To either side are obelisks mounted in immense water-filled basins. At the highest point stands a slender granite cross.

The lawn is defined by sections of granite walling which are an extraordinary example of the skill of stone masonry. Two pairs of pavilions, linked by vine-clad pergolas, denote the entrances to the rose gardens. One of these tiny 'bookrooms' houses the memorial record – a roll of honour, with decoration by Harry Clarke, listing the Irishmen who died in the war. In another is found the Ginchy Cross, which stood near Ginchy, northern France, from 1917 to 1926, commemorating the loss of 4354 men of the 16th Irish Division in just six days of September 1916.

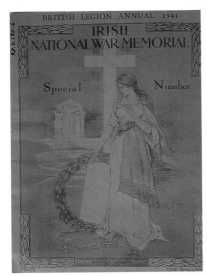

By the early 1980s the condition of the Islandbridge garden had greatly deteriorated, owing to a combination of vandalism, dutch elm disease and natural weathering. In 1986 a programme of restoration was devised between the trustees of the Memorial Committee and the OPW, and was jointly funded.

The restoration involved resurfacing the pathways, restoring the stonework of the bookrooms and pergolas, and the construction of a tempietta to Sir Edwin Lutyens's original plan. (Along with a three-arch bridge spanning the Liffey, which would link the memorial with the Phoenix Park, the tempietta was deferred in the 1930s due to lack of funding.) Extensive landscape restoration included replanting, according to the Lutyens's original design, avenues of yew, cherry, elm, poplar and birch, as well as thousands of rose bushes, where possible using old varieties.

The original dedication ceremony was postponed by the Taoiseach of the time, Éamon de Valera, in 1939, on account of the 'Emergency' (World War II). The event finally took place on 10 September 1988, following phase I of the restoration project, when Roman Catholic, Presbyterian and Methodist church leaders blessed the war memorial.

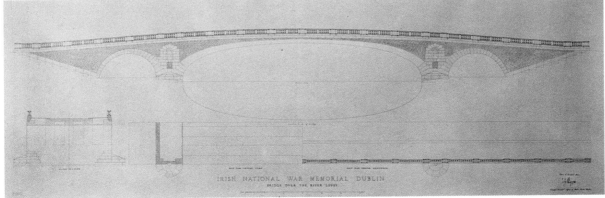

IRISH NATIONAL WAR MEMORIAL DUBLIN
BRIDGE OVER THE RIVER LIFFEY

Mount Congreve
Co Waterford

The lands of Mount Congreve estate, near Waterford city, were purchased in the early eighteenth century, and the present Palladian-style mansion was constructed *c*1725. The Congreve family, who are still in residence there, came to Ireland originally at the time of King Charles I.

The gardens at Mount Congreve are internationally famous. Earlier this century,

Ambrose Congreve and Lionel de Rothschild began cultivating 250 acres of land, and established an outstanding collection of exotic plants and flowering shrubs from around the world, forming a valuable scientific and cultural resource.

In 1979, the estate and house were vested in four trustees, one of whom is the OPW, eventually to become the absolute property of the state.

Heywood Gardens
Ballinakill, Co Laois

Heywood was a private garden designed for Colonel and Mrs Hutcheson Poë, completed by Lutyens in 1912 (below right, 1917). A long terrace links the various elements of the design, the jewel of which is the enclosed oval garden, approached via a lime walk and ornate wrought iron gates. A series of terraces leads to a sunken elliptical fish pool. Originally eight bronze tortoises balanced on the rim of the pond gazing into the water, from the centre of which rises a daringly proportioned fountain basin. In its many witty details and subtle ornament, Heywood displays Lutyens's mastery in interweaving the natural and built environments.

Heywood House was destroyed by fire in 1950, but the garden was carefully maintained by the Salesian Fathers, until entrusted to the state in 1993. Gertrude Jekyll has been credited with the horticultural design, and a programme of replanting according to her original scheme was initiated by the OPW in 1994.

Inscription in loggia, Heywood Garden

*To smooth the Lawn,
to decorate the Dale,
To swell the Summit, or
to scoop the Vale,
To mark each Distance through
each opening Glade,
Mass kindred Tints or
vary Shade from Shade.
To bend the Arch, to
ornament the Grot,
In all – let Nature never
be forgot,
Her varied gifts with
Sparing Hand combine,
Paint as you plant and
as you work design.*
Alexander Pope (1688–1744)

Ilnacullin
Garinish Island, Co Cork

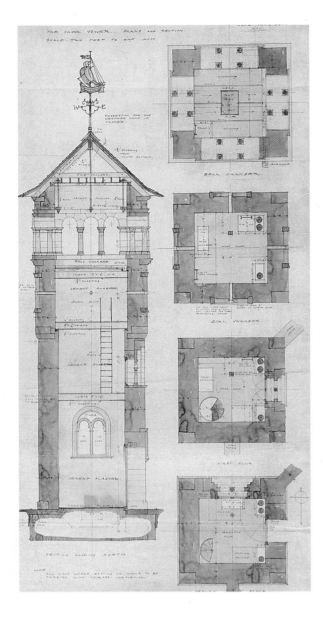

Situated in Glengarriff Harbour, Co Cork, Ilnacullin ('island of holly') was once a barren and exposed military outpost. Having purchased it from the British War Office in 1910, Annan Bryce MP engaged the eminent English architect, Harold Peto, to transform the island into an extraordinarily beautiful and varied garden, interwoven with architectural features. Entrusted to the state in 1953, Ilnacullin has continued to develop and mature, its mild and humid environment home to trees, plants and shrubs from all over the world. Considerable restoration and maintenance works have been carried out on the island, especially on the Italianate 'casita', and discreet visitor facilities have been provided.

Government Offices

Centralised and decentralised

The policy to decentralise government offices was based on the need for more widespread location of public service facilities and job opportunities. The ongoing programme was launched by the government in the late 1980s, making use of the design/build/finance arrangements which have resulted in very cost-effective buildings. Under the scheme, a substantial number of public servants have been able to settle outside the capital on a permanent basis, helping to counteract regional imbalances and relieve the pressure on Dublin. The towns to which public service staff have been moved reap the economic benefits, while the business, commercial and social life of the communities also receive a fresh impetus. Provincial 'centralised' offices house the central government agencies normally serving a town.

Thurles centralised government office, Tipperary 1983

Thurles government office was designed in the late 1970s and completed in 1983. The architects attempted to reflect the fact that the structure was intended for use as a civic building, and should appear as such. The two-storey concrete-framed building encloses a landscaped courtyard. An internal 'street' runs around the courtyard at ground-floor level, giving access to most of the departmental areas, while the first floor forms a gallery which overlooks this 'street'. The curtain wall contains aluminium panels finished in red, set in a black frame. Interior finishes are of painted plaster and brushed exposed concrete which contrasts with the brightly painted metalwork, carpets and ceiling tiles.

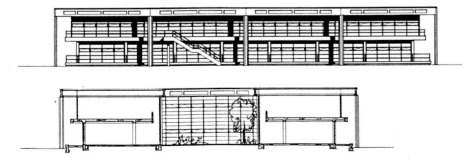

Decentralised office for Department of Defence, Galway, 1989

The transfer of 210 staff of the Department of Defence to Galway was part of the first stage of the official dentralisation programme. The building, which is curved in plan, overlooks Galway Bay.

The straight wings are given added interest by occasional convex sections rising through the first two storeys. Its pitched roof, rendered finish and subdued colouring enables the office development to assimilate with its mainly residential environment.

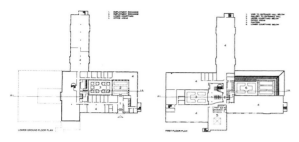

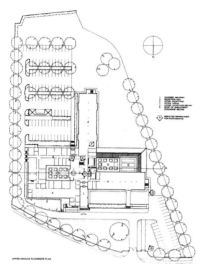

Longford 1994

Longford decentralised office is the product of a developer competition promoted by the OPW. The accommodation is grouped around two courtyards, whose different levels are determined by the contours of the site. The main entrance at upper ground floor level leads to the entrance hall, which is the principal architectural and organisational element in the building. The galleried, double-height hall is naturally lit by both banks of roof lights and a glazed wall overlooking the courtyard.

Portlaoise government office 1996

Consisting of some 50,000 square feet of office and public space, Portlaoise decentralised government office houses sections of the Departments of Agriculture, Social, Community and Family Affairs, Justice and the Revenue Commissioners. The accommodation is arranged as three storeys around a garden court with a full-height entrance hall overlooked by public galleries. The deeply projecting roof structure contains a café/dining facility, and a particular feature of the building's construction is its emphasis on low maintenance finishes combined with low energy consumption, achieved through high insulation

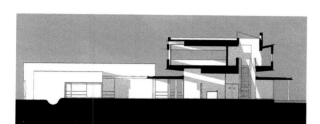

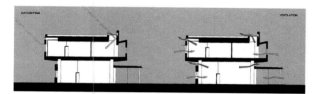

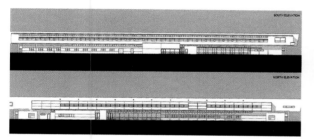

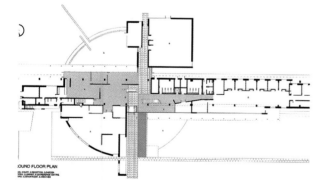

GROUND FLOOR PLAN

Environmental Protection Agency HQ, Johnstown Castle, Co Wexford 1998

A design competition for the new Environmental Protection Agency HQ was initiated by the OPW in 1996. The chosen location was Johnstown Castle estate, which is managed by Teagasc, the Agricultural and Food Development Authority, as a major agricultural research centre and tourist attraction. The architectural brief required a two-storey building with accommodation for five distinct divisions of the EPA, a library, restaurant, and conference room to cater for 150 people. Construction materials were to be chosen taking account of renewable resources, life-cycle characteristics and energy conservation. The winning design by Henry J Lyons & Partners satisfies these criteria within a novel plan which provides an environmentally responsive, brightly daylit, well-ventilated workplace of superior quality.

BUILDING FOR GOVERNMENT

Schools

The OPW assumed responsibility for the design of new national schools, as well as for supervising their construction and their maintenance, in 1857. The Department of Education took over complete responsibility for the provision and maintenance of schools in 1985.

The Education Act (1831), providing mass primary education in Ireland, was administered by the Board of National Education, which controlled the financial grant to each locality applying for a new school. Attempts to standardise architectural plans were generally unsuccessful, as the Board continued to accept designs submitted by applicants. In addition, the deteriorating position of the Board's finances severely restricted the development of OPW designs in line with new ideas on school planning.

On the whole, rectangular schoolrooms were the most common type, consisting of an entrance vestibule, small fuel store and one room in which pupils of all ages were taught (above right). In character they were similar to dwelling houses (1899, Derrycreagh National School, Co. Cork, above). From the 1880s, a second, smaller classroom became usual, in which a monitor (student teacher) would hold classes, the pupils seated on raked benches forming a gallery for easy supervision.

Apart from national schools, workhouse schools, district model schools and various types of agricultural schools were constructed and maintained by the OPW, though few new works of this kind were necessary in the twentieth century. William A Scott was commissioned to design a new complex for Athenry Agricultural College in 1906 (below), though the art nouveau scheme was never executed.

The OPW was also responsible for the maintenance of buildings forming the Royal University and Queen's Colleges in Belfast, Cork and Galway up to 1909. In the 1920s, 'preparatory colleges' were established, in which children selected by examination might be prepared for admission to teacher training colleges. This involved the adaptation of seven properties, two in Dublin and five in Gaeltacht areas.

1920s–50s

The major programme of school building, which commenced in the late 1920s, was largely based on the replacement or improvement of earlier schools. The new designs were standardised according to the attendance numbers, and share many characteristics. Generally single-storey symmetrical buildings with a rough-cast render, a water tower, covered playsheds and enclosing walls with stiles completed the arrangement. The provision of central heating and much improved sanitation, ventilation and lighting were important innovations. Where the school management wished to commission a private architect, these plans were submitted to the OPW for approval.

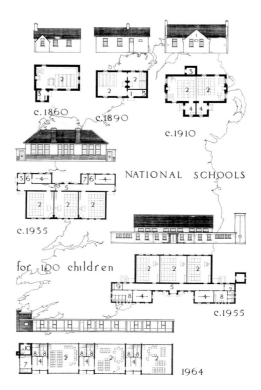

1	Entrance Porch	7	Teachers' Room
2	Classroom	8	Lavatories
3	Fuel Store	9	Electrical Heating
4	Cloakroom		Control Room
5	Corridor	10	Boiler Room
6	Ablution facilities		

1960s standard plans

In the 1960s, there were striking advances in the design of schools and the method of their erection. To deal with a growing backlog of schools in need of modern facilities, and to meet urgent political and social demands, a renewed drive was launched, reaching a peak in 1966 with 130 new buildings and sixty-six major improvement schemes. Special research into school planning was conducted, which informed the new designs that emerged in this decade. Characteristic of this new approach was the concept of self-contained classroom-toilet-cloakroom modules which could be multiplied according to specific needs. The module system allowed for the use of prefabricated parts, whose walls and roofs were clad with laminated timber panels, which did not require special lifting gear to erect. The sub-structure and bearer walls were of traditional construction.

In addition, developments in the approach to facilities for children with disabilities prompted the construction of several new schools adapted to their specific needs.

Duagh National School

Duagh central school, Co Kerry, completed in 1971, replaced five older two-room schools in the parish. This principle of centralisation afforded a higher standard of amenities than would be possible in small schools. For example, as well as eight classrooms, Duagh incorporated a library, a kitchen, staff rooms and a large general-purpose hall for assemblies, stage presentations and physical education. Constructed on the modular system, the building was insulated, internally sound-proofed and centrally heated. Mobile, stackable furniture was introduced in this period as an integral part of the new design philosophy.

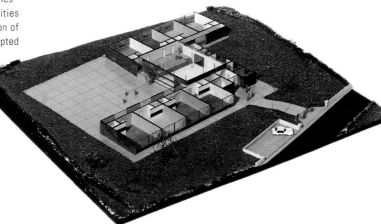

A new Department of Education design brief was issued in 1978, stating strict requirements for both the site and school building. These requirements are evident at Ashbourne, Co Meath 1988 (below). The general purpose area, the largest single space, is the central organising element of the scheme. Three two-storey blocks of four classrooms radiate from the central area. Externally the walls are exposed masonry cavity with two bands of heather-coloured blocks on each floor. Internal walls are plastered and painted white, with brightly coloured furniture, floor finishes and paintwork. The site is landscaped with trees and flowering shrubs, as well as ballcourts and playing fields.

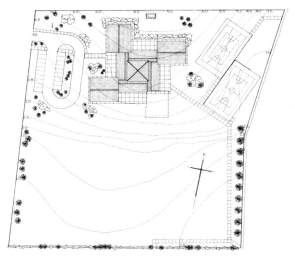

St Laurence's School, Finglas

St Laurence's industrial school was completed in 1971. It is a residential centre for adolescent boys who have been committed by a court. Fourteen acres were set aside for the project in this residential area to provide adequate space for outdoor activities, and to create an open environment without the remoteness from normal family living conditions sometimes associated with establishments of this nature.

The buildings were designed with a view to education and rehabilitation rather than constraint. The school is built around two quadrangles for junior and senior boys respectively, with a connecting administrative block. Classrooms and recreational spaces are found on the ground floor, with dormitories and showers above. A separate suite includes an infirmary and surgery, and the permanent staff live in a self-contained residential unit. The chapel forms a distinctive feature of the complex; the raking concrete beams from ground level to roof apex contrast with the vertical lines of the main block.

MAIN ENTRANCE ELEVATION

Irish Embassy to the Holy See
Villa Spada, Rome, *c* 1958

Irish embassies abroad

The purpose of Dáil Éireann's first representation abroad, at the Paris peace conference in 1919, continued to be the primary concern of Irish diplomats in the 1920s and 1930s: international recognition of Ireland's independent status. This is reflected in the strategic location of early diplomatic missions: Washington (1924, above), Paris (1929), and the Vatican (1929). In these years, suitable premises for the chancery (offices) and residence were normally leased, sometimes in the same building, depending on individual circumstances. Responsibility for the acquisition, furnishing and maintenance of embassy buildings lay with the OPW until 1989, when it was transferred to the Department of Foreign Affairs.

Following World War II, Ireland's representations abroad increased steadily, and in the period *c* 1950–*c* 1970, a policy of acquisition was pursued resulting in a number of prestigious buildings coming into state ownership.

In 1964, plans were drawn up for a combined chancery and residence in Lagos, Nigeria, before it was decided to purchase alternative accommodation. As a result, it was not until 1981 that Ireland's first purpose-built embassy opened, in Canberra, Australia, designed by a local architect in association with the OPW.

Diplomatic relations are maintained with 106 countries through a network of forty-two embassies worldwide, as well as multilateral missions to the European Union (Brussels), United Nations (Geneva and New York), OSCE (Vienna), OECD (Paris), the Council of Europe (Strasbourg), and six consulates.

The Villa Spada, high on the Janiculum hillside, commands spectacular views out over the city of Rome. Built in 1639, it is a scheduled national monument of considerable historical and artistic importance.

The Irish representation to the Holy See, distinct from that to the Italian state, was established in 1929. The Villa Spada was purchased by the OPW in 1946, the year in which the mission was raised to the status of embassy. The previous owners, the Uzielli family, had sensitively modernised the house in 1938–9, adding a nursery wing, elegant bathrooms and bedrooms, and a swimming pool in the 1.75 acre garden. Dr Vacchini, a local architect who was then directly responsible for the fabric of St Peter's Basilica, reported that 'this building is fairly preserved, and has no serious deficiency of static or aesthetic character'.

Refurbishment

A programme of refurbishment was initiated in 1952. Already furnished with a tasteful blend of antiques and reproductions, new additions were in keeping with the prevalent style, as 'any attempt to introduce modern furniture into the principal rooms in this Embassy would be nothing short of vandalism', according to an OPW furniture clerk. The project involved painting, retouching and new upholstery.

The ambassador, Joseph P Walshe, forwarded this carefully worded advice to the OPW in May 1953:

[T]he functions of the Embassy to the Holy See suppose that the great majority of the guests and visitors will always be priests, with a sprinkling of laymen. It is therefore well to have in mind rather the male than the female reaction to colour and materials. You will remember that the Venetian Room was so effeminate in its colours as almost to keep the men out. The purple material in the large reception room also rather suggested a background for renaissance ladies' costumes...

When the work was completed, the ambassador relayed to the Principal Architect that 'all my visitors, Irish and Italian, are full of praise for the way in which the Villa has been restored to its late renaissance elegance without a single fault in style or proportion'.

The Venetian room

The villa is constructed on a steep gradient, forcing a complex arrangement of floors and mezzanine levels. It has a Roman tiled roof and was rendered and finished in the typical 'tinta romana' – a limestone wash dyed with a natural earth pigment ranging from yellow ochre to Pompeiian red. Fine stucco details and dressings are carved from peperino, a volcanic stone popular in this part of Italy. French doors lead directly into the immense *grande salone* (above), off which is located the Venetian room. Its jasper green walls are complemented by McGrath's specially designed Donegal carpet. The former owners of the villa, the Uziellis, fitted the seventeenth-century painted and gilt doors depicting scenes of Venice.

The dining room

The dining room has one of the most outstanding interiors in the villa. Three large baroque paintings in shades of brown and indigo decorate the walls, while the coved ceiling features a fresco of Cupid and Bacchus dating from the period of construction. The carpet here is similar in design to that in the Venetian room, but shaded rich blue, lavender and gold to harmonise with the other strong decorative features.

Irish Embassy to France

12 Avenue Foch, Paris, 1956

Sanction to acquire the Hôtel de Breteuil at a cost of 150 million francs (approx. £150,000) was granted by the Minister for External Affairs, Frank Aiken, in his capacity as Acting Minister for Finance. The building was purchased in 1954 from the elderly Princesse de Faucigny-Lucinge, to accommodate the chancery and residence of the Irish Embassy to France. The cost was considered exorbitant at the time, but the mansion has proved a worthwhile investment, much admired by ambassadors, dignitaries and guests over several decades.

Situated on the corner of Avenue Foch, in the heart of Paris, the embassy overlooks the leafy park bordering that thoroughfare. The townhouse was built in the 1890s by the eighth Marquis de Breteuil, to the design of Ernest Sanson, using honey-coloured Caen sandstone. Its sculptural flourishes, ironwork and general character hark back to French rococo style of the eighteenth century.

When it was purchased by the Irish state, no structural alterations were necessary, apart from the addition of a barrel-vaulted glass and concrete roof over the small courtyard for parking facilites. The princess sold little of her furniture, and as a result the adaptation for embassy use principally involved furnishing and decorating.

The dining room

Because of the superior quality of the interior, the gracious *escalier d'honneur*, stone carvings and extensive parquetry, it was decided to furnish the building in the French style, while utilising Irish glassware, bedlinen, cutlery and carpets. This synthesis is demonstrated in the dining room. The wood panelling is part of a remarkable collection of Louis Quinze *boiseries* at the Hôtel. The hand-tufted carpet was designed by Raymond McGrath for the room, the main colours of which are 'the Corinthian reds found in Greek vases'. The table is from the State Apartments in Dublin Castle, and the oil paintings, on loan from the National Gallery of Ireland, are by the eighteenth-century Irish artist George Barret.

Salon d'introduction/ singerie

Five interconnecting reception rooms are contained on the first floor, the remaining levels occupied by the residence and offices of the chancery. The *salon d'introduction* is also known as the *singerie* (opposite) on account of the wood panelling, delicately painted with musical monkeys. The carpet is one of seven in the building designed by McGrath, which were hand-tufted, using pure Irish wool, by the renowned Donegal Carpets Ltd. It is a variation on that in the ballroom of Iveagh House, Dublin, also by McGrath.

The grand salon

The *boiseries* in the *grand salon*, originally from a house on the Rue de Richelieu, were regilded. They form a point of comparison with the oak panelling in the dining room and *fumoir*, which are entirely unpainted.

Four vibrant over-door panels depicting allegorical scenes on the theme of love are attributed to Louis Lagrenée, and date to 1768. McGrath's savonnerie-style carpet takes its inspiration from rococo decorative patterns, while incorporating the Irish harp and riverine heads. Its 'traditional Du Barry colours' of rose, gold, moss green and cornflower blue are picked up in Irish silk brocade drapes and upholstery.

Irish Embassy to Saudi Arabia
Riyadh, 1986

The Department of Foreign Affairs of Saudi Arabia transferred its headquarters in 1977 from the coastal city of Jeddah, 1000 miles inland to the oasis city of Riyadh, from where the ruling Saud family united the country at the start of the century. This necessitated the relocation of all foreign embassies, to a designated diplomatic quarter outside the city. The design for all the embassies in the area had to be approved by the Riyadh Development Authority, whose stipulations included that there should be no more than two storeys, and that the buildings should reflect the traditional architectural character of Central Arabia.

Climatic considerations were also crucial in shaping the final design of the chancery, and residences for the ambassador and first secretary. Courtyards, wide pergolas, undercroft spaces and small window openings provide shade, privacy and protection from the sand-laden winds.

Government Jet
1991

The Gulfstream IV jet was purchased by the Irish Air Corps Ministerial Air Transport Service in 1992, and, along with a Super King Air, currently meets the official international travel needs of the President, Taoiseach and government ministers.

Constructed in Savannah, Georgia, the jet was fitted-out in California, under the direction of the OPW project architects and the Air Corps. This involved the selection of suitable materials, choice of colour scheme, fittings and much of the equipment to represent, where possible, the highest standards of Irish industry and craftsmanship. Other criteria influenced their choices, such as low maintenance, passenger comfort and the creation of an environment conducive to productive work, so that passengers can arrive at their destination briefed, rested and ready to go directly to a meeting or conference. All materials used in an aircraft must be approved as safe, particularly fabrics, which must have stringent fire-retardant properties, and the total weight of the interior furnishings must be kept to a minimum. The overall colour scheme is burgundy and rich blue, with sycamore doors and details. Up to fourteen passengers can be accommodated, served by an Air Corps crew of four.

The galley
Meals and refreshments are prepared in the compact galley (below left). Glassware was hand blown in Ireland to conform to very practical specifications. The Air Corps brief for the crockery was also very exacting and several series of prototypes were designed, before a co-ordinated range was produced. Additional Irish products supplied for the Government Jet, many of them specifically designed, include aircraft blankets and pillows; hand towels, paper napkins and coasters incorporating the Irish Air Corps logo.

Art Works

The Irish Free State inherited numerous art works and furniture in 1922, as a result of the transfer of State buildings from the British Crown. Since then, the OPW has successfully managed the commissioning of official portraits and acquisition of other art works, which now number over four thousand.

The government is committed to a policy of incorporating an arts dimension into every government building project. The OPW's funding for art in state buildings comes in the main from the 'Per Cent for Art Scheme' for capital projects. Begun by the OPW in 1978, this scheme involves setting aside one per cent of all construction budgets, subject to limits, for an artistic feature.

A wide range of media is now represented, including painting, print, sculpture, textile, ceramic and music. Special provisions are made for commissions and competition is an essential part of this process. The selection panel in such cases normally consists of representatives of the OPW, the client (ie building user), the Arts Council, and the Artists Association of Ireland.

The Art Management Group, established in 1991, is responsible for implementing OPW's functions in relation to state art. The OPW is required under the Asset Register to account for all works of art in the care of the state. A major part of the Art Management Group's role is to catalogue, research and exhibit these art works. 'Art of the State', an annual themed exhibition drawn from the state's permanent collection, tours various venues in Ireland and abroad. Access to this information is available to researchers, curators and the general public. The OPW's expertise is also available to government departments and other public bodies for advice on the purchase, acquisition, maintenance, commissioning, restoration and valuation of art works.

Further reading:
OPW Art Management Handbook (1998)
Art in State Buildings 1970–85 (1998)
Art in State Buildings 1985–95 (1996)

'Night Fires LXXXVI' 1993 by Tim Goulding
'Night Fires LXXXVI' was selected by the Minister for Arts, Culture and the Gaeltacht in 1993 for that department's head office at Mespil Road, Dublin.

'Control' 1997 by Killian Schurmann
'Control' was commissioned in 1997 for the new Land Registry office in Waterford city. The art work is composed of five stained glass panels illuminated from behind.

**'Incommunicado' 1989
by Eileen McDonagh,
The Moat, Dublin Castle
Conference Centre**

This idea originated from a study of some jewellery found on the old Viking site in the vicinity of the Castle. From there it developed to a more simple form to its present shape. Bearing in mind the confined nature of the site with its many decorative architectural features in the form of arches, patterned railings and large areas of glazing, I felt it was necessary that the sculpture should be sharp, minimal and simple... The sculpture with its splitting effect reveals the natural break from the bed-rock where it was formed... This contrasts with the polished surface and is a symbol of time and evolution as the Castle and its surroundings have also evolved to what is there today.

Eileen McDonagh, Sculptor

'Dreach na Fódhla' by James Scanlon

'Dreach na Fódhla' (left) is a large-scale stained glass window in the foyer of the new building for the Council of the European Union in Brussels. In a competition held in 1993, the OPW invited Irish artists to submit proposed art works suitable for the building, from which a number of art works were commissioned by the EU using the 'Per Cent for Art Scheme'. The Council building incorporates works by artists from each of the member states.

An Turas, Blasket Island Visitor Centre

This immense screen wall, 5 x 12.5 metres (above), was commissioned for the Great Blasket Centre in Dún Chaoin, Co Kerry (1994). Designed by Róisín de Buitléar, and executed by Kawala Glass Studios, it is known as 'An Turas' ('The Journey') and is the largest secular glasswork in Ireland. It suggests in abstract form the natural and created environment of the Blasket islands: field patterns, *naomhóga* (currachs), fishing and seascapes.

National Famine Memorial

To honour the memory of all those who died, suffered and emigrated during the Great Irish Famine (1845–51), and the victims of all famines, the government's Famine Commemoration Committee selected an enlarged bronze version of a sculpture by John Behan. Overlooking Clew Bay in Murrisk, Co Mayo, the Famine Ship (1997, opposite) is a forceful reminder of the nightmare of famine, past and present.

Social Welfare Local Offices

Established in 1947, the Department of Social Welfare (now called the Department of Social, Community and Family Affairs) is responsible for the delivery of a range of social insurance and social assistance schemes, including pensions, benefits, allowances and other supports. The Department's services are provided through main offices in Dublin, Sligo, Letterkenny, Longford and Waterford, 57 local offices and 72 branch offices countrywide.

As part of the Strategic Management Initiative, launched in 1994, the department accelerated its programme of upgrading and improving office accomm- odation, with particular emphasis on customer privacy and access for people with disabilities.

The provision and refurbishment of public buildings for government departments is handled by the OPW's Architectural Services under a building programme agreed by the government.

Lower Gardiner Street, Dublin

Dundalk

Athlone

Lord Edward Street, Dublin

Social Welfare Local Office
Tallaght, 1995

The Tallaght Social Welfare Local Office is one of the first prototype 'one stop shop' facilities, integrating the functions of the Department of Social Welfare, FÁS – the Training and Employment Authority – and the Eastern Health Board in a single location. The office is run on a cashless basis and, in keeping with the drive by the Department of Social Welfare to make its new-generation outlets more user-friendly, considerable effort was put into the design of the public spaces within the building. The new counter design, in particular, achieves a balance between security, unobtrusiveness and privacy, and has been adopted for use in the future upgrading of other social welfare local offices throughout the country.

The specific needs of the wheelchair-bound, the partially sighted and the hard of hearing were incorporated into the architectural design. In recognition of this, Tallaght SWLO was awarded the International Symbol of Access by Rehabilitation International.

The office opened in 1995, and is situated near The Square, Tallaght Town Centre and the modern Garda District Headquarters. At an early stage, the Cork-based sculptor Vivienne Roche was commissioned to design an art work for the forecourt. Her corten steel piece 'The Duality of Three' reflects the routes frequently taken by locals traversing the busy plaza.

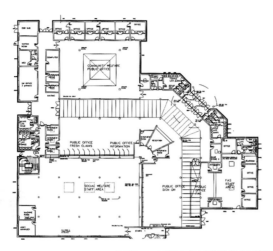

It is spacious and bright and there is no queuing outside. And one great thing is it is clean. There are no long queues and there are 19 hatches for people to sign on. The most I have to wait now is a half an hour but at least there are seats. There are lots of information leaflets around and the staff even seem happier. I definitely got the sense that the staff are more interested in pleasing the customer. I still wish to God I didn't have to sign on but at least it is more dignified.
Frank Scott quoted in the *Irish Independent*, 1 February 1996

Social Welfare Local Office

Hanover Street, Cork, 1990

This new 'one stop shop' for all social welfare services in Cork city is located on the site of a former factory and mill, and has an extensive river frontage. Convenient to public transport, pedestrian and vehicular traffic, the building presents a three-storey block of office functions to Hanover Street, with a two-storey block of greater scale, containing public functions, fronting on to the river. A long glazed lobby on this frontage gives access to the disparate section of the office. White 'forticrete' masonry blockwork is the chosen material. On the river front, smooth faced blocks are stack-bonded to give a formal collonade effect, while on the other elevations it is combined with grey split blocks, for contrast in colour and texture.

In the large public spaces, the design intention was to break down the scale by delineating bays which reflect the structure and organisation of the building.

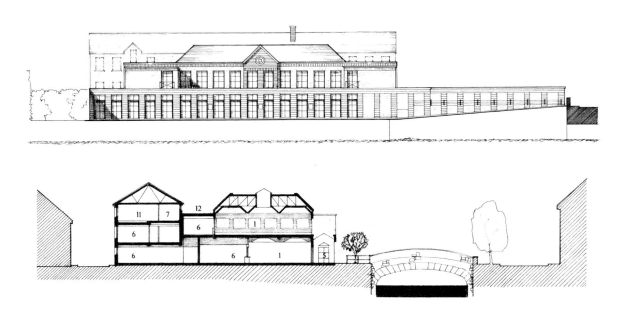

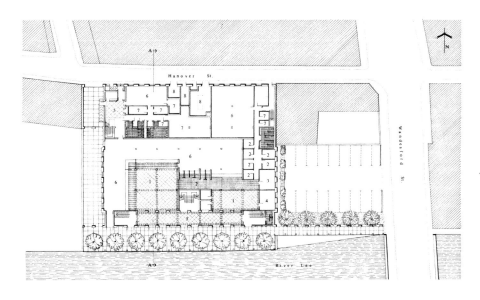

Ionad an Bhlascaoid Mhóir/Great Blasket Centre
Dún Chaoin, Co Kerry, 1994

All visitor centres are managed by the Department of Arts, Heritage, Gaeltacht and the Islands

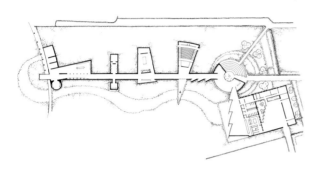

Situated a mile west of Slea Head in the Corca Dhuibhne Gaeltacht, the Great Blasket island, formerly home to an extraordinarily vibrant literary culture, has been uninhabited since 1953.

The Great Blasket Centre is the result of a fruitful collaboration between the OPW and the Blasket Island Foundation.

The sensitive question of location was carefully considered, and the low stone- and plaster-clad building harmonises with the natural contours and appearance of the landscape. In plan, the building resembles the geometric shorthand of Celtic Ogham script. This is intended as a reference to local Ogham stones and to the antiquity of the Irish language.

The spinal passage known as 'Slí an Bhlascaoid Mhóir' appropriately terminates in a glass pavilion overlooking the Blasket archipelago. Off the Slí is a succession of linked themed areas and exhibition spaces, such as the wedge-shaped audio-visual theatre.

The circular arrival space combines an external amphitheatre and an enclosed concave building providing shelter from the elements and space to ponder the floor inscription, quoted from *An tOileánach* by Tomás Ó Criomhthain: *Dúirt sé go mb'fhearr dom scríobh fad is a bheinn beo chun go mbeinn beo is mé marbh.* ('He told me I should write during my lifetime so that I might live after my death.')

Art works form an integral part of the building design. Works include Brendan Brennan's leather-bound and tooled doors; plaster reliefs by Brian King; and Cork artist Michael Quane's outdoor sculpture of Tomás Ó Criomhthain.

Céide Fields Visitor Centre
Ballycastle, Co Mayo, 1993

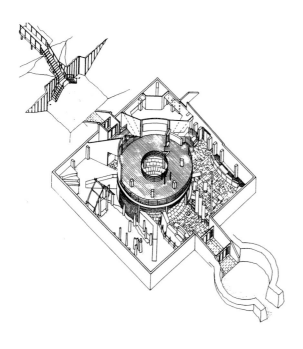

Between Céide Hill and Ballyknock Hill, on the north coast of County Mayo, a vast network of stone walls has been discovered deep beneath the thick blanket bog, providing evidence of a thriving farming community in this area more than 5000 years ago. Not a stone of these walls has been touched since growth of the bog gradually made the land unsuitable for cultivation and it was abandoned millennia ago.

Placing a building in this sensitive natural environment presented a considerable challenge. The pyramid shape was chosen as a natural extension of the landscape, a unified peak growing out of the bog like the nearby Stags of Broadhaven. The bog is folded around the sides of the pyramid, and ascends almost to the apex along the line of a stepped ramp, which brings visitors up to commanding views in all directions from external and internal viewing galleries. Natural, organic and durable materials – such as limestone, peat sods, stainless steel and glass – were selected, to ensure that the centre will mature gracefully.

The visitor approaches the pyramid axially from the clifftop viewing point, via the car parking area, to the sunken court surrounded by peat banks. From this subterranean level, the visitor enters the full volume of the pyramid, naturally lit by the glazed apex. A 5000-year-old pine tree,

uncovered during excavation nearby, forms the centrepiece of the building, to which numerous commissioned artists, craftspeople and masons have contributed. The project architects designed the interior in detail, and conceptualised the exhibition's spatial and material organisation so that it highlights the unique geology and bogland ecology of the area, as well as the Stone Age settlements and their discovery.

The Céide Fields Visitor Centre has won several prestigious national and international architectural awards, including the RIAI Triennial Gold Medal for Architecture 1992–4.

Muckross House
Killarney, Co Kerry

To the south and west of Killarney town lies Killarney National Park, over 10,000 hectares in extent, comprising the famous three lakes of Killarney and the mountains and woodlands which surround them.

With its varied habitats of mountain, moorland, woodland and lake, the park is rich in wildlife. In the upland areas, especially on the slopes of Torc and Mangerton, roams the only native herd of red deer remaining in the country. Now numbering over 850, this herd has had a continuous existence since the return of the red deer into Ireland at the end of the last Ice Age, 10,000 years ago.

The nucleus of the park is the 4300-hectare Bourn Vincent Memorial Park, formerly the estate of Muckross House, which was presented to the nation in 1933. In 1981, the park was designated by UNESCO as a biosphere reserve, part of a world network of natural areas which have conservation, research, education and training as major objectives.

The Herbert family of Wales was first granted lands in the Killarney district by Queen Elizabeth I in 1586. The present-day Muckross House was completed in 1843 for Henry Arthur Herbert and his wife Mary, at a cost of £30,000. It was designed by William Burns, an Edinburgh architect famed for his designs of Victorian country houses.

Lord Ardilaun of the Guinness brewing family purchased Muckross in 1899, renting out the property to parties for fishing, stalking and game. In 1911, William Bowers Bourn, a wealthy American, bought the property as a wedding gift for his daughter Maud and her husband Arthur Rose Vincent of Summerhill, Co Clare. Four years after Maud's death in 1929, her husband and parents presented Muckross House and its estate, renamed the Bourn Vincent Memorial Park, to the Irish nation. Today, the house is the focal point of Killarney National Park, accommodating the visitor centre, craft studios and numerous exhibitions of rural life.

Muckross House opened to the public in 1964 as a folk museum, jointly managed by the Office of Public Works and the Trustees of Muckross House (Killarney) Ltd. Muckross Gardens and Arboretum adjoining the house are world-renowned for their fine collections of rhododendron species and hybrids.

The first stage in the programme of restoration and redecoration of many of the important rooms commenced in 1983, to commemorate the golden jubilee of the state's ownership of the house. The second phase was undertaken between 1990 and 1995, and included the redecoration of the Boudoir, Queen's bedroom and dressing room, the Billiard Room and the Dining Room. The Boudoir was part of a suite of rooms reserved exclusively for Queen Victoria during her visit in 1861. The furnishings and decor are based on photographs of the room taken in 1865 (above). As in many of the other rooms, surviving furniture was restored and supplemented by suitable period furniture of the Victorian era (above right).

This phase of works also allowed for a visitor centre (1992).

The location of a restaurant and workshops will draw attention to the Victorian walled garden, currently undergoing restoration by the OPW (right). This complex of buildings will incorporate existing nineteenth-century stone and slate outhouses into a new structure which will use the natural materials of stone, glass and timber to create a complementary composition in a modern idiom. It will accommodate craft studios, a craft shop and a restaurant with an outdoor seating area overlooking the walled garden. The chief aim of this project is to relieve pressure on the existing services by moving them to a purpose-built complex removed from the Victorian house, freeing up more rooms for restoration in the next phase of work.

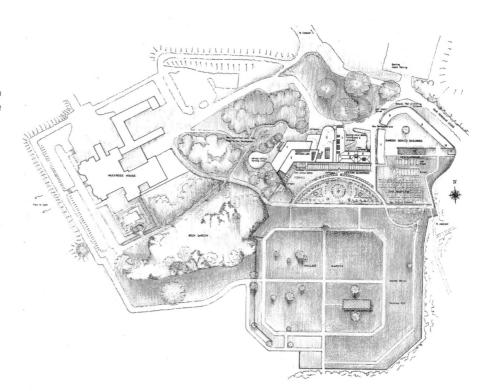

John F Kennedy Arboretum
New Ross, Co Wexford, 1968

The John F Kennedy Arboretum and Forest Park incorporates some 623 acres on the slopes of Slieve Coillte, a hill rising above the Kennedy ancestral home at Dunganstown, Co Wexford. It contains a plant collection of international standing with 4500 types of trees and shrubs from all temperate regions of the world, one special feature being the ericaceous garden where more than 500 rhododendron species and hybrids are represented.

The core of the park is the former demesne of Ballysop House, probably dating to the 1830s. The house was demolished in order to construct the visitor centre, which occupies exactly the same site.

The long, low buildings include an information centre, audio visual/lecture room and offices. They are connected by ambulatories, which provide a covered circulation area, and serve as excellent observatories from which to view the arboretum and countryside. Appropriately, the buildings are predominantly timber: western red cedar mounted clear of the ground on concealed tubular steel posts. The infill walls are of grey Liscannor stone, and the floor of the information centre is of green Connemara marble.

Jan de Fouw designed a number of plaques for the information centre, including large copper representations of 'plant life' and 'the plant kingdom'. The Dublin granite fountain in the open-sided internal courtyard is by the stone carver Michael Biggs and contains, in raised relief, the former President's famous entreaty – 'Ask not what your country can do for you – ask what you can do for your country.'

The centre and park were officially opened by President Éamon de Valera on 29 May 1968.

Corlea Trackway Visitor Centre

Kenagh, Co Longford, 1994

Corlea Trackway is the largest of over sixty ancient timber pathways, or *toghers*, discovered in County Longford, and the most extensive in Europe. It was constructed in 148 BC, during the Irish Iron Age, and rendered the dangerous and waterlogged bogland passable for pedestrians, animals and vehicles. Two parallel runners are set directly onto the bog, traversed by tightly packed oak planks, 3 to 4 metres in length.

The medium in which the trackway has lain for over 2000 years was a near-perfect preservative, and the togher has emerged as a remarkably intact example of large-scale Iron Age craftsmanship. In 1991, an 18-metre section of trackway was removed and underwent a series of preservative techniques before being replaced in its identical location and sequence. A hall designed to maintain suitable climatic conditions for its conservation encloses this section.

The Corlea Bog Visitor Centre leads off this structure. A glass-vaulted rotunda houses the main exhibition, which explores the region's many toghers, the history and industry of boglands, and their archaeological significance. The reception hall, audio-visual theatre and café radiate from the rotunda to complete the cross-shaped ground plan. The remainder of the trackway, undisturbed by modern investigation, lies up to 1.5 metres below the modern ground level. A new path from the building imitates the width and direction of the covered section.

Ashtown Visitor Centre and Tower House
Phoenix Park, Dublin, 1992

Ashtown Tower House
(c 1593)

When James Butler, First Duke of Ormonde, designated the Phoenix Park a royal deer park in 1662, Ashtown Tower House became home to the keeper of the park. The small sixteenth-century tower was incorporated into the British Under-Secretary's Lodge, built in the 1770s, which was later the official residence of the Papal Nuncio in Ireland.

By the 1970s the Georgian structure was in an advanced state of decay and was demolished. In the process, Ashtown Tower House was revealed and has been reinstated, in conjunction with the adjacent visitor centre.

Visitor centre

The creation of Ashtown Visitor Centre involved the adaptation and extension of the eighteenth-century stables and nineteenth-century outhouses of the former Under-Secretary's residence. The new structures are distinct from the old, contrasting both in material and method of construction.

The overall scheme draws inspiration from the traditional Irish farmyard design of masonry outbuildings and lightweight-steel barns surrounding a courtyard. The new exhibition building parallel to the former stables and the new Fionn Uisce café are, however, clad not in steel but in native Douglas fir – a sensitive response to the leafy environment of the Phoenix Park. The permanent displays chart the eventful history of the park from 3500 BC to today, and focus on the flourishing wildlife in Dublin's 'green lung'.

Waterways Visitor Centre
Grand Canal Dock, Ringsend, Dublin, 1993

The aim of the Waterways Visitor Centre is to explain the significance, of a network of eighteenth-century man-made inland waterways, designed to encourage industrial development.

The Newry Canal was completed in 1742, linking Lough Neagh to the Irish Sea at Newry, the first summit level canal in Britain or Ireland. Soon, Dublin was linked to Waterford, Limerick, and the lakes of Leitrim and Roscommon. However, with the development of railways in the first half of the nineteenth century and later automobiles, the canals became obsolete and were gradually closed to navigation.

The OPW had been responsible since 1846 for the maintenance of the Shannon Navigation; then, in 1986, in recognition of their value as important artefacts of our industrial heritage and potential as a recreational resource, authority for all inland waterways (over 720km) was transferred to the OPW. A programme of restoration commenced, and to date 650km of canals and navigations have been reopened, enjoyed by sailors, anglers, walkers and wildlife enthusiasts. In 1995, the waterways were transferred to the care of the Department of Arts, Heritage, Gaeltacht and the Islands, and will now form part of the proposed cross- border body 'Waterways Ireland'.

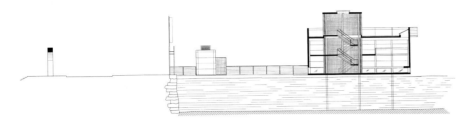

The visitor centre is located on the waters of the Grand Canal Basin in Ringsend, where the canal begins its long journey to Shannon Harbour. The gravel substrate to the canal basin required a lightweight structure, hollow steel piles being used to support a precast platform upon which sits a steel super-structure. The design is an amalgam of the primary elements of square, circle and triangle, drawing its inspiration from the simple geometrical forms of nearby buildings, such as the cylindrical gas works. A boating theme is also apparent, especially in the choice of materials – white aluminium panels forming the exterior, demountable Irish oak veneer on internal walls, and hardwood ships' decking being used for floor finishes.

The visitor passes through a quayside services building and along a timber boardwalk to reach the centre. The cube of the building is eroded at the corner to expose the glass block cylinder that is the entrance. Within this light-filled capsule, the staircase ascends to the roof deck, affording unique views of the canal and docklands. From here, external cantilevered stairs jut over the water and lead back to the boardwalk.

Half the exhibition hall is double-height to allow for a variety of small- and large-scale exhibitions, including a working model of a lock, and a diving suit dating from 1905, which was used by OPW divers in the Shannon for many years. Light is a crucial element in the centre, which benefits from the reflective properties of water. At night, the building is internally lit, glass skirting at the base of the walls creating the illusion of a structure hovering over the water.

Clonmacnoise Visitor Centre
Co Offaly 1995

The sixth-century monastery at Clonmacnoise was founded by St Ciarán, at the meeting point of Ireland's two major transport routes: the River Shannon and the Eiscir Riada, a natural gravel ridge traversing the boggy midlands. The monastery grew rapidly in importance, and flourished in spite of raids from Vikings and native Irish alike. It was renowned throughout Europe as a centre of learning and craftsmanship, and enjoyed royal patronage until reforms within the Irish church in the twelfth century marked the start of the dramatic decline of the monastery. In 1552 it was plundered by the English garrison at Athlone, after which the annals record 'There was not left moreover, a bell, small or large, an image, or an altar, or a book, or a gem, or even glass in a window, from the wall of the church out, which was not carried off.'

In 1877, the various ruins and carvings were taken into state care by the OPW, and in 1955 the remainder of the monastic site was transferred to the state by the Representative Church Body.

The new visitor centre is located west of the monastic complex, in a garden to the rear of a farmhouse which was retained and incorporated into the scheme. The form of the centre is designed to reflect the type of structures which would originally have surrounded the monastery. The scheme is a single-storey construction in natural materials, designed alongside the existing trees to minimise its visual impact. It takes the form of a staggered rectangular development terminating in a cluster of three circles. A reception, audio-visual area and café are housed in the centre, as well as an exhibition on the monastic site.

The Cross of the Scriptures is one of the finest surviving high crosses in Ireland, and probably dates to the early tenth century. Dedicated to the High King of Ireland, Flann Sinna, every surface has been decorated with carvings, most of which have been identified as biblical scenes. On completion of the adjoining visitor centre in 1995, the Cross of the Scriptures, the North Cross (*c* 800) and the South Cross (probably ninth-century) were transferred indoors to ensure their future safety, and facsimile copies were placed in their original positions. The centre also houses some of the 600 pre-Norman graveslabs found in the burial ground.

Connemara National Park Visitor Centre
Letterfrack, Co Galway, 1992

Connemara National Park, opened in 1980, comprises over 2000 hectares of heaths, bogs, grasslands and scenic mountains which form part of the famous Twelve Bens range. The visitor centre is located in Letterfrack, and incorporates the outhouses of the former industrial school, established by the Christian Brothers in the late nineteenth century. In 1992, the centre was enlarged and replanned to provide additional exhibition space and improved visitor facilities.

The new entrance, at first-floor level, is accessed via a circular courtyard. A similarly shaped desk forms the focal point of the reception. Connecting the new and old sections of the building is a glazed bridge over an existing stream. This affords the visitor excellent views of Barnaderg Bay to the east, and, inland, Diamond Hill. Exhibits explain the development of the park's landscape from the Ice Age onwards; the unique habitat provided by blanket bogland; and the Irish tradition of turf-cutting. The centre also functions as a starting-point for hill-walkers exploring the park, providing maps and practical advice, as well as tea-rooms, a picnic area for visitors.

The Architecture of State Buildings. OPW: Ireland 1900–2000

Part 3: Listings

OPW Projects of the Twentieth Century
OPW Personnel
Project Teams
Index

OPW Projects of the Twentieth Century

This listing aims to record all the new works and major extension/refurbishment projects undertaken by the Office of Public Works between 1900 and 1999. Projects appear under the date of completion. The extent of records varies greatly over the century, but the listing attempts to be as comprehensive as possible, given the constraints. The OPW acknowledges that this area is open to further study.

Abbreviations
CGS: Coast Guard station
DMP: Dublin Metropolitan Police (station) (pre-1925)
GS: Garda Siochána (station) (post-1922)
NS: National school
PO: Post office
RIC: Royal Irish Constabulary (pre-1922)

1900

Clonmel PO, Tipperary
St George's NS, Sherrard Street, Dublin
Ringsend NS, Dublin
Lunatic Asylum, Portrane, Dublin
Ballycrovane CGS, Cork
Dunny Cove CGS, Cork
Laytown CGS, Meath
Arthurstown CGS, Wexford
Curragh Camp PO, Kildare
Westport PO, Mayo
Dundalk PO, Louth
Enniskillen PO, Fermanagh
Carlow Convent NS, Carlow
St Malachy's NS, Belfast
St Matthew's NS, Belfast
St Mary's NS, Drogheda, Louth
St Malachy's NS, Dundalk, Louth
Fortwilliam NS, Antrim
St Vincent de Paul NS, Limerick

1902

Castletownbere CGS, Cork
Enniscorthy PO, Wexford
Central Bridewell DMP, Dublin
Chapel ceiling replaced Royal Hospital Kilmainham
Clonmel PO, Tipperary
Sligo PO, Sligo
Abbeytown NS, Roscommon
Abbeycartron NS, Roscommon
Chapelizod NS, Dublin
Harold NS, Dalkey
Holycross NS, Belfast
Cork PO (extension), Pembroke Street, Cork
Cahir PO, Tipperary
Kilkeel CGS, Down
Knightstown CGS, Kerry
St Mary's Convent NS, Roscommon town
Armagh PO, Armagh
Castlebar PO, Mayo

Sligo PO, 1902

1903

Omagh PO, Tyrone
Birr PO, Offaly
Limerick PO (extensive alterations)
Millfield NS, Belfast
Baden Powell Street NS, Belfast
Holycross NS, Belfast
Lurgan NS, Armagh
Dromantee NS, Armagh
St Catherine's NS, Dublin
Macroom NS, Cork
St Joseph's Cove NS, Cork
St Joseph's Monastery NS, Boyle, Co Roscommon
Moate Convent NS, Westmeath
Cappoquin Convent NS, Waterford
Ormeau Park NS, Down
Milltown Rooms, National Gallery of Ireland, Dublin
Clones PO, Monaghan
St Mary's NS, Belfast
Carnlough CGS, Antrim

1904

Crookhaven CGS, Cork
Brandon Quay CGS, Kerry
Corkbeg CGS, Kerry
Kells PO, Meath
Skibereen PO, Cork
Queen's University Cork (new gate lodge)
Tranquilla NS, Dolphin's Barn, Dublin
St Paul's NS, Bray, Wicklow
Belturbet PO, Cavan
Bray PO, Wicklow

1905

New Ross PO, Wexford
Aranmore CGS & signal station, Donegal
Fanad Head CGS & signal station, Donegal
Whitestown CGS & war signal station, Louth

1906

Carrowkennedy NS, Mayo
Monaghan PO, Monaghan

Belturbet PO, 1904

Royal Dublin Fusiliers Arch, 1907

1907

Bandon PO, Cork
Royal Dublin Fusiliers Arch, St Stephen's Green, Dublin
Athenry Agricultural College *(proposed)*, Galway
Tralee PO, Kerry
Carrick-on-Shannon PO, Leitrim

1908

Sybil Point CGS & war signal station, Kerry
Portrush PO, Antrim

1909

Clontarf DMP, Strandville Avenue, Dublin
Blackhead war signal station, Antrim
Tullamore PO, Offaly
Tulsk NS, Roscommon
The Grange NS, Fermoy, Cork
Boyle PO, Roscommon
Navan PO, Meath
Fairview PO, Dublin
Blackrock PO, Dublin

1910

Athy PO, Kildare
Lower Rutland Street NS, Dublin
St Mathias' NS, Belfast
Convent NS, Mallow, Cork
Convent NS, Navan, Meath
St Mary's NS, Nenagh, Tipperary
Athlone Mixed NS, Westmeath
Inland Revenue office, Fenit, Kerry
Templebreedy war signal station, Cork

1911

Roscommon PO, Roscommon
George's Hall, Dublin Castle
Lyracrumpane NS, Kerry
Maharees NS, Kerry
Lettera NS, Galway
Faughanvale NS, Londonderry
Gorthaganny NS, Roscommon
Kilvine NS, Mayo
Rathmorgan NS, Mayo

Tiernasligo NS, Donegal
West wing of Viceregal Lodge, Phoenix Park, Dublin

1912

Land Registry, Four Courts, Dublin
Portrane CGS, Dublin
Bunbeg wireless telegraphy station, Donegal 1912
Aille NS, Galway
Tonragee NS, Mayo
Koilmore NS, Mayo
Knock NS, Mayo
51 St Stephen's Green (conversion), Dublin
Castlerea PO, Roscommon
Killucan PO, Westmeath
Laurence Cove CGS, Bere Island, Cork

Roscommon PO, 1911

1913

Mouth of the Boyne CGS, Louth
Borlinn NS, Cork
Coomhola NS, Cork
Reengaroga NS, Cork
Ballymichael NS, Donegal
Carrownaganonagh NS, Donegal
Skerries NS, Dublin
Doaghbeg NS, Donegal
Ardeevin NS, Galway
Bushey Park NS, Galway
Brackluin NS, Kerry
St John's NS, Cashlagh, Co Kerry
Ventry NS, Kerry
Gazebo NS, Kilkenny
Ahanlish NS, Leitrim
Soran NS, Longford
Currane NS, Mayo
Lowpark NS, Mayo
Pollathomas NS, Mayo
Rossport NS, Mayo
St Joseph's NS, Killasser, Mayo
Clonaghadoo NS, Laois
Cliffoney NS, Sligo
Miltownpass NS, Sligo
Ballymena PO, Antrim
Tuam PO, Galway
Fitzgibbon St DMP, Dublin

1914

Petrie memorial, Mount Jerome cemetery, Dublin

1915

Ballycotton CGS, Cork
Lord Edward Street labour exchange, Dublin
Ballsbridge PO (extension), Dublin
Great Brunswick Street Dublin DMP, Pearse St, Dublin

1916

GPO (remodelled), Dublin

1919

Gormanstown aerodrome, Dublin
Tallaght aerodrome, Dublin

1921

Rialto NS, S C Road, Dublin

1922

Bagenalstown PO, Carlow
Royal College of Science and Government Buildings,
 Merrion Street, Dublin

1923

Killester housing for ex-servicemen, Dublin
Housing for ex-servicemen, Dún Laoghaire, Dublin

1924

Kill o' the Grange DMP (reconstruction), Dublin
Sligo Custom House (reconstruction), Sligo
Reconstruction of former RIC Barracks as GS
Borris-in-Ossory, Laois
Brittas, Dublin
Bruff, Limerick
Castlecomer, Kilkenny
Clarecastle, Clare
Drumbane, Tipperary
Dungarvan, Waterford
Hollymount, Mayo
Kildysart, Clare
Killorglin, Kerry
Lanesboro, Longford
Manorhamilton, Leitrim
New Ross, Wexford
Partry, Mayo
Sligo no.1, Sligo
Collins Barracks (reconstruction), Cork

1925

Fenit CGS reconstructed as GS, Kerry
Reconstruction of former RIC Barracks as GS
Abbeydorney, Kerry
Achill Sound, Mayo

Ardrahan, Galway
Ballickmoyler, Laois
Ballinamore, Leitrim
Ballindine, Mayo
Ballinlough, Roscommon
Ballinure, Tipperary
Ballymoghanny, Sligo
Bansha, Tipperary
Blackwater, Wexford
Camolin, Wexford
Carna, Galway
Carrowkeel, Donegal
Clonevan, Wexford
Coole, Westmeath
Union Quay, Cork
Duleek, Meath
Dunshaughlin, Meath
Ennis, Clare
Ferrybank, Waterford
Frenchpark, Roscommon
Glenisland, Kilkenny
Golden, Tipperary
Hospital, Limerick
Kanturk, Cork
Kilbrittain, Cork
Kill, Kildare
Lisdoonvarna, Clare
Maam, Galway
Millstreet, Cork
Oola, Limerick
Robertstown, Kildare
Roscommon
Rosmuc, Galway
Stoneyford, Kilkenny
Tralee, Kerry
Tyrrellspass, Westmeath
Clonakenny GS, Tipperary
Lahardane GS, Mayo
Scartaglin GS, Kerry
Ballinrobe GS, Mayo
Barran NS, Cavan
Ardcrone NS, Donegal
Drumcondra NS, Dublin
Blackrock NS, Dublin
Sallynoggin NS, Dublin
Carra NS, Mayo
Rathlee NS, Mayo
Ballinderry NS, Galway
Drishaghaun NS, Galway
Glaun NS (reconstructed), Cork
Clontarf telephone exchange, Dublin
Clonakilty PO (adaptation of former Presbyterian church),
 Cork

1926

Bruckless NS, Donegal
Garafin NS, Galway
Leenane NS, Galway
Ardrigole GS, Cork
Ballyferriter GS, Kerry
Ballylooby GS, Clare
Boston GS, Clare

Carrigaholt GS, Clare
Cloghane GS, Kerry
Corrinshigagh GS, Monaghan
Dereen GS, Kerry
Leinster House (adaptation), Dublin
Liscasy GS, Clare
Oylegate GS, Wexford
Reconstruction of former RIC barracks as GS
Balla, Mayo
Ballina, Mayo
Ballincurrig, Cork
Ballyduff, Kerry
Ballyduf, Waterford
Ballymacarbery, Waterford
Ballymoe, Galway
Ballywilliam, Wexford
Baltimore, Cork
Boherbue, Cork
Borris, Carlow
Buttevant, Cork
Cabinteely, Dublin
Callan, Kilkenny
Carron, Kerry
Castletownconyers, Limerick
Clogher, Donegal
Clonakilty, Cork
Clonmel, Tipperary
Cong, Mayo
Granard, Longford
Hollywood, Wicklow
Inchigeela, Cork
Innishannon, Cork
Kenmare, Kerry
Kerrykeel, Donegal
Killann, Wexford
Killenagh, Waterford
Kilmovee, Mayo
Leenane, Galway
Lennybrien, Waterford
Listowel, Kerry
Lough George, Galway
Macroom, Cork
Milford, Cork
Morris Mill, Clare
New Inn, Tipperary
Nobber, Meath
Passage East, Waterford
Rathowen, Westmeath
St Luke's, Cork 1926
McCurtain Street, Cork
Dromahair, Leitrim
Dundrum, Dublin
Farnaght, Leitrim
Glenamaddy, Galway
Glencolumbkille, Donegal
Glenville, Cork
Goresbridge, Kilkenny
Shrule, Mayo
Skerries, Dublin
Skibbereen, Cork
Stradone, Cavan
Tipperary town
Tullow, Carlow

Dromod GS, 1927

Virginia, Cavan
Waterville, Kerry
Araglen GS, Cork
Rathduff GS, Cork
Telephone exchange, Rere of 25/26 Upper Merrion St, Dublin
Drung NS, Cavan
Killeshandra NS, Cavan
Lisheen NS, Clare
Knockbeha NS, Clare
Long Island NS, Cork
St John the Baptist NS, Kildare
St Canice's NS, Kilkenny
Longwood NS, Meath
Smithboro' NS, Monaghan
Ferbane NS, Offaly
Philipstown NS, Offaly
Inchmore Island NS, Westmeath
National Library of Ireland, Kildaire St (extension)

1927

Ballinamult GS, Waterford
Camp GS, Kerry
Campile GS, Wexford
Galbally GS, Limerick
Goleen GS, Cork
Headford GS, Kerry
Kilmessan GS, Meath
Knock GS, Mayo
Leitrim GS, Leitrim
Moneygall GS, Offaly
Moycullen GS, Galway
Newtownsandes GS, Kerry
Rockchapel GS, Cork
Smithboro' GS, Monaghan
Sneem GS, Kerry
Templeorum GS, Kilkenny
Cnoc-na-Naomh NS, Donegal
Meenbanad NS, Donegal
St Patrick's NS, Lurgybrack, Donegal
St Columba's NS, Buncrana Donegal
Ballyadams NS, Laois
Edenmore NS, Longford
Dromiskin NS, Louth
Kilcurley NS, Louth
Kilmaine NS, Mayo
St John's NS, Breaffy, Mayo
Turlough NS, Mayo
Shanacashel NS, Kerry

Culleens NS, Sligo
St Mary's NS, Marino, Dublin
St Vincent's NS, Marino, Dublin
Ballycotton coast life-saving station, Cork
Ardnacrusha army barracks, Clare
1916 memorial, Glasnevin Cemetery, Dublin
Dalkey telephone exchange, Dublin
Reconstruction of former RIC barracks as GS:
Ballinakill, Laois
Ballygurteen, Cork
Ballyneety, Limerick
Cashel, Tipperary
Dromod, Leitrim
Drumshambo, Leitrim
Easkey, Sligo
Foynes, Limerick
Glengarriff, Cork
Paulstown, Kilkenny
Rathvilly, Carlow
Shanagolden, Limerick
Ballybunion, Kerry
Ballyheane, Mayo
Bennettsbridge, Kilkenny
Kilconly, Galway
Kinnity, Offaly
Maynooth, Kildare
Miltown, Galway
Mooncoin, Kilkenny
Oldcastle, Meath
Oulart, Wexford
Tynagh, Galway
Kilmeadon GS, Waterford
Smear GS, Longford
Coronea NS, Cavan
St Mary's NS, Bridge End, Co Donegal
Mulhuddart NS, Galway
Garafine NS, Kerry
Raheen NS, Laois
St Brendan's NS, Kilmeena, Co Mayo
Ballybay NS, Monaghan
Rathlee NS, Sligo
Cushenstown NS, Wexford

1928

Reconstruction of former RIC barracks as GS
Adare, Limerick
Carrick-on-Shannon, Tipperary

Bennettsbridge GS, 1927

Castletowngeoghegan, Westmeath
Clonark, Roscommon
Drimoleague, Cork
Eyrecourt, Galway
Farranfore, Kerry
Leitrim town
Mountshannon, Clare
New Pallas, Limerick
Tarbert, Kerry
Thomastown, Kilkenny
Ballyvary GS, Mayo
Barnadery GS, Galway
Carrowkennedy GS, Mayo
Coachford GS, Cork
Dolla GS, Tipperary
Dungourney GS, Cork
Fanore GS, Clare
Portmagee GS, Kerry
Redhills GS, Cavan
Skreen GS, Sligo
Kilferagh NS, Clare
Barrahaurin NS, Cork
Glassan NS, Donegal
St Mary's NS, Cockhill, Donegal
Fahan NS, Donegal
St Oran's NS, Sladran, Donegal
St Patrick's NS, Carrowmenagh, Donegal
St Brendan's NS, Killester, Dublin
St Brigid's NS, Killester, Dublin
Boheshill NS, Kerry
Kilmeedy NS, Limerick
Culmore NS, Mayo
Killala NS, Mayo
Nobber NS, Meath
Latnamard NS, Monaghan
Boher NS, Offaly
Collooney NS, Sligo
Kinageally NS, Sligo

1929

Colaiste Íde, Burnham House (adaptation and extension), Ventry, Kerry
Annascaul GS, Kerry
Cloyne GS, Cork
Corbetstown GS, Kilkenny
Crookstown GS, Cork
Doonbeg GS, Clare
Finea GS, Longford
Glenfarne GS, Leitrim
Ring GS, Ballingall, Waterford
Santry GS, Dublin
Tallaght GS, Dublin
Creeslough NS, Donegal
Reconstruction of former RIC barracks as GS
Castleisland, Kerry
Castletownberehaven, Cork
Glin, Limerick
Loughrea, Galway
Swinford, Mayo
Tierlahood NS, Cavan
Doochary NS, Donegal
Gortahork NS, Donegal

Loughanure NS, Donegal
Meenagowan NS, Donegal
Newtowncunningham NS, Donegal
O'Gallagher NS, Donegal
St Michael's NS, Keogh Square, Dublin
Loughshinny NS, Dublin
Newcastle NS, Dublin
Claregalway NS, Galway
Kilbaha NS, Kerry
St Caitlin's NS, Kilvicadonig, Kerry
Allenwood NS, Kildare
Dunamaggan NS, Kilkenny
Drumdiffer NS, Leitrim
Barna NS, Limerick
St Brigid's NS, Tooreen, Mayo
Kilbride NS, Meath
St Joseph's NS, Dunsany, Meath
Annyalla NS, Monaghan
Kinnitty NS, Offaly
Naomh Ceitheach NS, Roscommon
Coolbock NS, Sligo
Gainstown NS, Westmeath
Ballintubber NS, Roscommon
Ballybunion NS, Kerry
14/15 Upper O'Connell Street Dublin (reconstruction as income tax offices)
Restaurant, Leinster House, Dublin
Custom House (reconstruction), Dublin

1930

Elizabeth Fort (reconstruction of old military barracks as GS), Cork
Lifford PO (fit out), Donegal
Allihies GS, Cork
Ballinspittle GS, Cork
Kilcrohane GS, Cork
Reconstruction of former RIC barracks as GS
Muinebeag, Carlow
Ballyfeard, Cork
Eglinton Street, Galway
Mullingar, Westmeath
Macaire NS, Clare
Bunaninver NS, Donegal
Drumnaraw NS, Donegal
St Garvan's NS, Donegal
St Patrick's NS, Carndonagh, Donegal
Corpus Christi NS, Dublin
St Theres' NS, Dublin
Tallaght NS, Dublin
Newtown NS, Galway
Leixlip NS, Kildare
Rathcoffey NS, Kildare
Staplestown NS, Kildare
Dunbell NS, Kilkenny
Graigue Boys' NS, Kilkenny
Kilmallock NS, Limerick
St Mary's NS, Drumlish, Longford
Claremorris NS, Mayo
Murrisk NS, Mayo
St Columba's NS, Carrownedan, Mayo
Tullabawn NS, Mayo
Cannakill NS, Offaly

Scoil Padraig NS, Churchview, Roscommon
St Teresa's NS, Borrisoleigh, Tipperary
Glencairn NS, Waterford
Duncormack NS, Wexford
Kiltealy NS, Wexford
St Brigid's NS, Blackwater, Wexford
15/16 Upper Merrion St (adapted & redecorated for Department of Agriculture), Dublin

1931

Officers' Mess, Baldonnel Aerodrome
Donnybrook GS, Dublin
Tullyvin GS, Cavan
Ballydehob GS, Cork
Durrus GS, Cork
Eyeries GS, Cork
Corofin GS, Galway
Tullogher GS, Kilkenny
Louth GS, Louth
Rhode GS, Offaly
Templetuohy GS, Tipperary
Shevry GS, Tipperary
Rathgormack GS, Waterford
Reconstruction of former RIC barracks as GS stations
Ballon, Carlow
Ballyglass, Mayo
Brosna, Kerry
Ennistymon NS, Clare
Coppeen NS, Cork
Brackey NS, Donegal
Lower Fahan NS, Donegal
Naomh Brighid NS, Glenmakee, Donegal
Naomh Colmchille NS, Craigtown, Donegal
Scoil Brighde Moville, Donegal
Stillorgan NS, Dublin
St Vincent's Convent NS, Loughrea, Galway
Ballybunion Boys' NS, Kerry
Sacred Heart Convent NS, Tralee, Kerry
St Brendan's NS, Blennerville, Kerry
Ballycallan NS, Kilkenny
Mooncoin NS, Kilkenny
Strangsmills NS, Kilkenny
Erriff NS, Mayo
Tristia NS, Mayo
Tumgesh NS, Mayo
Clonbulloge NS, Offaly
Edenderry NS, Offaly
Eochaille Ara NS, Tipperary
Portlaw NS, Waterford
Walshestown NS, Westmeath
Oylegate NS, Wexford
Four Courts (restoration), Dublin

1932

Leinster House (extension), Dublin
General Post Office (reconstruction), Dublin
Castlebar income tax office, Mayo
Ballyclough GS, Cork
Glantane GS, Cork
Gurrandulla GS, Galway
Dunmore GS, Galway

Athea GS, Limerick
Newtowncashel GS, Longford
Keadue GS, Roscommon
Tulsk GS, Roscommon
Castlebridge GS, Wexford
Gorey GS, Wexford
Ardrigole NS, Cork
Skibbereen NS, Cork
Naomh Baoithin NS, Donegal
Rahoon Convent NS, Galway
Shindilla NS, Galway
Fionán Noamhtha NS, Baile an Ghoilín, Kerry
Clontubrid NS, Kilkenny
Ashford NS, Limerick
Derry NS, Mayo
Doocastle NS, Mayo
Fletcherstown NS, Meath
St Philomena's NS, Tullamore, Offaly
Attyrory NS, Roscommon
Corbally NS, Tipperary
Clash NS, Tipperary
Cloran NS, Westmeath
Clochar Mhuire NS, Wexford
Bray Boys' NS, Wicklow
Rathnew NS, Wicklow
Old fever hospital (adapted for NS), Castleisland, Kerry
GPO (restoration), Dublin

1933

Athlone high power wireless station, Westmeath
Fr Cullen Memorial NS, Carlow
Kanturk NS, Clare
Parteen NS, Clare
Castletownbere NS, Cork
Dunderrow NS, Cork
Lisgriffin NS, Cork
Carrowreagh NS, Donegal
Naomh Buadain NS, Donegal
Bloomfield Avenue NS, Dublin
Crumlin NS, Dublin
Cregmore NS, Galway
St Mary's NS, Lerhin, Galway
Ballyseedy NS, Kerry
St Canice's Convent NS, Kilkenny
Drumaney NS, Leitrim
St Canice's NS, Laois
Askeaton NS, Limerick
Bunnacurry NS, Mayo
Lahardane NS, Mayo
Urbleshanny NS, Monaghan
Killurine NS, Offaly
Kilmactranny NS, Sligo
Cahernhallia NS, Tipperary
Loughmore NS, Tipperary
Ballycomoyle NS, Westmeath
Coralstown NS, Westmeath
Kilmacoo NS, Wicklow
Naomh Sheosaimh NS (formerly fever hospital), Ballyshannon, Donegal
Collinstown NS (adaptation), Westmeath
Ballynoe GS, Cork
Newmarket GS, Cork

Finglas GS, Dublin
Kilmeedy GS, Limerick
Hackballscross GS, Meath
Ballynabola GS, Wexford
Curravagh NS, Cavan
St Nicholas' NS, Claddagh, Galway
Dunfanaghy NS (formerly fever hospital), Donegal

1934

Terenure telephone exchange, Dublin
Rathmines PO and telephone exchange, Dublin
St Mullens' GS, Glynn, Carlow
Shercock GS, Cavan
Beaufort GS, Kerry
Glenbeigh GS, Kerry
Lixnaw GS, Kerry
Milltown GS, Castlemaine, Kerry
Celbridge GS, Kildare
Carrigallen GS, Leitrim
Glenamoy GS, Mayo
Ballinagh NS, Cavan
Maghera NS, Cavan
Moneygashel NS, Cavan
Shragh NS, Clare
Sixmilebridge NS, Clare
Blackrock NS, Cork
Boherbue NS, Cork
Carrig Ui Ula NS, Cork
Cathedral NS, Cork
Clonkeen NS, Cork
Coomleigh NS, Cork
Munifluigh NS, Cork
St Colmogs NS, Cork
Sullivan's Quay NS, Cork
Fothar NS, Donegal
Kilclooney NS, Donegal
Knockfola NS, Donegal
Bluebell NS, Donegal
Christ the King NS, Cabra, Dublin
Ahascragh NS, Galway
Ardrahan NS, Galway
Aughagloragh NS, Galway
Carrabeg NS, Galway
Fossa NS, Kerry
Ranalough NS, Kerry
St Joseph's NS, Rathmore, Kerry
Coolcullen NS, Kilkenny

Newmarket GS, 1933

Aughawillan NS, Leitrim
Creevalea NS, Leitrim
Ahane NS, Limerick
Sexton Street Convent NS, Limerick
Coogue NS, Mayo
Naomh Padraig NS, Carrowmore, Mayo
St Michael's NS, Monaghan
Carnaleck NS, Sligo
Lugawarry NS, Sligo
Carniglea NS, Waterford
Kilwatermoy NS, Waterford
Cossan NS, Westmeath
Kilcomeragh NS, Westmeath
St Peter's Convent NS, Athlone, Westmeath
Scoil Padraig NS, Crossbeg, Wexford
Templetown NS, Wexford
Tomhaggard NS, Wexford
St Kevin's NS, Glendalough, Wicklow
Galway employment exchange (adaptation of former
    Piscatory School), Galway
Cashel PO, Tipperary
Colaiste na Mumhan, Ballyvourney, Cork c 1934
Coláiste Éinne preparatory college, Galway c 1934

1935

Casino, Marino (basic conservation), Dublin
Blanchardstown GS, Dublin
Claremorris GS, Mayo
Clonaslee GS, Laois
Rathkineely NS, Roscommon
Daingean GS, Offaly
Kill GS, Waterford
Lusk GS, Dublin
Miltown Malby GS, Clare
Recess GS, Galway
Tarleton GS, Cork
Mullagh GS (adaptation of former RIC barracks), Cavan
Clarecastle NS, Clare
Kilmurry NS, Clare
Ballymartle NS, Cork
Alt NS, Donegal
Earnain Naomhtha Ballintra NS, Donegal
Naomh Brighid NS, Ballylar, Donegal
Scoil Phadraig Dore, Donegal
Naomh Colmcille NS, Drumoghill, Donegal
St Patrick's NS, Meereagh, Donegal
Roshin NS, Donegal
St Peter's & St Paul's NS, Balbriggan, Dublin
Inishbarra Island NS, Galway
Knockatee NS, Kerry
Boolyglass NS, Kilkenny
St Patrick's NS, Ballylinan, Laois
Drumshambo NS, Leitrim
Loughross NS, Leitrim
Cappamore Boys' NS, Limerick
Ballinrobe Christian Brothers NS, Mayo
Cloughbrack NS, Mayo
Shanvaghera NS, Mayo
Shrule NS, Mayo
Carnaross NS, Meath
St Teresa's NS, Ballynagearn, Monaghan
Drumgoose NS, Monaghan

Gortmore NS, Monaghan
Sreenty NS, Monaghan
Moneygall NS, Offaly
Rahan NS, Offaly
Ardkeenan NS, Roscommon
Ballyweelin NS, Sligo
Derrylihan NS, Sligo
Meenmore NS, Sligo
Rathcormac NS, Sligo
Kill NS, Waterford
Drumcondra GS, Dublin

1936

Kanturk NS, Cork
Crossmolina GS, Mayo
Rosses Point GS, Sligo
Dromore West GS, Sligo
Roundfort NS, Mayo
Carlow CBS NS, Carlow town
Liscannor coast life-saving station, Doolin Head, Clare
Durrow Presentation Convent NS (adaptation of former
    Durrow Castle), Laois
Carrickbyrne GS, Wexford (c 1936)
Miltown Malbay GS, Clare (c 1936)
Glynn GS, Carlow (c 1936)
Clonaslee GS, Offaly (c 1936)
Timoleage GS, Cork (c 1936)
Castleknock GS, Dublin (c 1936)
Kilcullen GS, Kildare (c 1936)
St Mary's NS, Sandford, Dublin
Kiltormer GS, Galway
Kanturk NS, Cork
Castlebar GS (adaptation of former military barracks), Mayo

1937

Bishop Foley Memorial NS, Carlow
Hacketstown NS, Carlow
Ballyhea Boys and Girls NS, Cork
Carriganimma NS, Cork
Durrus NS, Cork
Glasheen Girls' NS, Cork
Laharn NS, Cork
St Mary's Convent NS, Carrigtwohill, Cork
St Patrick's Boys' NS, Cork
Glenagivney NS, Donegal
Meentimadea NS, Donegal
Cealltriagh NS, Kinclare, Galway
Coldwood NS, Galway
Kinclare NS, Galway
Muckalee NS, Kilkenny
St Fiacre's NS, Ullard, Kilkenny
Killanure NS, Laois
Crecora NS, Limerick
Shountrade NS, Limerick
Ballymahon Convent NS, Longford
Ardee Monastery NS, Louth
Accony NS, Mayo
Cill Chronaigh NS, Louth
Ardagh NS, Mayo
Ball Aluinn NS, Mayo
Glendoon NS, Mayo

Rathmore GS, 1937

Louisburgh Convent NS, Mayo
Shraheens NS, Mayo
Cortown NS, Meath
Monaghan CBS NS, Monaghan
Cnoc a' Chuilinn NS, Roscommon
Rahara NS, Roscommon
Golden NS, Tipperary
Clongeen NS, Wexford
Blessington Boys' & Girls' NS, Wicklow
Garryhill NS, Carlow
Lisroe NS, Clare
Drumkeen NS, Donegal
Killycreen NS, Donegal
St Columba's NS, Kilamcrenan, Donegal
Inchicore South Boys' NS, Dublin
Saggart NS, Dublin
St Nicholas Without NS, Dublin
St John's Girls' & Infants' NS, Kilkenny
Abbeyfeale Convent NS, Limerick
Glenroe NS, Limerick
St John the Baptist's Boys' NS, Limerick
St Brigid's NS, Loughill, Longford
Cill Chronaigh NS, Louth
Drogheda CBS NS, Louth
Kilmore NS, Mayo
Lankill NS, Mayo
Cushentown NS, Meath
Rathcarne NS, Meath
Killeigh NS, Offaly
Pollock NS, Offaly
St Caillin's NS, Rashina, Offaly
Ballycutranta NS, Sligo
Clonmellon Boys' NS, Westmeath
Downs NS, Westmeath
Multyfarnham NS, Westmeath
Ballyduff NS, Wicklow
Ballintubber GS, Roscommon
Rathcoole GS, Dublin
Rathmore GS, Kerry
Shanaglish GS, Galway
Timoleague GS, Cork
Tullamore GS, Offaly
Johnstown GS, Kilkenny
Foxford GS, Mayo
Carrigaline GS, Cork
Ballinasloe GS, Galway
St Oliver Plunkett Boys' NS, Moate, Westmeath
Wexford GS, Wexford
Shannon Airport, Clare
Kilmainham GS, Dublin

1938

Single men's quarters, Baldonnel aerodrome
Baldwinstown GS, Wexford
Ballycullane GS, Wexford
Carrowreagh GS, Roscommon
Kilcullen GS, Kildare
Louisburgh GS, Mayo
Scarriff GS, Clare
Coney Island NS, Clare
Carrick NS, Cavan
Críost an Rí NS, Cork
Cullen Boys' & Girls' NS, Cork
Dame Mary O'Connell NS, Cork
Edeninfagh NS, Donegal
Leitir Crann NS, Donegal
Letterbrick NS, Donegal
Crumlin Convent Girls' & Infants' NS, Dublin
Harold's Cross Boys' and Girls' NS, Dublin
St Joseph's (North Lotts) NS, Dublin
St Laurence O'Toole's CBS NS, Dublin
Monkstown Junior Boys' NS, Dublin
Castlefrench NS, Galway
Ballinasloe Boys' NS, Galway
Claran NS, Galway
St Brigid's NS, Ballycastle, Mayo
Ennismore NS, Kerry
Kiltallagh NS, Kerry
Bornafea NS, Kilkenny
Coone NS, Kilkenny
Reary NS, Laois
Diffreen NS, Leitrim
Drumnamore NS, Leitrim
Athlacca NS, Limerick
Kilcolman NS, Limerick
Longfield NS, Longford
Ballycastle Girls' NS, Mayo
Carra NS, Mayo
Mulranny NS, Mayo
Rathnamagh NS, Mayo
Kilmainham Wood NS, Meath
Killfargy NS, Monaghan
Rathcroghan NS, Roscommon
Castletowngeoghegan NS, Westmeath
Clonbonny NS, Westmeath
Kilbeggan Boys' NS, Westmeath
Coolgreany NS, Wexford
Tacumshane NS, Wexford
Mucklagh NS, Wicklow
Border custom office Clones, Monaghan

1939

Athlone PO
Athlone government buildings
Custom office, Moybridge
Custom office, Tullynagrow
Custom office, Bridgend
Ballylanders GS, Limerick
Hollyfort GS, Wexford
Kilmore Quay GS, Wexford
Rathcormac GS, Cork
Rathfarnham GS, Dublin

Enniskerry NS, 1939

Leighlinbridge GS, Carlow
Keelagh NS, Cavan
Shannow NS, Cavan
Balhuskey NS, Cork
Dripsey NS, Cork
Galladoo NS, Cork
Gortalassa NS, Cork
Knockskeagh NS, Cork
Inishannon NS, Cork
Umeraboy NS, Cork
Cloontiagh NS, Donegal
Crumlin CBS NS, Dublin
St Vincent's CBS NS, Glasnevin, Dublin
Star of the Sea NS, Sandymount, Dublin
Mullagh NS, Galway
Galmoy NS, Kilkenny
Graiguenamanagh Convent NS, Kilkenny
Inistioge NS, Kilkenny
Augharan NS, Leitrim
Edenville NS, Leitrim
Largy NS, Glebe, Leitrim
Tullaghan NS, Leitrim
Knockainy NS, Limerick
Dundalk CBS NS, Louth
Bohermeen NS, Meath
Moynalty NS, Meath
Carrickmacross Monastery NS, Monaghan
Monaghan CBS NS
Clegna NS, Roscommon
Elphin Boys NS, Roscommon
Cashel CBS NS, Tipperary
Killeen NS, Tipperary
Garranbane NS, Waterford
Newtown NS, Waterford
Blessed Oliver Plunkett NS, Westmeath
Boher NS, Westmeath
Corry NS, Rathaspic,
Lacken NS, Westmeath
Rathowen NS, Westmeath
Bannow NS, Wexford
Ferns NS, Wexford
Wexford CBS NS, Wexford
Dunganstown NS, Wicklow
Enniskerry NS, Wicklow
Damastown NS, Dublin
St Thomas' Boys' NS, Roscommon
Donoughmore NS, Donegal
Dundalk employment exchange, Louth
Custom House, Galway
Insitioge GS, Kilkenny
Islandbridge war memorial, Dublin

1940

Mail sorting office, Cork city
Killeagh NS, Cork
Tournafulla GS, Limerick
Store Street GS, Dublin
Kilmainham GS, Dublin
Scarriff GS, Clare
Carrigaline GS, Cork
Ballinsloe GS, Galway
Shanaglish GS, Galway
Killarney GS, Kerry
Kilcullen GS, Kildare
Johnstown GS, Kilkenny
Foxford GS, Mayo
Louisburgh GS, Mayo
Ballintubber GS, Rocommon
Wexford GS, Wexford
Athenry GS, Galway
Carrick-on-Shannon GS, Leitrim
Carrowreagh GS
Tipperary GS
Baldwinstown GS
Ballycullane GS, Wexford
Killybegs GS, Donegal
Creggs GS, Galway
Blackrock GS, Cork
Salthill GS, Galway
Inistioge GS, Kilkenny
Kilcock GS, Kildare
St Brigid's NS, Tonyduff, Cavan
Cloonanaha NS, Clare
Ovens NS, Cork
Togher NS, Dunmanway, Cork
St Anne's Convent NS, Charleville, Cork
Broadpath NS, Donegal
Laghey Bar NS, Donegal
Magheraroarty NS, Donegal
Munterneece NS, Donegal
Clonshough NS, Dublin
St Louis' Convent NS, Rathmines, Dublin
St Mary's Boys' NS, Haddington Road, Dublin
Athenry Boys' NS, Galway
Ballinakill NS, Galway
Castledaly NS, Galway
Creagh NS, Galway
Laurencetown NS, Galway
Lavally NS, Galway
Moyglass NS, Galway
Clashnagarrane NS, Kerry
Castlecomer Boys' NS, Kilkenny
Conahy NS, Kilkenny
Mullinavat Boys' NS, Kilkenny
Ballina Convent & Infants' NS, Mayo
Meath Hill NS, Meath
Laggan NS, Monaghan
Béal Átha na gCarr NS, Roscommon
Cloonfad NS, Roscommon
St Michael's NS, Clegna, Roscommon
Carney NS, Sligo
Forthill Boys' & Girls' NS, Sligo
Killaraght NS, Sligo
Ballysloe NS, Tipperary

Redwood NS, Tipperary
Tipperary CBS NS, Tipperary
Rath NS, Westmeath
Tara Hill NS, Wexford
Rathdrum Boys' NS, Wicklow
St Michael's Convent NS, Rathdrum, Wicklow
Canteen and mess, Baldonnel aerodrome
Stores block, Baldonnel aerodrome
Hostel for cadets, Baldonnel aerodrome
Sluagh (military training) halls
Castleblayney, Monaghan
Drogheda, Louth
Midleton, Cork
Swords, Dublin
Lahinch, Clare

1941

Tuam CBS NS, Galway
Clontarf NS (adaptation of Belgrove House), Dublin
Mount Merrion NS (adaptation of Manor House), Dublin

1942

Hoey's Court employment exchange, Dublin
Administration block, Baldonnel aerodrome
Leighlinbridge GS, Carlow
Lahinch GS, Clare
Dingle GS, Kerry
Ballytore GS, Kildare
Tounafulla GS
Kilkenny City GS, Kilkenny
Kinlough GS, Leitrim
Dublin Airport
Department of Industry & Commerce, Dublin

1943

Stradbally GS, Laois
Kimmage GS, Dublin
Shanagolden NS, Limerick
Aughrim GS, Wicklow
Collon GS, Louth
Quin GS, Clare

1944

Mullinavat GS, Kilkenny
Foynes GS, Limerick
Commons Road GS, Cork city
Durrow GS, Laois
Harcourt Terrace GS, Dublin
Sundrive Road GS, Harold's Cross, Dublin
RC Chapel, Baldonnel aerodrome

1945

Murroe GS, Limerick
Carlingford GS, Louth
Film censor's office, Dublin
Davis memorial *(proposed)*, St Stephen's Green, Dublin

1946

Development plan *(proposed)*, Dublin Castle
Oatquarter NS, Aran Islands, Galway
Skryne NS, Tara, Meath
Veterinary College of Ireland, Pembroke Road, Dublin
Pumping station, Phoenix Park, Dublin
Ballygar GS, Galway
Carraroe GS, Galway
Arva GS, Cavan
Caherconlish GS, Limerick
Drumcollogher GS, Limerick
Murroe GS, Limerick
Clara GS, Offaly
Edenderry GS, Offaly
Gymnasium, Baldonnel aerodrome

Film censor's office, 1945

Gymnasium, Baldonnel, 1946

1947

Killucan GS, Westmeath
Redcross (Barnaderg) GS, Wicklow
Castletownsend GS, Cork
Summerhill GS, Meath
Athlone Garda District HQ, Westmeath

1948

Rotunda concert hall *(proposed)*, Dublin
St Andrew's Street PO, Dublin
Kilmainham NS, Dublin
Falcarragh NS, Donegal
Whitegate GS, Cork
Avoca GS, Wicklow
Athleague GS, Roscommon
Ballybay GS, Monaghan
Kilmaine GS, Mayo
Lucan GS, Dublin
Mountbolus GS, Offaly
Stillorgan GS, Dublin
**Cahirciveen employment exchange and custom office
    *(proposed)***
Carrick-on-Suir Castle (restoration), Tipperary (1948–60)
Glangevlin GS, Cavan

1949

Kilnaleck GS, Cavan
Achill Sound GS, Mayo
Ballycastle GS, Mayo
Bellacorrick GS, Mayo
Ballintogher GS, Sligo
Summerhill GS, Meath
Dunleer GS, Louth
Rush GS, Dublin
Connolly GS, Clare
Doolin GS, Clare
Knocknagree GS, Cork
Liscarroll GS, Cork

1950

Ardnacrusha GS, Clare
Ardcath NS, Meath
Caislean Geal NS, Sligo
Trim GS, Meath
Convoy GS, Donegal
Harcourt Terrace GS, Dublin
Leinster Lawn obelisk, Dublin

1951

Drogheda PO and telephone exchange, Louth
Enniscrone GS, Sligo
Bundoran GS, Donegal
Thurles GS, Tipperary
Freshford GS, Kilkenny
Watergrasshill GS, Cork
Roundstone GS, Galway
Kilkelly GS, Mayo
Churchill GS, Donegal

Finglas GS, Dublin
Kilmaine GS, Mayo

1952

Irish embassy to the United Kingdom (adaptation), London
Letterkenny PO and telephone exchange, Donegal
New Ross GS, Wexford
Newmarket-on-Fergus GS, Clare
Telephone exchange Stillorgan, Dublin
Employment exchange, Waterford
Castletown NS, Laois
Castledermot NS, Kildare
Woodland NS, Donegal
Duleek NS, Meath
Mount Sackville NS, Dublin
Crumlin NS, Dublin
Shantalla NS, Galway
Curraha NS, Meath
Rush Boys' NS, Dublin
Killossory NS, Dublin
Kiltale NS, Meath
Portarlington NS, Offaly
Spiddal NS, Galway
Mountrath GS, Laois
Drumsna GS, Leitrim
Portumna GS, Galway
Roundwood GS, Wicklow
Irish pavilion, Frankfurt, Germany
Employment exchange, Westport *c* 1952

1953

Mullingar telephone exchange, Westmeath (*c* 1953)
Sligo telephone exchange, Sligo (*c* 1953)
Limerick telephone exchange, (*c* 1953)
Macroom PO, Cork (*c* 1953)
Girls' Convent NS, Ballyshannon, Donegal
Telephone exchange, Foxrock, Dublin
Goresbridge NS, Kilkenny
Swanlinbar GS, Cavan
Lanesborough GS, Longford
South Anne Street PO, Dublin
Tacumshane Windmill (restoration), Wexford (1953–73)

1954

St Francis NS, Manorhamilton
Liscarroll GS, Cork
Kilgarvan GS, Kerry
Knocknagoshel GS, Kerry
Cloghan GS, Offaly
St Columba's NS, Clady, Donegal

Carraroe NS, 1955

1955

Hollywood NS, Wicklow
Daingean GS, Offaly
Boyle GS, Roscommon
Ardfinnan GS, Tipperary
Moate GS, Westmeath
Carraroe NS, Galway
Aughnafarcon NS, Monaghan
Menlough NS, Galway

1956

Glenmore GS (improvements), Kilkenny
Irish Embassy to France (adaptation), Paris
Irish Embassy to Portugal (adaptation), Lisbon
Drogheda PO and telephone exchange, Louth
Bruff GS, Limerick
Ardee GS, Louth
Lanesboro GS, Longford
Custom House memorial, Dublin
Irish embassy to the Netherlands, (adaptation), The Hague
Irish embassy to the US (adaptation), New York
Holy Trinity NS, Dunfanaghy, Donegal
Ballina employment exchange, Mayo

1957

Girls' Convent NS, Kilmacud, Dublin
Royal Hospital Kilmainham (restoration), Dublin (1957–*c* 1965)
Booterstown NS, Dublin
Horseleap NS, Westmeath
Cloghan GS, Offaly
Mountmellik GS, Laois

Holy Trinity NS, Dunfanaghy, 1956

1958

Loughrea PO, Galway
Tarmon NS, Leitrim
Castlefinn Girls' NS, Donegal
St Mary's Boys NS, Ferbane, Offaly
Memorial seat to Louie Bennett, St Stephen's Green, Dublin
Kinsale GS, Cork
Kilmacrennan GS, Donegal
Pettigo GS, Donegal
Carna GS, Galway
Irish embassy to the Holy Roman See (adaptation), Rome, c 1958

1959

St Mary's NS, Creeslough, Donegal Kiladysart NS, Clare
Carrigart GS, Donegal
Blanchardstown GS, Dublin
Garrison Church of St Brigid, Curragh Camp, Kildare
Newbliss GS, Monaghan
Moneygall GS, Offaly
Soil Research Station Johnstown Castle, Wexford
Brittas NS, Dublin
Kiltartan NS, Galway
Athenry Garda District HQ, Galway
Stillorgan Road telephone exchange, Dublin
Girls' NS, Walkinstown, Dublin
Dundrum telephone exchange, Dublin

1960

Limerick PO, Limerick
Galway PO, Galway
Beauparc PO and rural automatic exchange, Meath
Knockcroghery NS, Roscommon
Glanmire telephone exchange, Cork
Baltinglass GS, Wicklow
Wellington Road telephone exchange, Cork
Finglas sorting office, telephone exchange, ancilliary stores, workshops, Dublin
Athenry GS, Galway
Stepaside GS (improvements), Dublin
Beggars Bush government offices, Dublin
Áras an Uachtaráin (alteration and redecoration), Dublin, c 1960

Knockcroghery NS, 1960

1961

Roscommon Garda Divisional HQ
Newbridge PO, Kildare
School for Blind Boys Drumcondra, Dublin
Al Centre Abbotstown, Dublin
Falcarragh GS, Donegal
Drogheda GS, Louth
Kinsale GS, Cork
Cahir GS, Tipperary

1962

Government offices, Wexford (c 1962)
Comhlucht Siúicre Éireann Teo., Earlsfort Terrace, Dublin
Bantry Garda District HQ, Cork
Grangemockler GS, Tipperary
Glynn GS, Carlow
Leenane GS, Galway
Rathmullan GS, Donegal
Ahascaragh GS, Galway
Banagher GS, Offaly
Castlebellingham GS, Louth
Clontibret GS, Monaghan
Cloone GS, Leitrim
Collooney GS, Sligo
Killala GS, Mayo
Enfield GS, Meath
Kingscourt GS, Cavan
Portumna GS, Galway
Rochfortbridge GS, Westmeath
Shannon Airport GS, Clare
Grange NS, Sligo
Glenamaddy NS, Galway
Cootehill PO, Cavan
National Library (stonework restoration), Dublin (c 1962)
Tralee government offices, Kerry
St Joseph's NS, Templeboy, Sligo
Valentia Observatory, Kerry

1963

Cabra GS, Dublin
Camus NS, Galway
Abbeydorney NS, Kerry
Naomh Lorcan NS, Kilmacud, Dublin
Castlefin GS, Donegal
Strokestown GS, Roscommon
Killeshandra GS, Cavan

1964

Shelter, People's Garden, Phoenix Park, Dublin
Irish Embassy to Nigeria (proposed), Lagos
1916 memorial, Arbour Hill, Dublin
Scoil Naomh Éanna, An Cheathru Rua, Sligo
JFK memorial concert hall (proposed)
Coolock-Raheny sorting office, Dublin (c 1964)
Agricultural research buildings, Backweston Farm, Kildare (c 1964)
Youghal PO, Cork (c 1964)

1916 memorial, 1964

1965

Quarantine station, Spike Island, Cork
Metropolitan sorting office, Amiens Street (formerly the Sally Gardens), Dublin
Ballyconnell GS, Cavan
Rothe House (restoration), Kilkenny
Dame Court telephone exchange, Dublin
Ballyboghill NS, Dublin
Ballybay GS, Monaghan
Kilgarvan GS, Kerry
Tubbercurry GS, Sligo
Blacklion GS, Cavan
Cootehill GS, Cavan
Ballingary North GS, Tipperary
Inagh GS, Clare
Labasheeda GS, Clare
Ballivor GS, Meath
Clontibret GS, Monaghan
Tubbercurry GS, Sligo
Rochfortbridge GS, Westmeath
Castletownroche GS, Cork
Kinsale GS, Cork
Rosscarbery GS, Cork
Youghal GS, Cork
Courtown GS, Waterford
Castlebellingham GS, Louth
Abbeyleix GS, Laois
Ardara GS, Donegal
Brockagh GS, Donegal
Carndonagh GS, Donegal
Killala GS, Mayo
Slane GS, Meath
Rathdrum GS, Wicklow
Athgarvan NS, Kildare

Athgarvan NS, 1965

Garden of Remembrance, 1966

Davis memorial, 1966

Garda memorial, 1966

Portmarnock NS, Dublin
Crookstown NS, Kildare
Ballyconnell GS, Cavan
Killeshandra GS, Cavan
Donoughmore GS, Cork
Burtonport GS, Donegal
Crumlin GS, Dublin
Ahascragh GS, Galway
Ballinamore GS, Leitrim
Broghagh GS, Donegal
Newbridge GS, Kildare
Castleconnell GS, Limerick
Dunboyne GS, Meath
Enniscorthy GS, Wexford
Veterinary field station, Abbotstown, Dublin
Athenry Agricultural College, Galway
Clonakilty Agricultural College, Cork
Westport NS, Mayo
Foundation Stock Farm, Abbotstown, Dublin

1966

Scoil Náisiúnta Mhuire, Knock, Mayo
Dundrum GS, Dublin
Garden of Remembrance, Parnell Square, Dublin
Slieverue NS, Kilkenny
Nenagh telephone exchange, Tipperary
Davis memorial, College Green, Dublin
Ardnacrusha GS, Clare
Ennistymon Garda District HQ, Clare
Roundstone GS, Galway
Fethard GS, Tipperary
Enniscorthy Garda District HQ, Wexford
Killimor GS, Galway
Clones GS, Monaghan
Colehill GS, Longford
Portlaoise GS, Laois
Ballickmoyler GS, Laois
Crossakeel GS, Meath
Gortnalee GS, Tipperary
Delvin GS, Westmeath
Aglish GS, Waterford
Pallas GS, Offaly
Shinrone GS, Offaly
Shannonbridge GS, Offaly
Ballinafad GS, Sligo
Newport GS, Mayo
Williamstown GS, Galway
Ballacolla GS, Laois
Garda memorial, Garda Síochána HQ, Phoenix Park, Dublin
Lismoyle NS, Roscommon
Wellington Road telephone exchange, Cork
Fern house, National Botanic Gardens, Dublin

Wolfe Tone memorial, 1967

1967

St Paul's Infant NS, Athlone, Westmeath
Droichead Nua GS, Kildare
Wolfe Tone memorial, St Stephen's Green, Dublin,
Shankill GS, Dublin
Kilfenore GS, Clare
Ballydesmond GS, Cork
Mallow GS, Cork
Railyard GS, Kilkenny
Clane GS, Kildare
Urlingford GS, Kilkenny
Loughglinn GS, Roscommon
Kinnegad GS, Westmeath
Carnew GS, Wicklow
Gortnahoe GS, Tipperary
Rathowen GS, Westmeath
Coolgreaney GS, Wexford
Duncannon GS, Wexford
Courtown GS, Wexford
Rathkeele GS, Tipperary
Keenagh GS, Longford
Kevin Street GS, Dublin
Clondalkin GS, Dublin
Terenure GS, Dublin
Cashel School for mildly handicapped children, Tipperary

1968

Computer Centre, Inchicore, Dublin
Clifden GS, Galway
Castleconnell GS, Limerick
Limerick GS, Limerick
National Gallery of Ireland (new wing), Dublin
Carlow government offices
John F Kennedy arboretum, Wexford
Land Registry (extension), Four Courts, Dublin
Enniscorthy school for mildly handicapped children, Wexford,
(c 1968)
Thurles school for mildly handicapped children, Tipperary,
(c 1968)
State Apartments (reconstruction), Dublin Castle
Leinster House (extension), Dublin

1969

Ballyfermot GS, Dublin
Myshall GS, Carlow
Arless GS, Laois
Curry GS, Sligo
Brockagh GS, Donegal
Asdee NS, Kerry

1970

Coolock GS, Dublin
Car ferry terminal, St Michael's Wharf, Dún Laoghaire, Dublin
Aclare GS & residence, Sligo
Taney NS, Dundrum, Dublin
Glasslough GS, Monaghan
Creeslough GS, Donegal
Peterswell GS, Galway
Valencia GS, Kerry
Cloonacool GS, Sligo
Puckaun GS, Tipperary
Cahir Castle (restoration), Tipperary

1971

Rathmines GS, Dublin
Dungloe GS, Donegal
Portroe GS, Tipperary
Raheny GS, Dublin
Killenaule NS, Tipperary
Kilrush GS, Clare
Birr GS, Offaly
Dundrum GS, Dublin
Kevin Street GS, Dublin
Ballymun GS, Dublin
St Brigid's NS, Duagh, Kerry
Ballinasloe NS, Galway
Dublin Institute for Advanced Studies
Ennistymon GS & residences, Clare
Ballivor GS, Meath
St Joseph's NS, Ballinasloe, Galway
St Laurence's School, Finglas, Dublin
Duagh NS, Kerry

1972

Ballyshannon Garda District HQ, Donegal
William Street GS, Limerick
Cavan PO and telephone exchange
Garden for the blind, St Stephen's Green, Dublin

1973

Waterford Garda Divisional HQ, Waterford
Central GS, Cork city (north)

Irish embassy to Japan, 1974

1974

Revenue Commissioners 'stamping branch', Dublin Castle
Charles' Fort (conservation), Kinsale, Cork
Enniskerry GS (restored), Wicklow
Askeaton GS, Limerick
Belturbet GS, Cavan
Kanturk GS, Cork
Portlaw GS, Waterford
Bunbeg GS, Donegal
Bunclody GS, Wexford
Rosmuc GS, Galway
Multyfarnham GS, Westmeath
Kiltyclogher GS, Leitrim
Moate GS, Westmeath

1975

Culdaff GS, Donegal
Emyvale GS, Monaghan
Raphoe GS, Donegal
Kilkelly GS, Mayo
Mountjoy GS, Dublin
Garda technical bureau, Dublin
Rosslare Strand GS, Wexford
Skibbereen GS, Cork
Ballinahown GS
Ballynacargy GS, Westmeath
Knockcroghery GS, Roscommon
Irish embassy to Japan (adaptation), Tokyo
Bruree GS, Limerick
Castleblaney GS, Monaghan
Clonroche GS, Wexford
Shannonbridge GS, Offaly
Croom GS, Limerick
Dunmore Caves visitor centre, Ballyfoyle, Kilkenny
Store Street GS (remodelled), Dublin

1976

Limerick Garda Divisional HQ
Carraig na bhFear GS, Cork
Emly GS, Tipperary
Inchageela GS, Cork
Store Street GS (adaptations), Dublin
Kiltullagh GS, Galway
Cloughjordan GS, Tipperary

Granard GS, Longford
William Street GS, Limerick
Corofin GS, Clare
Ballinalee GS, Longford
Ballinamore GS, Leitrim
Castlefin GS, Donegal
Rosslare Pier GS, Wexford
Duncannon GS, Wexford
Newport GS
Kilkenny Castle (restoration phase I)

1977

Athlone government offices, Westmeath
Fresco Room, National Gallery of Ireland, Dublin
Newcastlewest Garda Divisional HQ, Limerick
Castlebar government offices, Mayo
Cliffoney GS, Sligo
Fenit GS, Kerry
Mullagh GS
Ardfert GS, Kerry
Swords GS, Dublin
Broadford GS, Clare
Tulla GS, Clare
Carrick-on-Bannow GS
Omeath GS, Louth
Creeslough GS, Donegal
Kill GS
Sligo GS, Sligo
Ballinagh GS, Cavan
Enfield GS, Meath
Millstreet GS, Cork
Castlerea Garda Divisional HQ & residence, Roscommon
Mitchelstown GS, Cork
Terenure GS, Dublin
Blessington GS, Wicklow
Cabra GS, Dublin
Virginia GS & residence, Cavan
Kiltealy GS, Wexford
Irish embassy to Australia, Canberra
Ballyheigue GS, Kerry
Oughterard GS, Galway
Kanturk Garda Divisional HQ, Cork
Garda Headquarters (refurbishment), Phoenix Park
Genealogical Office (refurbishment), Kildare Street

1978

Buttevant GS, Cork
Garda residences, Belmullet, Mayo
Irish embassy to Greece (residence adapted), Athens (c 1978)
IMS headquarters, Glasnevin, Dublin
Charlestown GS, Mayo
Loughglynn GS, Roscommon
Ardfinnan GS, Tipperary
Fermoy GS, Cork
Drumlish GS, Longford
Gurteen GS
Passage West GS, Cork
Duleek GS & residence, Meath
Finglas GS, Dublin
Drumlish GS & residences, Longford
Fermoy GS (adaptation), Cork

Kilchreest GS & residences, Galway
Boyle GS & residences, Roscommon
Shelbourne House, Ballsbridge, Dublin
Lahardane GS, Mayo
Rockcorry GS, Monaghan
Corduff NS, Dublin
Borrisoleigh GS, Tipperary (c 1978)
Bantry GS, Cork
Bridewell GS, Cork
Tipperary PO
Dundalk GS, Louth
Chapeltown NS, Valentia Island, Kerry
OPW Engineering Services, Hatch Street, Dublin

1979

Tyrrelspass NS, Westmeath (c 1979)
Castleisland Presentation Convent NS, Kerry (c 1979)
Geological Survey Offices and Labour Court, Beggar's Bush
    Barracks, Dublin
Taoiseach's residence (proposed), Phoenix Park
Rosleven telephone exchange, Athlone, Westmeath
Clonmel PO, Tipperary
Department of Agriculture Library, Agriculture House, Kildare St,
    Dublin
Irish embassy to Austria (residence refurbished), Vienna
Mallow telephone exchange, Cork
Fermoy GS, Cork
Gearhameen visitor centre, Killarney, Kerry
Abbey Street automatic telephone exchange, Naas, Kildare
Department of Finance (refurbishment), Merrion Street, Dublin

1980

Clonaslee GS, Laois
Millstreet GS, Cork
Youghal GS, Cork
Meteorological synoptic training centre, Galway
Irish embassy to China (adaptation), Beijing
Scoil Mhuire gan Smál, Easky, Sligo
Department of Marine HQ, Leeson Street, Dublin
Tuam automatic telephone exchange, Galway

1981

Ballylinan GS, Laois
Killaloe GS, Clare
Mitchelstown GS, Cork
Glenbrien NS, Wexford
Stationery Office (extension & refurbishment), Bishop Street,
    Dublin
National Concert Hall, Dublin

1982

Newtownforbes NS, Longford
State Laboratory, Abbotstown, Dublin
Glenbrook telephone exchange, Cork
Newtowngore NS, Leitrim
Dolphin House (fit out), East Essex St, Dublin
Irish embassy to Australia, Canberra

Irish embassy to Australia, 1982

1983

Thurles government offices, Tipperary
Government Publications sales offices, Molesworth St, Dublin
Syncrolift Tower, Howth Harbour, Dublin
Glebe House & Gallery, Churchill, Donegal
Mervue telephone exchange complex, Galway
St Peter's Boy Scouts Hall, Phibsborough, Dublin
Shannon telephone exchange, Offaly
Longford PO
Prison officers' housing, Portlaoise, Laois
Newcastle NS, Co. Wicklow
Muckross House (restoration phase I), Killarney, Kerry

1984

Glenveagh Castle (restoration), Donegal
Department of Forest and Fisheries, Leeson Lane, Dublin
National Vehicle Registration Centre, Shannon, Offaly
Limerick Model School (adaptation), Limerick city
Silver Springs Garda District HQ, Mayfield, Cork
Garda District HQ, Gurranebraher, Cork
Veterinary Diagnostic Units, Abbotstown, Dublin
Single officers' quarters, Cathal Brugha Barracks Dublin
Carrick-on-Shannon Garda District HQ and government
    offices, Leitrim
Castlebar telephone exchange, Mayo
Belmullet Garda District HQ, Mayo
Telecom Éireann sales office, College Green, Dublin
Telecom Éireann District HQ, Portlaoise, Laois
Priory Park telephone exchange, Stillorgan, Dublin
Government offices, Navan, Meath
Leinster House link bridge, Dublin

Newcastle NS,1983

Blackrock GS, Cork
Casino Marino (restoration), Dublin
Royal Hospital, Kilmainham (restoration), Dublin

1985

Spike Island (barracks adapted to prison), Cork
'The Treasury' exhibition space, National Museum
Parke's Castle (restoration), Leitrim
Brookfield NS, Tallaght, Dublin
Apollo House employment exchange, Tara Street, Dublin
Castlebar telephone exchange, Mayo
Central Meat Control Laboratory, Abbotstown, Dublin
Japanese Room, National Museum, Dublin
Phoenix Park Garda Divisional HQ (refurbished), Dublin
OPW Furniture Branch premises, Rialto, Dublin
Senate chamber (restoration and repairs), Leinster House
Blessington NS, Wicklow (c 1985)
Tralee GS, Kerry (c 1985)
Tallaght Garda District HQ, Dublin

1986

Hill House (conservation), Donegal
Dundalk NS, Louth
Bartlemy NS, Cork
Ballyhale NS, Galway
Killykeen holiday complex, Lough Oughter, Cavan
Curracloe NS, Wexford
Irish embassy to Saudi Arabia, Riyadh
St Colmcille's NS, Swords, Dublin
Glenveagh Castle visitor centre, Donegal
Monaghan Garda Divisional HQ, Monaghan

1987

Wheatfield Prison, Clondalkin, Dublin
Glenveagh visitor centre, Glenveagh National Park, Donegal
Cranmore Road government offices, Sligo
Roxboro Road Garda Divisional HQ, Limerick
Swinford GS, Mayo
Lucan GS, Dublin
Children's Courthouse, Smithfield, Dublin

1988

Duncannon NS, Wexford
Department of Agriculture, Cavan
Newcastle West SWLO, Limerick
Tuam GS, Galway
Ashbourne NS, Meath
Sligo decentralised office, Summerhill, Sligo
National Monuments Depot, Kilkenny
Glendalough Visitor Centre, Wicklow
Islandbridge war memorial (restoration), Dublin

1989

Tralee government offices, Kerry
Swiss Cottage (restoration). Cahir, Tipperary
Shankill GS, Dublin
Watercourse Road GS, Cork
Ballyheigue GS, Kerry
Buncrana SWLO, Donegal

Glenveagh visitor centre, 1987

Sligo government offices, 1987

'The Work of Angels' exhibition space, National Museum, Dublin
Bandon Garda Divisional HQ, Cork
Castle Hall and conference centre, Dublin Castle
Blocks 8–10 and undercroft, Dublin Castle
Chapel Royal (restoration), Dublin Castle
Mullingar GS (extension), Westmeath
Naas Garda Divisional HQ, Kildare
Department of Defence, Galway
Letterkenny Garda Divisional HQ, Donegal,
Merchant's Road SWLO, Galway
Childrens' playground, People's Park, Phoenix Park
Leinster House, Dublin (refurbishment of Senate)
Parke's Castle, Leitrim (restoration)

1990

Ballyfermot SWSO, Dublin
Hanover Street SWLO, Cork
Government Buildings (adaptation and restoration)
Natural History Museum (conservation and restoration),
    Merrion St, Dublin
Kilbarrack SWLO, Dublin
Rustic pavilions, St Stephen's Green
Athlone government office, Westmeath
Foynes GS, Limerick
Cork Garda Divisional HQ, Anglesea Street, Cork
Jerpoint Abbey visitor centre, Kilkenny
'Ar Thúir na Saoirse' exhibition space, National Museum,
    Dublin
Newbridge SWLO, Kildare

1991

National Archives (adaptation), Bishop Street, Dublin
Cavan Garda District HQ, Cavan
Killarney decentralised office, Kerry
Dún Laoghaire Garda Divisional HQ & courthouse, Dublin
Pump house (renovation), North Slob Wildlife Reserve, Wexford
Irish Museum of Modern Art, Royal Hospital, Kilmainham,
    Dublin
Letterkenny decentralised office Donegal
Limerick SWLO, Limerick
9/10 Upper O'Connell Street (refurbished for Revenue
    Commissioners), Dublin
Balbriggan Garda HQ, Dublin
Shannon Garda HQ, Clare
St John's Road computer centre, Clondalkin, Dublin
Ennis SWLO, Clare
Galway SWLO, Galway
Custom House (restoration), Dublin
Government jet (fit-out)

Rustic pavilion, St Stephen's Green, 1990

National Archives, 1991

1992

Finglas SWLO, Dublin
Treasury block (restoration), Dublin Castle
Ashtown visitor centre, Phoenix Park
Department of Industry & Commerce (restoration), Kildare St,
    Dublin
Knocksink National Conservation Education Centre,
    Enniskerry, Wicklow
Longford decentralised office, Longford
Limerick decentralised office (refurbishment), Limerick
Connemara National Park visitor centre, Letterfrack
OPW Library (refurbishment), St Stephen's Green, Dublin
Creche, Revenue Buildings, Lower Mount St, Dublin
Carlow Garda HQ, Carlow
Scattery Island visitor centre, Kilrush, Clare
Cahir District Garda HQ, Tipperary
'Ór – Ireland's Gold' exhibition, National Museum, Dublin
Kilkenny government offices, Kilkenny

Limerick SWSO, 1991

Coole Park visitor centre, Galway
Killarney National Park visitor centre, Muckross House,
    Kerry
Gate lodges, Custom House, Dublin
National Museum café, Kildaire St, Dublin
Irish Pavilion, Seville, Spain

1993

Waterways visitor centre, Ringsend, Dublin
Cork meteorology centre, Cork
Waterford meteorology centre, Waterford
Limerick meteorology centre, Limerick
Sligo meteorology Centre, Sligo
Dundalk meteorology centre, Louth
Dublin meteorology centre, Dublin
Navan Road SWLO, Dublin
Céide Fields visitor centre. Ballycastle, Mayo
Muckross traditional farms, Muckross House, Killarney, Kerry
Trim Castle (conservation), Meath
Milford Garda District HQ, Donegal
Midleton Garda District HQ (modernisation), Cork
Killeagh GS, Cork
Enniscorthy Garda District HQ, Wexford
Glassan GS, Westmeath
Ballymore GS, Westmeath
Kildorrery GS, Cork
Togher Garda HQ, Cork
Custom House conference suite, Dublin
Kildysart GS
Blackrock GS, Dublin
Caravaggio exhibition, National Gallery of Ireland
Anatomy exhibition, National Gallery of Ireland
Garda training college,Templemore, Tipperary

1994

Heywood gardens, Co Laois
14/15 Upper O'Connell St (refurbished for Revenue
    Commissioners), Dublin
Central Statistics Office, Mahon, Cork
Film censor's office (extension), Harcourt Terrace, Dublin
The Great Blasket Centre, Dún Chaoin, Kerry
Corlea Bog visitor centre, Longford
Kells Garda District HQ, Meath (c 1994)
Ballylynan GS, Laois (1990s)
Listowel GS (refurbishment), Kerry
Killorglin GS (refurbishment), Kerry
Castletownbere GS (refurbishment), Cork
Kinsale GS (refurbishment), Cork
Falcarragh GS (refurbishment), Donegal
Carlow government offices (extended and adapted), Carlow
Ordnance Survey office (adaptation), Phoenix Park, Dublin
Thurles Garda HQ (major extension), Tipperary
Fraud Squad HQ (refurbishment), Harcourt Street, Dublin
Longford decentralised office, Longford
Dublin Zoo (masterplan/redevelopment), Dublin
Drogheda Garda Divisional HQ, Louth
Newmills (restoration), Donegal
Kilkenny Castle (restoration phase II)
National Museum, Collins Barracks (phase I)

Kildorrery GS, 1993

1995

Former Model School (refurbished for court facilities),
    Anglesea Street, Cork
Ship Street Barracks (restoration), Dublin Castle
Coach house and Dubh Linn Garden, Dublin Castle
Tallaght SWLO, Dublin
Clonmacnoise visitor centre, Offaly
Regional passport office, Cork
Bruff Garda District HQ, Limerick
Ballymahon GS basic unit, Longford
Keel GS basic unit, Mayo
Roscommon GS (extension), Roscommon
Clogher GS basic unit, Louth
Douglas GS, Cork
Mountjoy GS (refurbishment), Dublin
Kilmainham Gaol visitor centre, Dublin

Boyne Valley visitor centre, 1995

Boyne Valley visitor centre, Meath
Self-service restaurant, Leinster House, Dubiln
Members' restaurant, Leinster House, Dublin
Muckross House (restoration phase II), Killarney, Kerry
Curvilinear Range (restoration), Botanic Gardens, Dublin
Stables and coach house (adaptation), Royal Hospital,
    Kilmainham, Dublin
Clock tower, Dublin Castle (restoration and adaptation)
National Library (roofworks phase I), Kildare Street, Dublin

1996

Eirinn Room and mural, Dublin Castle
Department of Defence GHQ, Infirmary Rd, Dublin
Tullamore decentralised office, Offaly
Clogherhead GS, Louth
Wexford decentralised office (phase 1), Wexford
Waterford decentralised office, Waterford
Limerick decentralised office, Limerick
Nenagh decentralised office, Tipperary
Ennis decentralised office, Clare
Cathal Brugh Barracks (refurbishment), Dublin
Castlebar Garda Divisional HQ, Mayo
Environmental Protection Agency, Monaghan
Barretstown Castle camp, Ballymore Eustace, Kildare
Royal Irish Academy (refurbishment), Dawson Street, Dublin
National Gallery of Ireland, Dublin (refurbishment)
Portloise government office, Co Laois
Castlerea Prison, Co Roscommon
World of Primates, Zoological Society of Ireland, Dublin

1997

National Library, new technical service building
Monaghan government offices, Monaghan
Carrick-on-Shannon courthouse, Leitrim
Library/Herbarium, Botanic Gardens, Dublin
'Ancient Egypt' exhibition, National Museum
The Hunt Museum, Limerick
Custom House visitor centre, Dublin
Doneraile GS, Cork
Keel GS, Mayo
Trim National Monuments district office & depot, Meath
Famine memorial, Murrisk, Mayo
Richmond courthouse, Dublin
Longford Garda HQ, Longford
Mellifont Abbey visitor centre, Louth
Riverbank court (adaptation), Dublin
National Library (roofwork & refurbishment), Dublin

Department of Defence GHQ, 1996

Mountjoy women's prison, Dublin
Thomas Street SWLO, Dublin
Ballyfermot SWLO, Dublin
Pearse Street GS (major refurbishment), Dublin
Four Courts, Dublin (major refurbishment)
National Museum, Collins Barracks (phase I)
National Museum, Collins Barracks (inaugural exhibition)

1998

Environmental Protection Agency HQ, Wexford
Emo Court (restoration and landscaping), Laois
Store Street Garda Divisional HQ, Dublin
Department of Finance (refurbishment), Merrion St, Dublin
National Photographic Archive (adaptation), Dublin
1798 memorial, Croppies' Acre, Dublin
Telescope (restoration) and visitor pavilion, Birr Castle
  demesne, Co Offaly
Anne Street government office, Wexford
Enniscorthy government office, Wexford
89 Merrion Square (for National Gallery), Dublin
Garinish Island visitor facilities, Cork
Douglas GS, Cork
Drogheda Garda HQ, Louth
Dunshaughlin GS (refurbishment), Meath
Kilmacow GS
Sacred Heart Oratory (restoration and conservation),
  Dún Laoghaire, Dublin
Newbridge Garda HQ
Blanchardstown GS, Dublin
Cork SWLO, Cork
Wexford government office (phase 2), Wexford
Limerick prison, D Wing, Limerick
Midlands prison, Portlaoise
'Viking Ships' exhibition, National Museum, Dublin
Restaurant and craft workshops, Muckross House, Killarney,
  Kerry
Waterford GS, Waterford
Lixnaw GS, Kerry
Terenure GS, Dublin
Clock tower, Department of Education, Marlborough Street
Talbot House, Department of Education, Marlborough Street
Building Unit, Department of Education, Marlborough Street
Attorney General's Office
1798 Exhibition, National Museum, Collins Barracks, Dublin
Valuation Office (refurbishment), Irish Life Centre, Dublin
Tulach a tSolais, Oulart Hill Memorial Project, Co Wexford
World of Cats, Zoological Society of Ireland, Dublin
89 Merrion Square for National Gallery, Dublin

Emo Court (resoration and landscaping), 1998

National Photograpic Archive, 1998

Refugee Applications Centre, Timberly House, Dublin
Clifden SWLO, Galway
Achill SWLO, Mayo
Belmullet SWLO, Mayo
Coosan Veterinary Laboratory, Athlone

1999 and current projects

Cloverhill prison and courthouse, Clondalkin, Dublin
Mayorstone Garda District HQ, Limerick
National Folklife Museum, Castlebar, Mayo
Osmonde House, Ship Street, Dublin
National Gallery (millennium wing) Clare Street, Dublin
Dunsink Observatory Dublin
Michael Davitt Museum, Straide, Mayo
Kilmacurragh House (restoration), Wicklow
Department of Education, Marlborough St, Dublin
Davitt House, Castlebar, Mayo
Northside Crêche, Department of Education, Marlborough
  Street
Templemore Garda Training College (extension), Tipperary
Galway Custom House (refurbishment), Galway
Dublin Custom House (refurbishment), Dublin
Government Supplies Agency (refurbishment), Harcourt Road,
  Dublin
Carlow Courthouse (refurbishment)
Chester Beatty Library (fit-out), Clock tower, Dublin Castle
Ely Court (refurbishment), Dublin
Iveagh Gardens, restoration of cascade
**National Library of Ireland, (extension of former NCAD
  building),** Dublin
Killarney National Monuments Depot, Kerry
Sligo Abbey Visitor facilities
Irish Pavilion, Hanover, Germany
Clonmel SWLO, Tipperary
Sligo SWLO
Cahirciveen SWLO, Kerry
National Botanic Gardens, visitor facilities
Dunmore East CGS, Waterford
Skellig Michael conservation, Kerry (1978–)
Rathfarnham Castle (restoration), Dublin (1987–)
Castletown House (restoration), Kildare (1994–)
National Museum (stone restoration), Kildare Street, Dublin
  (1995–)
Deputy Master's house, Royal Hospital, Kilmainham
  (adaptation), Dublin

Office of Public Works head office (refurbishment),
  St Stephen's Green, Dublin
Kilkenny Castle, Kilkenny (restoration phase III)
Kilkenny Hydrometric Station, Kilkenny
New Oireachtas building, Dublin
Yeats Room, National Gallery of Ireland, Dublin
Womens Prison, Dublin
Midlands Prison, Portlaoise
Muckross House visitor centre, (restaurant & workshops)
Farmleigh (adaptation), Dublin
Templemore Garda College, (education block), Tipperary
Fringes of the Arctic, Zoological Society of Ireland, Dublin
Dairy Science laboratory, Abbotstown Estate, Co Dublin
State laboratory, Abbotstown Estate, Co Dublin
2–3 Kildare Street (adaptation for National Library of Ireland),
  Dublin
National Museum, Collins Barracks – costume and jewellery
  exhibition, Dublin
National Museum, Collins Barracks, Building 19 (refurbishment),
  Dublin
Carrick-on-Shannon SWLO, Leitrim
Clifden SWLO, Galway
Tralee SWLO, Kerry
Mullingar SWLO, Westmeath
Dun Aengus vistor facilities, Galway
Carlow SWLO (extension), Carlow
Con Colbert House (refurbishment), Dublin
Rathmines GS, Dublin
Dundalk government offices, Louth
Lansdowne House (refurbishment for the Revenue Commissioners)
Frederick Court (refurbishment for the Department of Education
  and Science)
59 Dawson Street (refurbishment for the Department of Art,
  Heritage, Gaeltacht and the Islands)
Clonmel Place (fit-out for the Department of Justice, Equality and
  Law Reform)
Plaza, Tallaght, Dublin (fit-out for the Revenue Commissioners)
Agriculture House, Dublin (refurbishment for the Department of
  Agriculture)
Environmental Protection Agency, Belfield, Dublin
Talbot Premises, Santry (for the Garda Síochána)
Kealkil GS, Cork
Bray GS, Wicklow
Ballinskelligs GS, Kerry
Ballyfermot GS, Dublin
Entrance building & shop, Zoological Society of Ireland, Dublin
Sea lion pool, Zoological Society of Ireland, Dublin
African Plains, Zoological Society of Ireland, Dublin
New government offices, Tipperary
Ardfert Cathedral (conservation of nave), Kerry
Bridgend Revenue Offices, Donegal
National Botanic Gardens, education facility
Doneraile Court (conservation), Cork
Hawkins House (foyer), Dublin
Marine Emergency Services facility, Dunmore East, Waterford

Office of Public Works

Personnel 1900–99

Government Ministers with Reponsibility for the Office of Public Works since 1924

In 1922, the Office of Public Works was transferred from the British Treasury to the Department of Finance of the Irish Free State. The Ministers and Secretaries Act (1924) allowed for the appointment of a Parliamentary Secretary at the Department of Finance with special responsibility for the OPW. Henceforth, the OPW has taken instructions on executive matters from the Parliamentary Secretary or Minister of State (as they were called from 1977).

Parliamentary Secretaries

1924–5	John M O'Sullivan
1926–7	Eamon J Duggan
1927–32	James A Burke
1932–43	Hugo V Flinn
1943 (Feb–June)	Seán Moylan
1943–6	Patrick Smith
1947–8	Seán O'Grady
1948–51	Michael Donnellan
1951–4	Patrick Beegan
1954–7	Michael Donnellan
1957–8	Patrick Beegan
1958–9	Gerald Bartley
1959–61	Joseph Brennan
1961–5	Donogh B O'Malley
1965–9	James Gibbons
1969–73	Noel T Lemass
1973–5	Henry Kenny
1975–7	Michael Begley

Ministers of State

1977–9	Pearse Wyse
1979–81	Thomas McEllistrim
1981–2	Joseph Bermingham
1982 (Mar–Dec)	Sylvester Barrett
1982–6	Joseph Bermingham
1986–7	Avril Doyle
1987–9	Noel Treacy
1989–91	Brendan Daly
1991 (Feb–Nov)	Vincent Brady
1991–2	John O'Donoghue
1992–3	Noel Treacy
1993–4	Noel Dempsey
1994–5	Phil Hogan
1995 (Feb–May)	Jim Higgins
1995–7	Hugh Coveney
1997–	Martin Cullen

Commissioners of the Office of Public Works 1900–99

Chairmen appear in bold.

1900–1	**Thomas Robertson**
	Richard O'Shaughnessy
	George A Stevenson
1901–3	**George C V Holmes**
	Richard O'Shaughnessy
	George A Stevenson
1903–13	**George C V Holmes**
	George A Stevenson
	Philip Hanson
1913–21	**George A Stevenson**
	Philip Hanson
	Thomas Philip Le Fanu
1921–2	**Philip Hanson**
	Thomas Philip Le Fanu
1922–3	**Philip Hanson**
	Thomas Philip Le Fanu
	Andrew Robinson
1923–6	**Philip Hanson**
	Thomas Philip Le Fanu
1927–8	**Philip Hanson**
	J J Healy
1928–32	**Philip Hanson**
	Pierce Kent
1932–4	**Philip Hanson**
	Pierce Kent
	Diarmuid Ó h-Éigeartaigh
1935–43	**Joseph Connolly**
	Pierce Kent
	Diarmuid Ó h-Éigeartaigh
1944–50	**Joseph Connolly**
	Diarmuid Ó h-Éigeartaigh
	George P Fagan
1950–7	**Diarmuid Ó h-Éigeartaigh**
	George P Fagan
	Thomas J Morris
1958–9	**George P Fagan**
	Thomas J Morris
	Henry J Mundow
1959–70	**Henry J Mundow**
	Cornelius Farrell
	Jeremiah Cullinane
1970–2	**Cornelius Farrell**
	Bernard Fanning
1972–7	**Cornelius Farrell**
	Seán Breathnach
	John J McCarthy
1977–9	**John J McCarthy**
	Seán Breathnach
	John Allen
1979–81	**John J McCarthy**
	John Allen
	Philip McCabe
1981–2	**John Allen**
	Philip McCabe
	M Paschal Scanlon
1982–8	**M Paschal Scanlon**
	Philip McCabe
	Brendan Scully
1988–9	**John Mahony**
	Philip McCabe
	Brendan Scully
1989–95	**John Mahony**
	Brendan Scully
	Brian (Barry) Murphy
1995–	**Brian (Barry) Murphy**
	Brendan Scully
	Seán Benton

Principal Architects 1900–99

1891–1918*	John Howard Pentland
1900–11*	Thomas J Mellon
1900–09*	Robert Cochrane
1911–13*	Samuel Kerr Kirker
1909–23*	Andrew Robinson
1923–39	Thomas Joseph Byrne
1939–48	John M Fairweather
1948–68	Raymond McGrath
1968–76	Gerald McNicholl
1976–80	Martin D Burke
1980–90	Noel de Chenu
1990–	Michael O'Doherty

In the early years of the century, the rank of principal architect (then known as principal surveyor) was shared.

OPW Principal Officers 1954–99

The grade of principal officer was formed in 1954 to replace a number of older civil service grades. Current members of staff appear in bold type.

1954–9	Jeremiah Cullinane
1954–9	Cornelius Farrell
1954–70	J Fassbender
1959–70	Tom Connolly
1959–70	Bernard Fanning
1962–77	Phil G Furlong
1964–9	John J McCarthy
1964	P S Ó Céarnaigh
1965–72	Seán Breathach
1969–77	John Allen
1970–6	Sean Coughlan
1970–81	James O'Halloran
1970–9	Con W Heuston
1970–81	A G (Hugh) MacAlastair
1970–7	David F O'Connor
1972–84	Tom O'Dea
1974–9	Philip McCabe
1976–9	Sean Ingoldsby
1977–9	J J (Sheila) Gillan
1977–82	D Cyril Griffith
1977–81	M Paschal Scanlon
1978–82	Des Doyle
1979–88	Meta Hastings-Doyle
1979–93	D Noel Lynch
1979–82	Seamus McIntyre
1980–1	Sean S Barrett
1980–5	Patrick C Condon
1980–6	James G Dunne
1980–1	Noel S Murphy
1981–8	John Berkery
1981–93	Jimmy P Dunlea
1982–96	Fergus Gilmore
1982–	**Percy C Kenny**
1982–94	Dermot McCann
1982–88	Brendan Morrisey
1985–91	Kathleen Brewster
1986–8	John F Mahony
1987–90	N O'Keefe
1988–96	Michael Canny
1988–91	Fergus O'Gorman
1990–	**Una Redmond**
1991–6	Dermot Burke
1991–	**Tom Costello**
1991–	**Tom Sherlock**
1993–	**June Thompson**
1994–	**Joe Farrell**
1996–	**J Paul Molloy**
1999–	**Jim Blighe**

Assistant Principal Architects 1900–99

Current OPW personnel appear in bold.

1884–1911	Samuel Kerr Kirker
1905–10	Patrick Joseph Lynch
1905–9	Andrew Robinson
1910–23	Alfred Kirke Browne
1910–23	William Mortimer Paton
1922–35	Harry Allberry
1939–42	Martin Joseph Burke
1942–47	William Henry Howard Cooke
1942–4	Gerald McNicholl
1947–69	Basil Raymund Boyd-Barrett
1947–72	Sidney Francis James Maskell
1953–64	Thomas Francis Williamson
1959–84	Leo Mary Carroll
1964–72	Thomas James McCarthy
1967–76	Martin Desmond Burke
1968–74	Arthur Seymour Rice
1969–88	Cornelius Alphonsus Manahan
1971–80	Oscar Leach
1972–87	Francis Thomas Du Berry
1974–80	Michael John Curran
1976–80	Roger Noel de Chenu
1976–90	Brian P Hayden
1978–87	John W B Cumming
1979–87	Thomas O'Sullivan
1980–4	Michael F Crowe
1980–8	Patrick J Fearon
1980–90	James F Green
1980–90	Michael O'Doherty
1984–5	W Harold P Higginbotham
1987–8	John Sweetman
1989–	**Michael Denis Haugh**
1990–	**Liam Egan**
1990–	**Nicholas (Klaus) G Unger**
1991–	**Patrick J Cooney**
1996–	**Finbarr P Wall**
1997–	**David Lindsay Byers**

Project Teams

The following project teams relate to the projects described in Parts 1 and 2 in the order in which they appear in the text. In general, the project teams for works described in the text appear in this listing. Dates used here indicate the year of completion. OPW personnel appear in roman text, while consultants and contractors appear in italics. From 1987, all projects (with the exception of National Monuments) have been managed using standardised procedures outlined in the Project Management Plan. For this reason, the terms 'project head', 'project co-ordinator' and 'design team leader' have been used after that date.

OPW Head office

1912
Client: The Office of Public Works

Royal College of Science and Government Buildings

1922
Client: Department of Education/Department of Local Government/Department of Agriculture & Technical Instruction
Project architects: *Sir Aston Webb and Thomas Manly Deane*
Monitoring architect: John Howard Pentland
Quantity surveyors: *Patterson & Kempster*
Main contractors: *McLoughlin & Harvey*

1990
Client: Department of the Taoiseach
Project head: Barry Murphy
Project co-ordinator: Una Redmond
Design team leader: Klaus Unger
Architects: David Byers, Angela Rolfe, Michael Carroll and Helen O'Neill
Consultant architect: *Noel de Chenu*
Architectural assistants: Kevin McKenna and Mary O'Boyle
Structural engineers: *Denis O'Leary & Partners*
Mechanical and electrical engineers: *Varming Mulcahy Reilly Associates*
Quantity surveyors: *Mulcahy McDonagh & Partners*
Design consultants on rear engineering building: *P & A Lavin Associates*
Main contractors: *McInerney Contracting Ltd*

National Gallery of Ireland

1903
Client: Department of Education
Project architect: *Thomas M Deane and Son*
Main contractors: *Michael Meade & Sons*

1968
Client: Department of Education
Project architects: Frank T du Berry and Michael F Crowe
Mechanical and electrical engineers: *Delap and Waller*
Quantity surveyor: *Thomas C Whelan*
Main contractors: *Hugh O'Neill & Co. Ltd.*

1996
Client: Department of Arts, Heritage, Gaeltacht and The Islands
Project head: June Thompson
Project co-ordinator: Frank Fingleton and Kevin Connolly
Design team leader: Stephen Kane
Architect: Kate Quinn
Structural engineers: *Lee McCullough* (main building), *Kara Taylor* (oval stairs and lift), Tony Smyth (houses)
Mechanical and electrical engineers: *Delap and Waller* (main building) and *Peter Deer & Associates* (oval stairs and lift)
Quantity surveyors: *Healy Kelly* (main building) and Aidan Quinn (oval stairs and lift)
Main contractors: *Mahon McPhillips* (main building) and *G & T Crampton* (oval stairs and lift)

Yeats Room: 1999
Client: Department of Arts, Heritage, Gaeltacht and the Islands
Project head: June Thompson
Project co-ordinator: Kevin Connolly
Design team leader: Stephen Kane
Architectural assistants: Robert Carty
Structural engineer: *Lee McCullough & Partners*
Mechanical and electrical engineer: *Delap & Waller*
Quantity surveyor: Aidan Quinn
Main contractors: *Rohcon Ltd*

Millenniun wing 1999–
Client: Department of Arts, Heritage, Gaeltacht and The Islands
Project head: Sean Benton
Project co-ordinator: June Thompson
Design team leader: *Benson & Forsyth*
Monitoring architect: Klaus Unger
Structural engineers: *O'Connor Sutton Cronin*
Mechanical and electrical engineer: *Oscar Faber*
Quantity surveyors: *Rogerson Reddan Associates*
Main contractors: *Michael McNamara & Co*

Leinster House

Repairs to Senate chamber 1989
Client: Oireachtas
Design team leader: Geoffrey Johnson
Architect: Paul McMahon
Structural engineers: *McCabe, Delaney & Associates*
Quantity surveyors: *D Laurence Martin & Associates*
Main contractors (initial investigation): *P J Quigley Ltd*
Main contractors (repairs): *John Paul Construction*
Plaster work restoration: OPW Building Maintenance Services
under the direction of Val Ryan

Office and restaurant block 1962–8
Client: Oireachtas
Project architect: Joseph P Alcock
Assistant architects: Brian P Hayden and Brigid Hanna
Structural engineer: *C H Clifton*
Mechanical and electrical engineer: *Gerard J Larchet*
Quantity surveyors: *F D Shortall & Co*
Main contractors: *E Stone & Sons Ltd*

Self-service restaurant 1995
Client: Oireachtas
Project management: OPW Project Management Services
Design team leader: *P & A Lavin Associates*
Monitoring architect: Liam Egan
Mechanical and electrical engineer: Jim O'Sullivan
Main contractors: *Pierse Building Services*

Members' restaurant 1995
Client: Oireachtas
Project management: OPW Project Management Services
Design team leader: *P & A Lavin Associates*
Monitoring architect: Liam Egan
Structural engineer: Ian Wolfe
Mechanical and electrical engineer: Jim O'Sullivan
Main contractors: *Michael McNamara & Co*

New Oireachtas building
Client: Oireachtas
Project head: Sean Benton
Project co-ordinator: Una Redmond
Design team leader: Michael O'Doherty
Architects: David Byers and Mary MacKenna
Support architects: *Dolan & Donnelly Architects*
Historic stonework consultant: *Paul Arnold*
Structural engineer: *O'Connor Sutton Cronin*
Mechanical and electrical engineers: Jim O'Sullivan with assistance
from *Callaghan Engineering Ltd; Draftech Ltd*; and *Varming Mulcahy
Reilly Associates*
Quantity surveyors: *Keogh & McConnell*
Main contractors: *Michael McNamara & Co*

General Post Office

Remodelling 1904–16
Client: Department of Posts and Telegraphs
Project architect, phase I, Henry Street: Robert Cochrane
Project architect, phase II, Prince's Street: Robert Cochrane
Main contractors, phase II, Prince's Street: *Alexander Hull & Co*
Project architect, phase III, main block: John Howard Pentland
Main contractors, phase III, main block: *J & W Stewart*

Reconstruction 1924–32
Client: Department of Posts and Telegraphs
Project architect: T J Byrne, assisted by J M Fairweather, H G Leask,
W H H Cooke and D M Turner
Consultant architect for Henry Street elevation: *P J Munden*
Main contractors: *Alexander Hull & Co*

The Custom House

Restoration 1926–9
Client: Department of Local Government and Public Health/
Revenue Commissioners
Project architect: T J Byrne
Architects: W H H Cooke, J M Fairweather, William Ward,
J A Geoghegan
Main contractors: OPW Direct labour and *J & P Good Ltd*

Restoration 1984–91
Client: Department of the Environment and Local
Government/Revenue Commissioners
Project management: OPW Project Management Services
Project architects: David Slattery and Alistair Lindsay
Structural engineers: *Thomas Garland & Partners*
Quantity surveyors: *Desmond McGreevy & Partners*
Main contractors: *John Sisk & Son Ltd*

Custom House conference suite 1993
Client: Department of the Environment and Local
Government/Revenue Commissioners
Project management: OPW Project Management Services
Design team leader: Barbara Kenny
Architectural assistants: William Sargent, Frances Fay
Structural engineers: *Thomas Garland & Partners*
Mechanical engineer: Jim O'Sullivan
Decorative plasterwork: OPW Building Maintenance Services
Main contractors: *Straffan Construction Co Ltd*

Custom House visitor centre 1997
Client: Department of the Environment and Local
Government/Revenue Commissioners
Project head: Una Redmond
Project co-ordinator: Niamh O'Regan
Design team leaders: Alistair Lindsay and Helen Blair
Architect: Caroline Leaden
Architectural assistant: Frances Fay
Structural engineer: Allen French
Mechanical and electrical engineers: *McArdle McSweeney
Associates*
Quantity surveyor: James Walsh
Main contractors: *Pierse Building Services*

The Four Courts

Reconstruction 1924–31
Client: Department of Justice
Project architect: T J Byrne
Architects: W H H Cooke, J M Fairweather, William Ward,
J A Geoghegan
Main contractors: *J & P Good Ltd*

Refurbishment 1994–7
Client: Department of Justice
Project head: Una Redmond
Project co-ordinator: Niamh O'Regan
Design team leader: *Costello Murray Beaumont*
Structural engineers: *Redmond Holloway*
Mechanical and electrical engineer: Pádraig Cronin
Quantity surveyors: *Duffy Gaffney Partnership*
Main contractors: *Duggan Brothers Contractors Ltd*

The Casino, Marino 1984

Client: OPW
Project architects: *O'Neill Flanagan & Partners*, in association with
Ian Bristow and David Newman Johnson
Mechanical and electrical engineers: *Varming Mulcahy Reilly
& Associates*
Quantity surveyor: OPW
Main contractor: OPW Central Building Maintenance Services
Painting contractors: *J F Keatinge & Sons Ltd*
Fireplaces: *Roe & O'Neill*
Interior decoration: *T Austin Dunphy, John Redmill*, Ian Bristow, with
advice from *Peter Thornton and John Hardy of V&A Museum, London*
Floors: *Modern Floors Ltd*
Roofing: *T C Walsh & Son Ltd*
Resident supervisors: John Ledwith and Stephen Grant

Dublin Airport 1942

Client: Department of Industry & Commerce
Architects: Desmond FitzGerald, Dermot O'Toole, Daithí Hanly,
Charles Aliaga Kelly, Kevin Barry, Harry Robson
Main contractors: *Murphy Bros (John J Murphy)*

Baldonnel Aerodrome

Church 1944
Client: Department of Defence
Project architect: W H H Cooke
Assistant architects: Oscar Leach and Vincent H O'Neill
Mechanical and electrical engineer: Thomas Illingworth
Quantity surveyor: *Francis D Shorthall*
Main contractors: *A Panton Watkinson*

Gymnasium 1946
Client: Department of Defence
Project architects: W H H Cooke and Oscar Leach
Mechanical and electrical engineer: Thomas Illingworth
Quantity surveyor: *Francis D Shorthall*
Main contractors: *T & J Macken*

Department of Industry and Commerce 1942

Client: Department of Industry & Commerce
Project architect: *J R Boyd Barrett*
Architectural assistants: *S J Docking, T G Nolan*
Structural engineers: *O'Connell & Hartley, Cork*
Quantity surveyors: *Patterson Kempster*
Main contractors: *John Sisk & Son Ltd*
Sculpture: *Gabriel Hayes*

Abbotstown Estate

Foundation Stock Farm 1958–65
Client: Department of Agriculture
Project architect: *Desmond FitzGerald*
Monitoring architect: Gerald McNicholl
Mechanical and electrical engineers: *Varming & Mulcahy*
Quantity surveyor: *Austin F Reddy*
Main contractors stage I: *Collins & Rooney*
Main contractors stage II & III: *Hannon Bros. Ltd*

Artificial Insemination Centre 1961
Client: Department of Agriculture
Project architects: Oscar Leach
Assistant architect: Vincent H O'Neill
Quantity surveyor: *Valentine Reynolds*
Main contractors: *Carey & Clarke Ltd*

Veterinary Field Station 1965
Client: Department of Agriculture
Project architect: J B Fox, assisted by Patrick L Dolan,
Sean Rothery and John O'Reilly
Mechanical and electrical engineer: Thomas Illingworth

The State Laboratory 1982
Client: Department of Agriculture
Project architects: Brigid Hanna, Klaus Unger, Michael Carroll
Architectural assisitant: Patrick McGuinness
Structural engineers: *Thomas Garland & Partners*
Mechanical and electrical engineer: Thomas Illingworth
Quantity surveyors: *John Cuddy & Partners*
Main contractors: *Hannon Bros. Ltd*

Veterinary Diagnostic Laboratories 1984
Client: Department of Agriculture
Project architects: Michael Haugh, Mary MacKenna and
Mark McSwiney
Architectural assistant: Maura Brennan
Structural engineer: *MacNeill & Associates*
Mechanical and electrical engineers: P Hannon, R Wynne
and R Lewis
Quantity surveyors: *Barry McHugh & Associates*
Main contractors: *Collen Bros. (Dublin) Ltd*

Central Meat Control Laboratory 1985
Client: Department of Agriculture
Project architects: David Slattery and John Tuomey
Architectural assistant: Brendan Walsh
Structural engineer: *Bernard LeCesne Byrne*
Mechanical and electrical engineer: *R N Murphy*
Quantity surveyor: Aidan Quinn
Main contractors: *P Kelly & Sons Building Contractors Ltd*

Garrison Church of St Brigid Curragh Camp 1959

Client: Department of Defence
Project architects: Gerald McNicholl, Thomas John Ryan
and Herbert Unger
Structural engineer: *Thomas Garland & Partners*
Mechanical and electrical engineer: Thomas Illingworth
Quantity surveyors: *F D Shortall & Co*
Main contractors: *M J Davis & Co*

Valentia Observatory 1962

Client: Department of Industry & Commerce
Project architects: Oscar Leach and Raymond McGrath
Assistant architect: Maeve Molloy
Quantity surveyor: *Noel Speidel*
Mechanical and electrical engineer: Thomas Illingworth
Main contractors: *John Cleary*, succeeded by *John O'Doherty*,
completed by *J J O'Sullivan*

Irish Meteorological Service Headquarters 1978

Client: Department of Tourism and Transport
Project architects: *Corr & McCormick Architects*
Structural engineers: *Thomas Garland & Partners*
Mechanical and electrical engineers: *Varming Mulcahy
Reilly Associates*
Quantity surveyors: *Seamus Monahan & Partners*
Main contractors: *Hugh O'Neill*; completed by *John Sisk & Son Ltd*

Kilkenny Castle

Phase I – 1969–76
Client: OPW
Project architect: M D Burke
Architects: John Cumming and David Slattery
Quantity surveyor: *Thomas D'Arcy*
Main contractors: *Castlecomer Joinery Ltd (later 'P Kelly & Sons Ltd')*
Landscape architects: Sidney F Maskell, F H Hilton
Landscape contractors: *Goulding Horticulture Ltd*
Main contractors for park: *W K Cleere & Son Ltd*

Phase II – 1990–4
Client: OPW
Project heads: Jimmy Dunlea and June Thompson
Project co-ordinator: Frank Fingleton
Design team leader: Patrick Gannon
Architectural assistant: William Sargent
Structural engineer: Tony Smyth
Mechanical and electrical engineer: Pat Hannon
Quantity surveyors: *Con Shanley Associates*
Main contractors: *Kevin Moore Building Contractors Ltd* and
Mahon McPhillips
Project archaeologist: *Ben Murtagh*

Phase III – 1998–9
Client: Department of Arts, Heritage, Gaeltacht and The Islands
Project head: June Thompson
Project co-ordinator: Kevin Connolly
Design team leader: Patrick Gannon
Architectural assistant: William Sargent
Mechanical and electrical engineer: Keith Milsom
Structural engineer: Kieran Walsh
Quantity surveyors: *Nolan Ryan*
Main contractors: *Noreside Construction Ltd*
Project archaeologist: *Ben Murtagh*

National Concert Hall 1981

Client: Department of the Taoiseach
Project architect: Michael O'Doherty
Architects: Allen Smith, Anthony O'Daly, Gregory Devlin
and Gerry Joyce
Architectural assistant: Joseph Sloane
Structural engineers: *Denis O'Leary & Partners*
Mechanical and electrical engineers: *Varming Mulcahy
Reilly Associates*
Acoustic consultant: *Dr Vilhelm Lassen Jordan*
Quantity surveyors: *Seamus Monahan and Partners*
Main contractors: *G & T Crampton Ltd*

Dublin Castle

Reconstruction of State Apartments 1958–68
Client: Department of the Taoiseach
Project architect: Oscar Richardson assisted by Raymond McGrath
Assistant architect: J B Maguire
Structural engineers: *Ove Arup & Partners*
Mechanical and electrical engineer: Charles Farnan
Quantity surveyors: *Leonard & Williams*
Main contractors: *W & J Bolger Ltd*

Development Plan 1946
Client: Department of the Taoiseach
Project architect: Raymond McGrath
Assistant architects: J D Fairweather, Alexander McRobbie,
Maeve Molloy, Frank du Berry,
Architectural assistant: George Sutton
Structural engineers: *Ove Arup & Partners*

Revenue offices 1974
Client: Department of the Taoiseach
Project architect: Frank DuBerry and Raymond McGrath
Mechanical engineers: *Lyons & Partners*
Electrical engineers: *McArdle, McSweeney, O'Malley*
Structural engineers: *Ove Arup & Partners*
Quantity surveyor: *Niall O'Kelly*
Main contractors: *Hugh O'Neill & Co. Ltd*

Restoration, conference centre and Castle Hall 1989
Client: Department of the Taoiseach
Project head: Meta Hastings
Project co-ordinator: June Thompson
Design team leader: Klaus Unger
Architects: David Byers, Angela Rolfe and Michael Carroll
Architectural assistants: Kevin McKenna, Joseph Sloane,
Ben Duignan, Jerry O'Shea and Cyril O'Brien
Structural engineers: *Ove Arup & Partners*
Mechanical and electrical engineers: *Varming Mulcahy
Reilly Associates*
Quantity surveyors: *Seamus Monahan & Partners*
Main contractors: *Mahon & McPhillips Ltd*

Blocks 8, 9, 10 and undercroft 1989
Client: Department of the Taoiseach
Project head: Meta Hastings
Project co-ordinator: Una Redmond
Design team leaders: David Slattery and Patrick Gannon
Structural engineers: *Ove Arup & Partners*
Mechanical and electrical engineers: *Robert Jacob & Partners*
Quantity surveyors: *Patterson Kempster & Shortall*
Main contractors: *John Paul Construction Ltd*
Archaeological team leader: Conleth Manning

Treasury Block, 1992
Client: Department of the Taoiseach
Project head: Meta Hastings
Project co-ordinator: Una Redmond
Design team leader: David Wall
Architect: John Cahill
Architectural assistant: Greg Hastings
Structural engineers: *Ove Arup & Partners*
Mechanical and electrical engineers: *Robert Jacob & Partners*
Quantity surveyors: *Desmond McGreevy & Partners*
Main contractors: *Mahon McPhillips*

Chapel Royal 1989
Client: Department of the Taoiseach
Project head: Tom Sherlock
Project co-ordinator: Austin Cunningham
Design team leader: David Wall
Architect: John Cahill
Architectural assistant: Jack McDonald
Electrical engineer: Jim O'Sullivan
Structural engineers: *Ove Arup & Partners*
Quantity surveyors: *Seamus Monahan & Partners*
Consultant on historic decoration techniques: *Dr Ian Bristow*
Furniture restoration: OPW Furniture Branch
Painters: *Treacy & Thomas Ltd*
Main contractors: *W & J Bolger Ltd*

Coach House and Dubh Linn Garden 1995
Client: Department of the Taoiseach
Project head: Una Redmond
Project co-ordinator: Redmond Aherne
Design team leader (Coach House): David Byers
Design team leader (Dubh Linn Garden): Ana Dolan
Structural engineer: *Tony Moore*
Mechanical and electrical engineers: *Callaghan Engineering Ltd*
Quantity surveyors: *Brendan Merry & Partners*
Main contractors: *Cleary Doyle Contracting Ltd*

Ship Street barracks 1995
Client: Department of the Taoiseach
Project head: Barry Murphy
Project co-ordinator: Una Redmond
Design team leader: Klaus Unger
Architect: Kevin Wolahan
Consultant architect: *Geoffrey Johnson*
Consultant assistant architect: *Mark Stewart*
Mechanical and electrical engineers: *McCarrick Woods*
Structural engineers: *Clifton, Scannell, Emerson*
Quantity surveyor: *F Junius Horne*
Main contractors: *Pierse Contracting Ltd*

Clock Tower 1995
Client: Department of the Taoiseach/ Department of Arts, Heritage,
Gaeltacht and the Islands
Project head: Una Redmond
Project co-ordinator: Niamh O'Regan
Design team leader: Klaus Unger
Architect: Angela Rolfe
Consultant assistant architect: *Brian O'Donnell*
Architectural assistant: Kevin McKenna
Structural engineers: *McCabe, Delaney & Partners*
Mechanical and electrical engineers: *Varming, Mulcahy,
Reilly Associates*
Quantity surveyors: *Brendan Merry & Partners*
Main contractors: *P Rogers & Sons*

Skellig Michael 1978–

Client: OPW/ Department of Arts, Heritage, Gaeltacht and the Islands
Conservation architect and project co-ordinator: Grellan D Rourke
Assistants: Richard Stapleton, Pauric Coffey, John O'Brien and
Declan Hodge
Archaeologists: Ann Lynch and Edward Bourke
Structural engineer: *Joss Lynam*
Main contractors: National Monuments Service workforce, Killarney

Royal Hospital Kilmainham

Restoration 1980–4
Client: Department of the Taoiseach
Project architects: *Costello Murray Beaumont*
Monitoring architect: M D Burke
Quantity surveyors: *Leonard & Williams*
Structural engineers: *Joseph McCullough & Partners*
Mechanical and electrical engineers: *John Egan Associates*
Main contractors: *John Sisk & Son Ltd*

IMMA 1991
Client: Department of the Taoiseach
Project head: Jimmy Dunlea
Project co-ordinator: Tom Sherlock
Design team leader: *Shay Cleary Architects*
Monitoring architect: Noel de Chenu
Structural engineers: *Joseph McCullough & Partners*
Mechanical and electrical engineers: *J N & G Traynor & Partners*
Main contractors: *Mahon & MacPhillips*

Coachhouse/stables 1995
Client: Department of Arts, Heritage, Gaeltacht and the Islands
Project head: June Thompson
Project co-ordinator: Frank Fingleton
Design team leader: Elizabeth Morgan
Architectural assistants: Thomas MacArdle
Structural engineers: John Gallagher
Mechanical and electrical engineer: Pat Savage
Quantity surveyors: John Brownlee
Main contractors: *Mahon & McPhillips*

Deputy Master's House 1999
Client: Department of Arts, Heritage, Gaeltacht and the Islands
Project head: June Thompson
Project co-ordinator: Kevin Connolly
Design team leader (exterior): Pat Cooney
Design team leader (interior): *Shay Cleary Architects*
Structural engineers: *Lee McCullough & Partners*
Mechanical and electrical engineer: *Delap & Waller*
Main contractors: *G&T Crampton*

Glebe House and Gallery 1983

Client: OPW
Project architect (House): Michael O'Doherty
Architect (House): John Cahill
Project architect (Gallery): Gregory Devlin
Architectural assistants: Donna Turner and William Sargent
Structural engineers: *T J O'Connor & Associates*
Quantity surveyor: *Raymond Donnelly*
Mechanical and electrical engineer: *Kevin Madden*
Landscape architect: *Anthony M O'Neill*
Main contractors: *Thomas MacMahon*

Killykeen Forest Park 1986

Client: Department of Energy
Project architects: Ciaran O'Connor and Noel de Chenu
Architectural assistants: Gerard O'Sullivan and Donna Turner
Quantity surveyors: *Séamus Monahan & Partners*
Mechanical and electrical engineers: *Hugh Munro & Co. Ltd*
Structural engineers: *Jennings & O'Donovan*
Main contractors: *Michael Reynolds & Sons Ltd*

Parke's Castle 1989

Client: OPW
Project architect: Paul McMahon
Architectural assistant: John O'Brien
Mechanical and electrical engineer: Seamus Farrelly
Main contractor: OPW National Monuments (Sligo District) Workforce

Newmills 1994

Client: OPW/ Department of Arts, Heritage, Gaeltacht and the Islands
Project architects: Paul McMahon and *Jacqui Donnelly*
Architectural assistant: John O'Brien
Structural engineer: John Gallagher
Mechanical and electrical engineer: Dick Wynne
Quantity surveyor: Aidan Quinn
Milling consultant: *Vincent Conaghan*
Main contractors: *Patrick J Doherty & Sons*

National Library of Ireland

Roofworks and refurbishment 1997
Client: Department of Arts, Heritage, Gaeltacht and the Islands
Project head: June Thompson
Project co-ordinator: Kevin Connolly
Design team leader (reading room refurbishment): Stephen Kane
Design team leader (roof): *John O'Reilly*
Architectural assistants: Mary Regan, Mary O'Boyle, Sean Moylan
Mechanical and electrical engineer: *J V Tierney & Co.*
Structural engineers: *Ove Arup & Partners*
Quantity surveyor: *Thomas Clear*
Main contractors: *Dunwoody & Dobson*

Former NCAD building refurbishment 1999–
Client: Department of Arts, Heritage, Gaeltacht and the Islands
Project head: June Thompson
Project co-ordinator: Kevin Connolly
Design team leader: Stephen Kane
Architects: Sean Moylan, Rory Murphy
Structural engineers: *Ove Arup & Partners*
Mechanical and electrical engineers: *J V Tierney & Partners*
Quantity surveyors: *Boyd & Creed*
Main contractors: *Rohcon Ltd*

Former Racquet Hall 1997
Client: Department of Arts, Heritage, Gaeltacht and the Islands
Project head: June Thompson
Project co-ordinator: Kevin Connolly
Design team leader: Stephen Kane
Architect: *Brian O'Donnell*
Structural engineers: *Denis O'Leary & Partners*
Mechanical and electrical engineer: *Declan Holmes*
Quantity surveyor: *Clifford Campbell*
Main contractors: *Rohcon Ltd*

National Museum of Ireland

Collins Barracks inaugural exhibition 1997
Client: Department of Arts, Heritage, Gaeltacht and the Islands
Project head: Michael O'Doherty
Project co-ordinator: June Thompson
Design team leader: Pat Cooney
Architects: Patrick Gannon, Des Byrne, Barbara Kenny, Elizabeth
Morgan, Ian Kelly and Caroline Leaden
Architectural assistants: Tom MacArdle and Leslie Walsh
Consultant architects: *Gilroy McMahon Architects*
Structural engineers: *Lee McCullough & Partners*
Mechanical and electrical engineers: *J V Tierney & Co.*
Quantity surveyors: *Mulcahy McDonagh & Partners*
Main contractors: *Pierse Contracting Ltd*

1798 Memorial 1998
Client: Department of Arts, Heritage, Gaeltacht and the Islands
Project head: Kevin Connolly
Project co-ordinator: Mary Heffernan assisted by Emer O'Mahony
Design team leader: Elizabeth Morgan
Assistant architect: *Deirdre Heffernan*
Stone carving: *Black Stone Studios Ltd*
Structural engineer: Kieran Walsh
Mechanical and electrical engineer: Declan Holmes
Quantity surveyor: John Brownlee
Main contractors: *C&M Construction Ltd*

Turlough Park House 1999–
Client: Department of Arts, Heritage, Gaeltacht and the Islands
Project head: June Thompson
Project co-ordinator: Kevin Connolly
Design team leader: Des Byrne
Architects: Mark Stewart and Terri Sweeney
Structural engineer: John Gallagher
Mechanical and electrical engineer: Pádraig Cronin.
Quantity surveyor: James Walsh
Main contractors: *JJ Rhatigan & Co*

Royal Irish Academy 1996

Client: Royal Irish Academy
Project head: Una Redmond
Project co-ordinator: Niamh O'Regan
Design team leader: *John J O'Connell*
Structural engineers: *Ove Arup & Partners*
Mechanical and electrical engineers: *Grant Tennyson*
Quantity surveyors: *O'Reilly Hyland Tierney & Associates*
Main contractors: *P Elliott & Co. Ltd*

The Zoological Society of Ireland

Entrance building 1999
Client: The Zoological Society of Ireland
Project head: Una Redmond
Project co-ordinator: John McMahon
Design team leader: *Scott Tallon Walker*
Monitoring architect: Angela Rolfe
Structural engineers: *P H McCarthy & Partners*
Mechanical and electrical engineers: *MacArdle McSweeney
Associates*
Quantity surveyors: *Brendan Merry & Partners*
Main contractors: *CLG Construction*

World of Primates 1996
Client: The Zoological Society of Ireland
Project head: Niamh O'Regan
Design team leader: Martin Heffernan
Architect: Mark Stewart
Structural engineers: *P H McCarthy & Partners*
Mechanical and electrical engineers: *MacArdle McSweeney
Associates*
Quantity surveyors: *Brendan Merry & Partners*
Landscaping: *Brady Shipman Martin*
Main contractors: *Cleary & Doyle Contracting Ltd*

Fringes of the Arctic 1997–9
Client: The Zoological Society of Ireland
Project head: Una Redmond
Project co-ordinator: Frank Shalvey
Design team leader: *Keane Murphy Duff*
Monitoring architect: Angela Rolfe
Structural engineers: *P H McCarthy & Partners*
Mechanical and electrical engineers: *MacArdle McSweeney
Associates*
Landscaping: *Brady Shipman Martin*
Quantity surveyors: *Brendan Merry & Partners*
Main contractors phase I: *Cleary Doyle Contracting Ltd*
Main contractors phase II: *Denphi Construction Ltd*

World of Cats 1998
Client: The Zoological Society of Ireland
Project head: Niamh O'Regan
Project co-ordinator: Frank Shalvey
Design team leader: Mark Stewart
Structural engineers: *P H McCarthy & Partners*
Mechanical and electrical engineers: *MacArdle
McSweeney Associates*
Quantity surveyors: *Brendan Merry & Partners*
Main contractors: *Eamonn Duffy (Rosemount) Ltd*

Castletown House 1994–

Client: Department of Arts, Heritage, Gaeltacht and the Islands
Project head: June Thompson
Project co-ordinators: Frank Fingleton and Kevin Connolly
Design team leader: John Cahill
Architectural assistant: Greg Hastings
Consultant architect: *John Redmill*
Structural engineers: John Gallagher, Kieran Walsh, Niall Jordan
Mechanical and electrical engineers: *Callaghan Engineering Ltd*
Quantity Surveyor: *Patterson Kempster & Shortall*
Main contractors (Phase I): *John Sisk & Son Ltd*
Main contractors (Phase II): *Rohcon Ltd*
Main contractors (Phase III): *Rohcon Ltd*

Rathfarnham Castle 1987–

Client: Department of Arts, Heritage, Gaeltacht and the Islands
Project head: June Thompson
Project co-ordinator: Kevin Connolly
Design team leaders: David Slattery, Alistair Lindsay and
Barbara Kenny
Design team leaders (kitchen wing): Alistair Lindsay and
Niall Parsons
Design team leader (rerendering): *Mel Reynolds*
Architectural assistants: Leonard Whyte and Leslie Walsh
Quantity surveyors: *T B Kennedy & Partners* and Aidan Quinn
Services engineer: *Derham & McPhilips* and OPW
Mechanical and electrical engineer: Keith Milsom
Structural engineer: Ian Wolfe
Main contractors: *Cleary & Doyle, Lissadel Construction, Patrick
Brock & Sons, Dick Roche Ltd* and other specialist contractors

National Botanic Gardens

Curvilinear Range 1995
Client: Department of Arts, Heritage, Gaeltacht and the Islands
Project head: June Thompson
Project co-ordinators: Frank Fingleton and Kevin Connolly
Design team leader: Ciaran O'Connor
Architect: Michael Carroll
Structural engineers: *Ove Arup & Partners*
Services engineers: Jim O'Sullivan and Larry McGettrick
Quantity surveyors: *D L Martin & Partners*
Main contractors: *John Paul Construction*

Library/Herbarium 1997
Client: Department of Arts, Heritage, Gaeltacht and the Islands
Project head: June Thompson
Project co-ordinator: Kevin Connolly
Design team leader: Ciaran O'Connor
Architects: Gerard O'Sullivan, Michael Carroll, *Sheila Foley* and *Gerard Harvey*
Structural engineers: *Donald Keogan & Associates*
Mechanical and electrical engineers: *Delap & Waller*
Quantity surveyors: *Seamus Monahan & Partners*
Main contractors: *McCabe Builders Ltd*

Barretstown Castle 1996

Client: The Barretstown Gang Camp Fund Ltd
Project head: Una Redmond
Project co-ordinator: Niamh O'Regan
Design team leaders: Martin Heffernan and Kevin Wolahan
Assistant architect: Mark Stewart
Architectural assistant: Robert Carty
Structural engineers: *Malony & Millar*
Mechanical and electrical engineers: *Varming Mulcahy Reilly Associates*
Quantity surveyors: *Mulcahy McDonagh & Partners*
Main contractors: *Pierse Contracting Ltd*

The Hunt Museum 1997

Client: The Hunt Museum
Project co-ordinator: Niamh O'Regan
Design team leader: Niall Parsons
Exhibition architect: Patrick Gannon
Architectural assistant: William Sargent
Quantity surveyors: *O'Reilly Hyland Tierney & Associates*
Structural engineers: *Michael Punch & Partners*
Mechanical and electrical engineers: *Don O'Malley & Partners*
Main contractors (building): *Michael McNamara & Co*
Main contractors (exhibition): *Gem Joinery Longford*

The Sacred Heart Oratory 1998

Client: Department of Arts, Heritage, Gaeltacht and the Islands
Project head: June Thompson
Project co-ordinator: Kevin Connolly
Design team leaders: Michael Haugh and Marie Fox
Architects: Deirdre Wolahan and *Conor Moran*
Architectural assistants: Leonard Whyte and Paul O'Leary
Structural engineer: Alan French
Mechanical and electrical engineer: Declan Holmes
Quantity surveyor: Aidan Quinn
Main contractors: *Patrick Brock & Sons*
Artwork conservators: *Karena Morton and Christoph Oldenbourg*

Farmleigh 1999–

Client: Department of the Taoiseach
Project head: June Thompson
Project co-ordinator: Kevin Connolly
Design team leader: David Byers
Architect: Peter Rogers
Art inventory: Jacquie Moore

RIC & Garda Síochána Stations

Pearse Street modernisation 1997
Client: Department of Justice
Project head: Una Redmond
Project co-ordinator: Niamh O'Regan
Design team leader: *Brian Hogan Architects*
Monitoring architect: Pat Cooney
Structural engineers: *Molony and Millar*
Mechanical and electrical engineers: *Delap and Waller*
Quantity surveyors: *Hickey Heritage & Associates*
Main contractors: *Mahon McPhillips*

Roscommon 1961
Client: Department of Justice
Project architect: Gerald McNicholl
Assistant architects: Thomas John Ryan and Robert R Smyth
Mechanical & electrical engineer: Thomas Illingworth
Quantity surveyor: *Noel J Dooley*
Main contractors: *Killian & Dervin, Roscommon*

Roscommon 1995
Client: Department of Justice
Project head: Una Redmond
Project co-ordinator: Niamh O'Regan
Design team leader: Ciaran McGahon
Structural engineers: *H G L O'Connor & Co*
Services engineer: Patrick Savage
Quantity surveyors: *Peter Costello & Partners*
Main contractors: *P Connelly & Sons*

Tallaght Garda District HQ 1985
Client: Department of Justice
Project management: OPW Project Management Services
Project architects: John Keoghan and Con de Burca
Structural engineers: *McCabe, Delaney & Associates*
Mechanical and electrical engineer: Patrick Savage
Quantity surveyors: *Kevin McArdle & Associates*
Main contractors: *P J McLoughlin & Sons*

Cork HQ Garda Divisional HQ 1990
Client: Department of Justice
Project head: Una Redmond
Project co-ordinator: Niamh O'Regan
Design team leaders: Kevin Wolahan and John Keogan
Structural engineers: *John O'Donovan & Associates*
Mechanical and electrical engineer: Patrick Savage
Quantity surveyors: *McGrath & McGrath*
Main contractors: *Michael McNamara & Co*

Templemore Garda Síochána College 1993

Client: Department of Justice
Project head: Barry Murphy
Project co-ordinator: Una Redmond
Design team leader: Finbarr Wall
Architects: Ciaran McGahon, Gerry Browner and Brian Kiernan
Architectural assistants: Terry Beagon, Dermot Cleary, Paddy Clifford and Jerry O'Shea
Structural engineers: *Michael Punch & Partners*
Mechanical and electrical engineers: *J V Tierney & Co*
Quantity surveyors: *Patrick Butler & Partners*
Main contractors: *Duggan Bros. (Contractors) Ltd*

Store Street Garda Divisional HQ 1998
Client: Department of Justice
Project head: Una Redmond
Project co-ordinator: Bríd Snow
Design team leaders: Fred McElwee with *Campbell Conroy Hickey Partnership*
Architectural assistants: Patrick Moloney and James Sweeney
Structural engineers: *Fearon O'Neill Rooney*
Mechanical and electrical engineers: *Homan O'Brien Associates*
Quantity surveyors: *Burton & O'Connor*
Main contractors: *Christopher Bennett & Son Construction Ltd*

Prisons

Castlerea Prison 1996
Client: Department of Justice
Project management: OPW Project Management Services
Project architect: OPW Architectural Services
Mechanical and electrical engineer: OPW Engineering Services
Quantity surveyor: OPW Quantity Surveying Services
Main contractors/developers: *Henry; O'Rourke Ltd*

Mountjoy Women's Prison 1999
Client: Department of Justice
Project management: OPW Project Management Services
Project architect: OPW Architectural Services
Structural engineers: *Thomas Garland & Partners*
Mechanical and electrical engineers: *Homan O'Brien Associates*
Quantity surveyors: *Desmond McGreevy & Partners*
Main contractors: *John Paul Construction Ltd*

Midlands 1999
Client: Department of Justice
Project management: OPW Project Management Services
Project architect: OPW Architectural Services
Professional architectural services to OPW: *Campbell Conroy Hickey*
Structural engineer: OPW Engineering Services
Mechanical and electrical engineer: OPW Engineering Services
Quantity surveyor: OPW Quantity Surveying Services
Main contractors/developers: *Henry; O'Rourke Ltd*

Cloverhill Remand Prison and Courthouse 1999
Client: Department of Justice
Project managment: OPW Project Management Services
Project architects: OPW Architectural Services
Mechanical and electrical engineer: OPW Engineering Services
Quantity surveyors: *Rogerson Reddan & Associates* and OPW Quantity Surveying Services
Main contractors/developers: *John Sisk & Son Ltd*

Courthouses

Smithfield Children's Courthouse 1987
Client: Department of Justice
Design team leader: John Tuomey
Architect: David Slattery
Architectural assistant: Brendan Walsh
Structural engineer: *Donald Keoghan*
Mechanical and electrical engineer: Tom Glynn
Quantity surveyor: Aidan Quinn
Main contractors: *Mahon & McPhilips*

Richmond Courts 1997
Client: Department of Justice
Project head: Una Redmond
Project co-ordinator: Niamh O'Regan
Design team leader: *Brian O'Halloran & Associates*
Monitoring architect: Michael Haugh
Structural engineers: *Donnelly Troy & Associates*
Mechanical and electrical engineers: *Jacobs Engineering*
Acoustics consultants: *National Environmental Services*
Main contractors: *Cedar Building Company Ltd*

Carrick-on-Shannon Courthouse, 1997
Client: Department of Justice
Project head: Una Redmond
Project co-ordinator: Una Cluxton
Design team leader: *Burke-Kennedy Doyle & Partners*
Monitoring architect: David Wall
Structural engineer: *HGL O'Connor & Co*
Mechanical and electrical engineer: Jim O'Sullivan
Quantity surveyors: *Patrick A Butler & Partners*
Main contractors: *JSL Group Ltd*

Anglesea St Courthouse, Cork 1995
Client: Department of Justice
Project head: Una Redmond
Project co-ordinator: Niamh O'Regan
Design team leader: Michael Haugh
Architect: Kevin Wolahan
Architectural assistant: Terence Beagon
Structural engineers: *John O'Donovan & Associates*
Mechanical and electrial engineer: Jim O'Sullivan
Quantity surveyors: *Sean McDermott Murphy & Partners*
Main contractors: *P J Hegarty & Sons*

Irish National War Memorial

1933–39
Project architects: *Sir Edwin Lutyens*, in association with T J Byrne
Gardening: *Sir Frederick Moore*, John William Besant (Keeper of the Botanic Gardens), A F Peterson (Assistant Superintendent of the Phoenix Park), *Robert Anderson*, Phoenix Park Forestry Unit
Structural engineer: Captain David Campbell, M C
Quantity surveyor: *W P Beckett*
Contractor: Unemployed ex-servicemen under Office of Public Works supervision

1987–8 Restoration
Client: OPW
Design team leader (stonework): Paul Sherwin
Design team leaders (tempietta): Paul Sherwin and David Byers
Main contractors (tempietta): *Glasnevin Cemetery Monument Works Ltd*
Main contractors (stonework): *Building Fabrics Ltd* and *Glasnevin Cemetery Monument Works Ltd*
Main contractors (roads): *Roadmaker Ltd*
Main contractors (fountains): OPW Building Maintenance Services
Gardens: OPW Parks Section
Metal seats: *Metweld Fabrications Ltd*

Decentralised and Centralised Government Offices

Thurles 1983
Client: Revenue Commissioners/Department of Labour/Department of the Environment/Department of Social Welfare/Department of Agriculture
Project architects: Stephen Kane, David Byers
Structural engineers: *Redmond Holloway Associates*
Mechanical and electrical engineer: Tom Glynn
Quantity surveyor: *Patrick F. Coveney & Son*
Main contractors: *Fethard Construction Ltd*

Galway 1989
Client: Department of Defence
Design team leader: *Frank Crowley & Partners*
Structural engineers: *Michael Punch & Partners*
Mechanical and electrical engineer: *MacArdle McSweeney Associates*
Quantity Surveyor: *Eugene Beglan & Associates*
Main contractors: *Rohan Construction Ltd*

Longford 1994
Client: Department of Social Welfare/Department of Agriculture/Department of the Environment/Ordnance Survey Office
Project head: Una Redmond
Project co-ordinator: Jim Roche
Design team leader: *Horan Keogan Ryan*
Mechanical and electrical engineers: *R N Murphy & Associate*
Structural engineer: *McCabe, Delaney & Associates*
Quantity surveyors: *Sweeney Fogarty & Co*
Main contractors: *P J McLoughlin & Sons Ltd*

Portlaoise 1996
Client: Department of Agriculture, Food & Forestry
Project head: Una Redmond
Project co-ordinator: Jim Roche
Design team leader: *Burke-Kennedy Doyle & Partners*
Structural engineers: *Molony & Millar*
Mechanical and electrical engineers: *Mercury Engineering Ltd*
Quantity surveyors: *Brendan Merry & Partners*
Main contractors/developers: *Irishenco*

Enviromental Protection Agency 1998
Client: Environmental Protection Agency
Project head: Una Redmond
Project co-ordinator: Niamh O'Regan
Design team leader: *Henry J Lyons & Partners*
Mechanical and electrical engineers: *R N Murphy & Associates*
Structural engineers: *Molony & Millar*
Quantity surveyors: *Kerrigan, Sheanon Newman*
Landscape architects: *Mitchell & Associates*
Developers and main contractors: *Pierse Contracting Ltd*

Irish Embassy to the Holy See *c* 1958
Client: Department of Foreign Affairs
Project architect: Raymond McGrath
Local architect: *Francesco Vacchini*
Mechanical and electrical engineer: Thomas Illingworth
External painting: *Aristedemo Cotani*
Wood treatment: *Lorenzo Pasqualli*
Redecoration: *Giulio Sordini*
Redecoration of chapel: *Lombardozzi Ferruccio & Co.*

Irish Embassy to France 1956
Client: Department of Foreign Affairs
Project architect: Raymond McGrath
Architectural assistant: Noel de Chenu
Local architect: *Alexandre Ziwès*
Conversion of courtyard: *Etablissements P. Dindeleux*
Main furniture, upholstery and curtain supplier: *Louis Koch & Son*
Upholstery: *Ronchetti*
Carpet laying and cleaning: *Pinton Frères*
Silk poplin curtain fabric: *Thomas Elliott & Sons*

Irish Embassy to Saudi Arabia 1986
Client: Department of Foreign Affairs
Project architects: *Arthur Gibney & Partners*
Monitoring architect: Con Manahan
Structural engineers: *Ove Arup & Partners*
Mechanical and electrical engineers: *J A Kenny & Partners*
Quantity surveyors: *Desmond McGreevy & Partners*
Main contractors: *Saudi McInerney Construction Company Ltd*
Resident engineer: *Seamus Mulhern*

Government Jet 1991
Client: Department of the Taoiseach
Completed: *Gulfstream Aerospace Corporation, Long Beach, California*
Project architects: Angela Rolfe, David Byers and Klaus Unger
Wilton carpets: *Munster Carpets Casdale Ltd*
Upholstery fabric: *Botany Weaving Mill*
Linen damask: *John England Textiles Ltd*
Decorative wall panels: *Cathy MacAleavy*

Social Welfare Local Offices

Tallaght 1995
Client: Deparment of Social, Community and Family Affairs
Project head: June Thompson
Project co-ordinator: Frank Fingleton and Kevin Connolly
Design team leader: Pat Cooney
Architectural assistant: Brendan Cormican
Structural engineer: *Malone O'Regan Engineers*
Mechanical and electrical engineer: *Noel Lawlor*
Quantity surveyors: *Dooley Leonard Bone*
Main contractors: *Rohcon Ltd*

Hanover Street 1990
Client: Deparment of Social, Community and Family Affairs
Project head: Jimmy Dunlea
Project co-ordinator: Tom Sherlock
Design team leader: Michael Haugh
Architectural assistants: Maura Brennan and Jerry O'Shea
Structural engineers: *Malachy Walsh & Partners*
Mechanical and electrical engineer: Tom Glynn
Quantity surveyors: *Denis King & Co*
Main contractors: *P J Hegarty & Sons*

Ionad an Bhlascaoid Mhóir/ Great Blasket Centre 1994

Client: OPW/ Department of Arts, Heritage, Gaeltacht and the Islands
Project heads: Jimmy Dunlea and June Thompson
Project co-ordinator: Frank Fingleton
Design team leader: Ciaran O'Connor
Architects: Gerard O'Sullivan and *Antoinette O'Neill*
Structural engineers: *Malachy Walsh & Partners*
Mechanical and electrical engineers: *Paul Twomey & Associates Ltd*
in association with *Martin Buckley & Associates*
Quantity surveyors: *John J Casey & Company*
Main contractors: *Murnane & O'Shea Ltd*

Céide Fields Visitor Centre 1993

Client: OPW/ Department of Arts, Heritage, Gaeltacht and the Islands
Project head: Una Redmond
Project co-ordinator: Niamh O'Regan
Design team leader: Mary MacKenna
Architectural assistants: Tony O'Shaughnessy, Andrew Cooke
Landscape architect: *Mitchell Associates*
Structural engineers: *Concannon, Healy, Heffernan*
Mechanical and electrical engineers: *Project Management Ltd*
Quantity surveyors: *Fergal Coghlan Associates*
Main contractors: *Kilcawley Building & Civil Engineering Ltd*

Muckross House

Restoration 1980–3
Client: OPW
Design team leaders: Anthony O'Daly and Barbara Kenny
Architectural assistant: Lindi Dingle
Decorating contractors: *Keogh Decorators, Killarney*
Joinery: *Muckross House Joinery Workshop*
Furniture restoration: OPW Furniture Branch

Restoration 1990–5
Client: OPW/ Department of Arts, Heritage, Gaeltacht and the Islands
Project heads: Jimmy Dunlea and June Thompson
Project co-ordinators: Frank Fingleton and Kevin Connolly
Design team leader: Helen Blair
Decorating contractors: *Keogh Decorators, Killarney*
Electrical contractors: *Flesk Electrical*

Visitor Centre 1992
Client: OPW
Project head: Jimmy Dunlea
Project co-ordinator: Frank Fingleton
Design team leader: Helen Blair
Exhibition design: Jim Larner, Killarney National Park
Mechanical and electrical engineer: Tom Glynn
Quantity surveyors: *Kane-Crowe Partnership*
Main contractors: *Ned O'Shea & Sons*

Restaurant and Workshops 1999
Client: Department of Arts, Heritage, Gaeltacht and the Islands
Project head: June Thompson
Project co-ordinator: Kevin Connolly
Design team leader: Helen Blair
Architect: Elizabeth Morgan
Structural engineer: Kieran Walsh
Mechanical and electrical engineer: Jim O'Sullivan
Quantity surveyor: *Kane-Crowe Partnership*
Main contractors: *Ned O'Shea & Sons*

John F Kennedy Arboretum 1968

Client: OPW
Project architects: S F Maskell, F H Hilton
Civil engineer: *Edward G Pettit*
Mechanical and electrical engineer: Thomas Illingworth
Quantity surveyor: *Francis Cross*
Main contractors: *John Sisk & Son Ltd*

Corlea Trackway Visitor Centre 1994

Client: OPW/ Department of Arts, Heritage, Gaeltacht and the Islands
Project head: Una Redmond
Project co-ordinator: Niamh O'Regan
Design team leader: Stephen Kane
Architect: Deirdre Wolahan
Structural engineers: *Joseph McCullough & Partners*
Mechanical and electrical engineers: *Robert Jacob & Partners*
Quantity surveyors: *Desmond McCreevy & Partners*
Main contractors: *Coffey Construction*

Ashtown Visitor Centre and Tower House 1992

Client: OPW
Project head: Una Redmond
Project co-ordinator: Niamh O'Regan
Design team leader: Ciaran O'Connor
Architect: Gerard O'Sullivan
Structural engineers: *O'Connor, Sutton, Cronin*
Mechanical and electrical engineers: *J W Hogan & Associates*
Quantity surveyors: *Rogerson Reddan & Associates*
Main contractors: *McCabe Builders Ltd*
Display design: Pat McCusker
Displays: *Arena Construction Ltd*
Restoration of Ashtown Tower House:
Client: OPW
Project architect: Willie Cumming

Waterways Visitor Centre 1993

Client: OPW
Project head: Pierce Pigott
Project co-ordinator: Tom Sherlock
Design team leader: Ciaran O'Connor
Architects: Gerard O'Sullivan and *Michelle Fagan*
Structural engineers: *Thomas Garland & Partners*
Mechanical and electrical engineers: *E G Pettit & Co*
Quantity surveyors: *Bruce Shaw Partnership*
Main contractors: *Mahon McPhillips*

Clonmacnoise Visitor Centre 1995

Client: OPW/ Department of Arts, Heritage, Gaeltacht and the Islands
Project head: Noel Lynch
Project co-ordinator: June Thompson
Design team leader: Paul McMahon
Architectural assistant: John O'Brien
Interior design: Helen O'Neill and Mary O'Boyle
Exhibition design: *Éigse*
Structural engineer: Tony Smyth
Mechanical and electrical engineer: Pat Hannon
Quantity surveyor: Aidan Quinn
Main contractors: National Monuments Service Athenry

Connemara National Park Visitor Centre 1992

Client: OPW
Project head: Dave Fadden
Design team leader: Des Byrne
Architect: *Donal MacNally*
Architectural assistant: Leonard Whyte
Structural engineer: Tony Smyth
Quantity surveyor: Tom Dooley
Mechanical and electrical engineer: Stan O'Grady
Main contractors: *Paddy Roe*

Index